## EARLY CHILDHOOD F

**Leslie R. Williams, Editor**

ADVISORY BOARD: Barbara T. Bowman, Ha
Doris Pronin Fromberg, Celia Genishi, St
Alice Sterling Honig, Elizabeth Jones, (                    ..eikart

*(Continued)*

# Serious Players in the Primary Classroom

Empowering Children Through Active Learning Experiences

## SECOND EDITION

## SELMA WASSERMANN

Teachers College, Columbia University
New York and London

Published by Teachers College Press, 1234 Amsterdam Avenue, New York, NY 10027

*Library of Congress Cataloging-in-Publication Data*

Wassermann, Selma.
   Serious players in the primary classroom : empowering children through active learning experiences / Selma Wassermann.—2nd ed.
     p. cm. — (Early childhood education series)
   Includes bibliographical references (p.   ) and index.
   ISBN 0-8077-3986-3 (pbk. : alk. paper)
   1. Education, Primary—Activity programs.  2. Play.  3. Creative activities and seat work.
4. Active learning.    I. Title.  II. Early childhood education series (Teachers College Press)
LB1537.W34   2000
372.13—dc21                                  00-028704

ISBN 0-8077-3986-3 (paper)

Printed on acid-free paper
Manufactured in the United States of America

07  06  05  04  03  02  01  00    8  7  6  5  4  3  2  1

For my most serious players,
Simon & Arlo

# Contents

## PART IV. AFTER PLAY

# Preface

It is almost a decade since I sent off the manuscript of the first edition of *Serious Players* to my editors at Teachers College Press. When one writes largely in isolation, head burrowed into the computer screen without noticing if it is day or night, one rarely considers how well the book will be received in the educational marketplace. The writing process is intense enough, concentration focused tenaciously on what needs to be said and how to say it. Only when the deed is done, only when one has labored long and hard, only when the finished product is wrapped, with trembling fingers, in the box that will transport it, does one dare to hope that someone, out there, will actually read what has been written.

It would not be an overstatement to say that I could not anticipate the hugely positive response generated by *Serious Players*. I was enormously gratified to learn that the book spoke to large numbers of teachers and student teachers in a way that touched both hearts and minds. In fact, during this decade, the way of organizing curriculum, *play-debrief-replay*, described extensively in this book, has so insinuated itself into the educational lexicon that it has risen to the heights of having its own acronym: P-D-R (sigh).

This book was written to help teachers bridge the gap between ideas and the application of those ideas in early childhood classrooms. It attempts, first, to create a theoretical framework, a structure that weaves together three threads: the importance of play in the social, psychological, and intellectual development of children; the human need for personal power—the gratification that challenge in active learning experiences brings to one's feelings of self-worth; and finally, the imperative of respect for children, respect for them and for their choices. The position taken in this book is that when certain conditions exist in primary classrooms, children are empowered. They grow in their feelings of self-respect, self-worth, and intellectual competence—that is, they are imbued with a *can-do* spirit. The threads that have been woven together to form the theory of empowerment will not be new to any student or practitioner in education. No one who is deeply concerned with the healthful development of children will reject this theory. Who, after all, will be the first to say that play is bad? Or that children should not be intellectually challenged? Or that they should not be treated respectfully? This is what all adults want for children, and we want this in our early childhood programs as well.

The wrinkle seems to lie in how these ideas are translated into active classroom life. It is one thing to believe in the importance of play, but another to consider how play may help to stimulate intellectual development in the classroom. It is one thing to believe in providing children with opportunities to develop a sense of personal power, but another to consider what teaching strategies and curriculum experiences enable this growth. It is one thing to believe in respect for children and for their choices, but another to know how the words we utter to them contribute to or diminish that respect. It is one thing to believe in the merit of *thinking* as a noble educational goal, but quite another to design an educational program that brings that goal to fruition.

In bridging the gap between theory and classroom practice, this book is strong in the "example department." It makes a clear and unambiguous statement about an approach to teaching for thinking called play-debrief-replay that provides a discernable structure for early childhood programs. It contains numerous examples of fully fleshed-out curriculum activities in math, science, language arts, and social studies, as well as in music, arts and crafts, and dramatic play, that will work to empower children. Suggestions for "playing with ideas" provide a framework for classroom discussions that examine moral and ethical issues, giving opportunity for character building and social development. Practical help is offered about setting up classrooms and preparing children for active learning. Chapters dealing with teacher-student interactions, and the kinds of evaluative practices that enable, rather than defeat, children are intended to further teaching effectiveness. In all of what is written, teachers are always encouraged to choose for themselves what they like and what they think will work for them. This is not a cookbook of strategies to embrace willy nilly, but a presentation of alternatives for teachers to reflect upon and choose what is appropriate. To me the right of children to choose and the right of teachers to choose is a key to empowerment.

What makes the play-debrief-replay approach so appealing is, I believe, the fact that it is consonant with what many early childhood teachers believe about how young children learn best. What's more, it gives teachers a "handle" on how to translate theory about child-centered classrooms into actual classroom practice, providing the tools and the understandings necessary to bridge the gap between *ideas* about constructivism, student control, power theory, and teaching for thinking, and their *applications* in the early childhood classroom. What also makes this pedagogy appealing is that teachers are easily able to observe that effectively implemented, P-D-R delivers on its promises with respect to learning outcomes.

The data gathered from educators and students over the years are compelling, and they reach beyond the early childhood classrooms to student learning at all instructional levels. Students enjoy and much prefer working under conditions where they are able to exercise control over their learning; students enjoy and much prefer working in environments where they and their choices are respected. Students point to their growth in their problem solving skills, their "can-do" spirit, and in their ability to take on new challenges. Their sense of self-worth is seen to be substantially strengthened. (See, for example, Kohn, 1998; and Wassermann, 1992)

Teachers' observations concur with these student findings. Moreover, teachers are quickly able to see that by "playing" first, following up the play with serious, intelligent discussion that provokes thoughtful inquiry, and following that with opportunities to extend investigative inquiries and gather additional information, learning is enhanced, and a strong knowledge base built. Concerns about the "non-motivated" student and students "on task" and "behavior" seem to melt away. And this appears to be true whether this pedagogy is used in primary or middle grades, in the strict content areas of the secondary school, in education courses, or in professional development workshops. In fact, under a different set of labels, the pedagogy may be seen in widespread use in the highly acclaimed case method approach of the Harvard Graduate School of Business. While all of this was reported in the first edition, the cumulative evidence from students and teachers over the years continues to substantiate earlier claims. (See, for example, Bracey, 1998; Gorman, Plucker, & Callahan, 1998; and Lewin, 1999)

In a realm outside of the classroom, data from studies on "learned helplessness" provided startling information about the psychological mindset of adults with "can-do" attitudes and the effect of those attitudes on overall physical health. In his book, *Learned Optimism*, Martin Seligman (1991) wrote:

> The defining characteristic of pessimists is that they tend to believe bad events will last a long time, will undermine everything they do, and are their own fault. The optimists, who are confronted with the same hard knocks of this world, think about misfortune in the opposite way. They tend to believe defeat is just a temporary setback. . . . Such people are unfazed by defeat. Confronted by a bad situation, they perceive it as a challenge to try harder. (pp. 4–5)

These data appear to be consonant with the views about the "can-do" and "can't-do" child, discussed in the first edition of *Serious Players*. Where Seligman's work takes us, however, is into the connection between "can-do" and "can't-do" mindsets, and physical health. His research shows that "learned helplessness ["can't-do" adults] doesn't just affect behavior; it also reaches down into the cellular level and makes the immune system more passive" (p. 173). When the immune system is thus weakened, the body becomes more susceptible to disease. Optimists ("can-do" adults) have better health; pessimists ("can't-do" adults) are more vulnerable to disease. Seligman supports these claims with an abundance of data from studies he conducted and supervised over the last 25 years.

The relationship between learned helplessness and longevity was substantially supported by data from Seligman's long-range research begun with a group of Harvard University male undergraduates, who were followed up through age 60. This study found that health, at age 60, was strongly related to optimism at age 25; pessimistic men began to come down with diseases of middle age earlier and more severely than optimistic men, and the differences in health by age 45 were already large. In this study, when many factors were entered into the equation, optimism stood out as the primary determinant of health, beginning at age 45 and continuing for the next 20 years.

In retrospect, it makes sense. A "can-do" mindset allows children and adults to believe they have control over their lives, that they can affect change for the better. They believe that they have the "power to do." They are able to take on challenges, and they thrive on challenge. A "can't-do" mindset communicates an inability to affect change in one's life; beliefs that the power "to do" lies not with self, but with others. Challenges are perceived as obstacles, and are responded to with passivity. As I have written in the first edition, the roots of "can-do" and "can't-do" attitudes are formed in early childhood; and teachers play pivotal roles in cultivating these mindsets in the early childhood grades. That embracing learning is a concomitant of a "can-do" spirit has already been demonstrated; that overall good health and longevity is also compromised by a "can't-do" attitude now gives greater weight to the urgency of the role teachers must play in promoting a sense of "can-do" in their young charges.

What then, might have been added to this new edition? Upon reflection, it seemed to me that, at the very least, two major additions were necessary. These thoughts were borne out by two helpful and provocative reviewers, Cheryl Macdonald and Patricia Nourot, to whom I owe a large debt of gratitude. First, it seemed important to examine the significant educational trends and issues of the past decade and make connections between them and the content of the text. For example, how would current thinking about issues like diversity, multiple intelligence, constructivism, authentic evaluation, and reflective practice relate to the theory and practices being advocated here? What role, for example, does the Reggio Emilia approach play in our thinking about early childhood education and to what extent is that approach consonant with P-D-R? How does performance assessment fit with this approach? Additions with respect to these issues are interwoven in relevant chapters, and new bibliographical references have been included.

Second, in these past few years, we have been witness to the most unspeakable examples of violence in our schools—shootings, murders, suicides—students going on rampages with guns and assault weapons, killing and maiming their schoolmates and teachers. The shock waves created by these occurrences reverberated throughout the international community, and teachers everywhere asked themselves, "What could we have done to prevent this?" It seemed to me that this book should also address issues of morality, character development, and social responsibility, and show how these could be incorporated within a P-D-R lens in a primary classroom. A new chapter, "Using Serious Play to Examine Moral/Ethical Dilemmas" (Chapter 12), assumes the burden of providing teachers with tools and teaching strategies for dealing with character development and social responsibility "head on" in the early childhood years.

In working on this new edition, I have tried to protect what has been valued in the original text, as well as including new material that addresses more current concerns. It is my earnest hope that the new edition will continue to "speak" to teachers, as well as provide them with the means to bridge the gap between what they *know* and what they *do*.

There are many whose contributions to both editions must be acknowledged, and I want to express my gratitude to all, individually and collectively: Jack, my husband of very many years, who is my chief ally, resource, and constant support; Susan Liddicoat, my indefatigable editor, whose efforts on behalf of both manuscripts helped to bring greater clarity to the ideas and to the writing; my very cool grandsons, Simon and Arlo, who remain delighted that they gave me their pictures to use when they were still toddlers; students and colleagues who allowed me to make use of their words—Bernie Kollishke, Deborah Dunn, Linda Muttit, Sonia O'Connor, Cheryl MacDonald, Heather McAllister, and Neil and Maureen McAllister; and Sol Pavony, whose question "What's important?" continues to keep me humble.

Maeve was glad to see the end of school in June. Her kindergarten year had been a highly structured, formal program, in which individual work on tasks, silence, workbook exercises, and formal lessons highlighted each day. A little "trooper," she went each morning, albeit reluctantly, into the mouth of the dragon, and "graduated" from kindergarten with a certificate of achievement. "Well, Maeve," asked her neighbor in mid-summer, "are you looking forward to starting Grade 1 in September?"

"No, thanks, Mrs. Moffatt," Maeve told her. "I'm through with school. I think I'd prefer home schooling much better."

This new edition is dedicated to those miraculous early childhood teachers who continue, in the face of adversity, to advocate for children; and whose work inspires children to find pleasure and satisfaction in learning so that they never want to be through with school.

Selma Wassermann
Vancouver, B.C.
November, 1999

# Part I

# PERSPECTIVES

# CHAPTER 1

# The Can–Do Child

"I'm not little. I'm four."

Never underestimate young children, for, if you do, you are bound to be surprised. Young children are more than just delightful. They are wise, thoughtful, and reflective. They are astutely observant and sensitively aware. They are highly intuitive, resourceful, and able to make cognitive leaps of insight that set adults agog. When Jennifer had once more pushed her mother's patience to the edge, her mother, pretending to be distraught, bantered, "Jennifer, if you don't start behaving right now, I'm going to put a 'For Sale' sign on you and stand you right outside on the road." Whereupon her 4-year-old brother Hans, immediately discerning the subtle humor, wittily countered with, "Why don't you take her down to the corner store? She'll sell much faster there."

We often wonder where children pick up these ideas. We are constantly amazed at the way they gather data through all of their senses and demonstrate again and again not only the ability to "receive" this information from the ebb and flow of life around them but to make some sense of it, by discriminating, synthesizing, and integrating it with a sophisticated intelligence that is frequently laced with dry humor.

By age 4, most children have already mastered one of the most complex and difficult tasks of their lives—the learning of oral language. Without formal teaching, they comprehend complicated instructions, nuances of tone and expression, and the subtle messages of affect conveyed by body language. Without formal teaching, they master new vocabulary and fit new words almost immediately into their language repertoire. "Come and tarry with me for a moment," Grandma invites 3-year-old Arlo as she taps her lap. He stops and reflects and then counters, "First, I'll tarry with my momma," and he follows his own advice and snuggles into his mother's lap. Without formal instruction, young children construct complex sentences with subjects and predicates, nouns and verbs, subordinate and subjunctive clauses, objective and subjective cases. They use metaphor and imagery like poets. "Look at the clouds, Mom. Like fluff, like fluff, like fluffy fluff in the sky," Shannon makes a poem as effortlessly as she describes that the milk is not *on top* of the cereal but *under* it. Many "smalls" also play with language and sounds, inventing new words because such invention and sound play delight them. "Caterpillars turn into butterflowers," chuckles Rachel, delighted at her word play.

Most young children, left to their own devices, can play resourcefully on their own or with small playmates for long periods. Often this play is investigative; they are the most ardent scientific inquirers, bent on discovering "what makes it work" or "how that happened." Replication of experiment is far from boring for them; they prefer repetition, taking pleasure in sameness as well as delight in variation. Simon, at 3, plays "tamp, tamp, tamp" with a rock in the shallows of a small stream, as he watches how the weight of the rock flattens the pile of mud he has mounded. The water washes over the flattened spot, obliterating it completely, and he says, "Ha!" and begins another mound. He mounds and tamps until his father comes to fetch him for lunch. A "short attention span" may be a label *we* have invented to explain why young children are not interested in doing the things *we* think they should do. It rarely applies to children who are purposefully engaged in inquiries of their own invention. We need only to observe young children at play to note their inventiveness, their experimental testing, their ability to "stick to it," their creative solutions.

Well-integrated, healthy young children have already established a strong sense of *can-do*. They *want* to do things for themselves, and they receive great satisfaction and ego affirmation when they are able to demonstrate that they can do. Sometimes they feel grievously affronted when adults intervene to do *for* children what they are quite able to do for themselves. For example, Teddy, at age 4, becomes hurt and angry when his mother, in a hurry, unbuckles his seat belt after she has parked the car. "I can do that for myself!" he storms, his pride offended. The unconscious action of his mother has inadvertently diminished him.

Carla watches her mother scrape carrots. "I can do it too," she says, meaning, *Give me a chance to learn.* As she engages in such tasks, her competence grows and her skills are extended. In the early childhood years, the need to demonstrate skill, accomplishment, and performance is very much tied in with ego development and the building of belief in self as able — what I call the can-do spirit.

We have heard young children say, "Let me try it," "I can do it," and "Look at me do it." Children are asking for opportunities to test their competence. When that competence is affirmed, perceptions of self as *able* grow and become building blocks in the developmental process of can-do. Ego is strengthened, self-esteem blossoms, and children's sense of personal power — that perceived ability to make a change in your environment or in yourself — is significantly advanced.

On the other hand, when can-do needs are thwarted, when adults "do for" young children and thus seriously reduce their options and their fields of endeavor, when children's efforts are met with impatience or ridicule, they learn that they *can't do*. They learn to rely on others to do for them and to help them in their life's work. The literature in human growth and development suggests that the seeds of can-do and can't-do adults are sown in the formative years of early childhood experiences (Elkind, 1978; Erikson, 1968; Gruen, 1986; Purkey, 1970). These data affirm that the growing of can-do children is the key to effective schooling, while the mental handicapping that produces the can't-do youngster must be avoided at all costs.

No responsible adult consciously sets out to handicap young children mentally. Yet it is clear that some children (and some young adults) suffer from crippling can't-do beliefs about themselves. While the most recent studies of babies have shown that they demonstrate sophisticated abilities to discriminate, to choose, to integrate information, and to manipulate the environment assertively to satisfy their needs (Quinn, 1982), beliefs still persist that young children are largely incapable and incompetent and that adults must "do for" them at every step of their learning experience.

Other kinds of adult interventions also reduce children's opportunities to develop a sense of can-do. Some adults may be overprotective or overcontrolling, and such behaviors acted out upon children seriously impair their ability to develop personal power. Some adults may have the misguided idea that, unless they do everything for young children, they will be thought of as neglectful. Who among us has not been sorely tempted to "help" as we watch a young child experiencing frustration at unwrapping a parcel, putting a key in a lock, or unbuttoning a raincoat? "Here, Danielle," we'd like to say. "Let me do that for you." It is very difficult for even the most sensitive adults to walk the thin line between doing too much and doing too little, knowing when to intervene and when to hold back. But, when we can thoughtfully allow children the full range of their own attempts to do for themselves, the foundations of can-do are demonstrably established, producing energetic, resourceful, inventive, capable, fully functioning adults. When we do not allow this growth to take its natural course, we get the opposite result: dependent, submissive, handicapped adults who are imprisoned by fears of failure, by their conviction that they can't do.

## DEVELOPING PERSONAL POWER

The word *power* has a bad reputation. When we think of power, we generally think of it in its negative sense. We associate it with unpleasant feelings and actions, with needs to dominate, control, and exert influence over others. Power has decidedly good sides, however; for example, the power of a play to move an audience to tears, the power of an orator to stir, the power of an idea to inspire action. The exhilaration one experiences from an extraordinary accomplishment — reaching the mountaintop after a long and arduous climb — is also related positively to power. This sense of *power-to* — what we feel as a result of something important accomplished for our own satisfaction — feeds the ego. The message given to self is: I can do this! There is something special about me!

A person who sits in a power seat with power over others is much to be feared and despised. We have seen numerous examples of the use of violent cruelty in the exercise of power over others, and we have seen the use of power over others to satisfy personal greed. In almost every circumstance, *power-over* means the use of resources to control the freedoms of others for personal satisfaction or gain (French, 1985).

Power-to, on the other hand, increases pleasure. It is related to ego strength, self-confidence, and heightened personal autonomy. Persons with a well-developed sense of power-to are adults who are able to be "in charge" of their lives. Carl Rogers (1961) has called these adults "fully functioning." We have seen how they operate in our professional circles, among our friends, and in the marketplace of life, and we admire them. There is a positive spirit about them. In tough situations they are able to take charge, and their actions reveal thoughtful and intelligent plans. When faced with a problem requiring some innovative procedure, they do not shirk but rather embrace the problem with a positive energy. We trust them to find solutions. *Their* confidence in *themselves* fills *us* with confidence in *them*. A very good example of such a person is Richard Feynman. That he took the Nobel Prize in physics is only one indication of his extraordinary can-do spirit. What is even more extraordinary is that he lived with an unshakable belief in his own capability to *do*, which allowed him to take on tasks far outside his original area of expertise. Safecracking and painting were just two of his other skills requiring quite diverse talents, and he succeeded in doing them with remarkable ease. When Feynman was faced with a problem that required an immediate solution and for which he had no previously developed talents, he invariably began with a positive attitude about his potential for finding a solution. Inevitably he found one (Feynman, 1985).

What kinds of growth conditions allow for the development of power-to? How can people grow to believe in themselves with such unshakable confidence? How is such positive growth turned inside out, resulting instead in an unsatiable need for power over others? What's the relationship between power-over and power-to?

There is some reason to believe that the development of a sense of personal power is an emotional-needs derivative. Like our basic human needs for love, belonging, and economic security, we may also have the need for power-to inherent in our human makeup. Glasser, writing in his book *Control Theory in the Classroom* (1985), tells us that "all of our behavior is always our best attempt to satisfy at least five powerful forces which, because they are built into our genetic structure, are best called basic needs" (p. 14). One is the physiological need to stay alive and reproduce; the other four, all psychological needs, are "belonging (which includes love), power, freedom and fun" (p. 14). Everything we do may thus be seen as aimed at satisfying one or more of these needs.

Children who grow up in environments in which they are loved, where they feel they belong, and where they feel safe and emotionally secure become emotionally healthy adults. Children who grow up in environments in which there is little or no emotional nurturance grow up "haywire," with very little chance of their becoming emotionally whole adults. In very extreme cases, loss of nurturing love has even resulted in the tragic deaths of otherwise physically healthy babies (Spitz, 1949). Serious neglect of a child's emotional needs may result in maladaptive behaviors that present grave problems for the child, the family, and the community at large. The data suggest that the potential and likely results of emotional-needs deprivation include extreme forms of aggression, obedient submission, withdrawal, acute psychosomatic symptoms of illness, and regression to more primitive forms of behavior (Raths, 1973/1998).

If the development of a sense of personal power or power-to is accepted as yet one more emotional need that forms a part of our basic human needs makeup, it also follows that it must be adequately satisfied in the early years of childhood if children are to grow into adults who believe in their own capability — can-do adults. Power-to needs are fed when adults allow children choices; when even very young children may exercise their own options in situations that genuinely matter to them. Allowing children options implicitly communicates that we believe in them and in their ability to do. When they are given options, when they are allowed to choose, when their choices are respected, they grow to believe in themselves. They learn that they can do. A sense of can-do and feelings of personal power are thus intimately connected. Children learn to believe that they have the power to make a change, that they have control over their environment. I'm not sure why it is so, but it is clear that exercising one's power-to is enormously satisfying. We can see it with even the youngest children, who wish to have their choice and who, when choice is given, are satisfied, even elated.

When the power to choose is taken away by others who exercise the options in their behalf, children become frustrated, even enraged. Kohn (1998) cites apathy and disengagement, as well as thoughtlessness and aggression as behavioral symptoms of powerlessness, resulting when adults take away students' control over what they are doing. Through such adult actions, children learn that they are not to be trusted to decide for themselves. They learn not that they can do, but that they can't do. They learn to doubt themselves. When their drives for power-to continue to be thwarted, children are likely to show increased frustration and anger that reveals itself in acts of aggression. It is no wonder that adults with frustrated power-to needs desire power-over.

Power-over needs are compensatory, in that they seek to make up for personal power deficits. They are also ways of acting out feelings of aggression. Maladaptive behaviors resulting from power-to needs deficits may take a variety of forms. The most extreme include very bizarre acts of aggression and terrorism we read about in the newspapers and in the history books, such as those committed by torturers, secret police forces, the Ku Klux Klan, terrorist groups, dictators, and, lamentably, children with guns. In all these cases, bodily harm, violence, and destruction become the route to power-over needs satisfaction. The more moderately aggressive forms of maladaptive behavior include that of "highly controlling" adults in positions of power who maintain control over the options of others. There are also the more mildly aggressive forms, expressed in the need for heavy-duty motorcycles or noisy, intrusive portable radios, where the operator can unleash a surge of power on the environment and its inhabitants. Whether mild or extreme, the message to the world is the same: "Look at me! I have power!" This indicates a desperate need to demonstrate power through external force and an acute lack of confidence that true power resides within.

Other subtle forms of behavior suggesting personal power deficits are found in the relentless acquisition of power accoutrements: the key to the executive washroom; higher positions in power hierarchies; and the acquisition of certain high-status material goods such as expensive cars, homes in fashionable or exclusive places, and designer clothes. These more subtle power trappings supposedly make an individual feel more powerful, yet the terrible need to demonstrate this once again signals inner deficits.

Unsatisfied needs for power-to can never be adequately met through power-over actions. A person caught up in a power-over drive may seek to increase a power-over base but will never be adequately satisfied. The more one has, the more one wants. Nor can power-to needs be met through the acquisition of power "toys." One may be caught up in an ever-increasing spiral of material acquisition, none of which every adequately compensates for inner power-to deficits.

While aggressive behaviors are one manifestation of inadequately satisfied power-to drives, at the other end of the behavioral spectrum are those adults who have given up. For whatever reasons, aggression has given way to obedient submission. As children, many of these adults learned habits of obedience, bowing to others' commands and turning to them to be "in charge" of them. Their courage to try, to take risks, to decide for them-selves has shrunk and "fear of doing" has become part of their essence. Instead of an inner core of can-do, of personal power, they are burdened with an overwhelming sense of personal defeat. As adults, their handicaps make them vulnerable to the power-over plays of others. In any circum-stance where you see obedient submission to a dominant, controlling au-thority, you see examples of adults who have been disempowered. The gamut of these submissive behaviors extends from the obedient and docile wife who must ask permission from her husband for any decision of conse-quence, to the incomprehensible suicides of the scores of adults and chil-dren who were ordered to take their lives by the "Reverend" Jim Jones. Seligman (1991) refers to this behavior as "learned helplessness" (p. 15).

People who have developed a sense of personal power, whose feelings of can-do are strong and highly developed, have little need to acquire power trappings for reassurance. Individuals who feel empowered do not need to exercise power over others nor allow others to control their lives.

## GROWING THE CAN-DO CHILD:
## BUILDING BLOCKS OF EMPOWERMENT

Adults — parents, teachers, and significant others — are the people who are largely responsible for the healthful development of young children. Like growing flowers, where certain specific conditions are provided to produce beautiful blossoms (e.g., good-quality soil, sunlight, water, fertilizer, prop-er temperature), adults provide the conditions that establish the growing ground for empowered children. These conditions include, of course, pro-vision for children's physical safety and well-being, as well as emotional nurturance, respect for children as persons and for their right to exercise their own choices, opportunities for active engagement in tasks that chal-lenge thinking, and opportunities for creative and investigative play. It is with these last three — the building blocks of personal power — that the rest of this chapter is concerned.

### Respecting Children as Persons and Respecting Their Choices

While physical safety and emotional nurturance stand at the head of any list of essential growth conditions for children, I put behaving respectfully right there at the top as well. When children feel respected, they strength-en that aspect of personhood upon which all healthful psychological growth rests: self-respect. Empowerment rests on self-respect; the absence of self-respect is diminishing.

Respect is shown when children receive recognition for who they are and what they do. In this way, we respect them as persons. Respect is also shown when children are allowed to choose for themselves, that is, when they are allowed to make decisions affecting their lives and when their decisions are acknowledged and valued. In this way, we show respect for their right to function on their own, apart from us, as separate, able persons. Children who are allowed to make their own choices grow to see themselves as independent persons who can influence the environment in which they live. They learn to see themselves as persons of worth.

This is not to suggest, of course, that children should have choices about everything they do; that would be absurd. We would not allow choices in life-threatening situations, nor would we allow choice where certain options are unwise or unwarranted or simply inappropriate. Choices do not have to be made from among unlimited options. Children may still have control over their choices when they are choosing from among three or four options. Opportunities for choice should be genuine, and offered when appropriate. Empowering children means increasing children's choices and respecting their decisions.

Respect for children is not shown by deferential treatment, by fawning, by patronizing them, by telling them that what they *know* to be true is false. Respect is not shown through excessive praise of everything a child does. On the contrary, excessive praise is likely to be as harmful as overt neglect, for it is phony.

Respect is shown through interactions that attend thoughtfully to what children have to say, through our attempts to understand what is being said and felt, and through our nonjudgmental acceptance of those feelings and thoughts. Respect is shown through interactions that are genuine. The communication of respect for children is not at all different from how adults communicate respect for other adults.

Primary classrooms that routinely provide many opportunities for children to choose, to decide on matters of substance, are places where children have greater opportunities to increase their personal power. Here's how respect for the child's choice might be observed:

The Grade 1 class is choosing activities for the morning's free-play time. One by one the children make a choice from the following options: puzzles, reading, cut-and-paste, drawing, Lego, games. When a choice has been made, the child then moves to that activity center. It's Jaime's turn to choose, and he picks Lego. It is the fifth time in a row that he has chosen Lego, and the teacher has a moment of concern that he may be limiting his own play experiences to a single activity. How does a teacher communicate these concerns, yet show respect for Jaime's choice?

"You must really love Lego, Jaime. You keep choosing it again and again."

Or, "Lego is always your first choice, Jaime. You don't seem to want to choose anything else."

In either response, Jaime's choice is respected and treated courteously. Both responses implicitly ask Jaime to think about that choice in relation to other options. Both allow Jaime to have the final say about his choice.

Disrespect for Jaime's choice is shown by rejecting it, by manipulating it, by taking away his option to choose:

"Jaime, you have had five turns at Lego this week. It's time for you to choose another activity."

Or, "Now, Jaime, don't you think you've had enough Lego for this week? Don't you think you should try something else?"

Or, "You haven't been to the puzzles yet, so you'd better go there today. You can't do Lego all the time, Jaime."

Communicating and showing respect for children occurs when adults can let go of their need to persuade children that they must always obediently "do as I say." When Claudia says, "I'm tired now. I don't want to do this work anymore," and her teacher urges, "You must finish it" or "Just do a little more" or "You won't be able to go out to play unless you finish," she communicates neither respect for the child's feelings nor acceptance of what she has said as having validity. On the contrary, such manipulation of children disempowers them.

It is easy to be disrespectful of young children. They are physically smaller than we are, and if push comes to shove, we have the upper hand. They have less ability to control their needs, and their needs, wants, and drives can be exceedingly tiresome. Because they have less experience, they need lengthier and more in-depth explanations, and this is especially annoying when adults are in a hurry (which we are a lot of the time). We attribute to children the need to be told, to be shown, to be directed, and to have their lives happily organized by us; and we believe that we have the right to do these things because we are smarter, know more, and know better what is best for them. It is easy for us to manipulate children successfully, to get them to do what we want them to do or think they *should* do, and lots of adults exercise such power over children a lot of the time. But the rewards we reap from such behavior, from such disempowerment, are grim. What's more, through such actions, we have given children powerful role models of how to behave when they get to be adults who may then exercise their power over others.

Listening to adults talk to children in different settings reveals how disrespect habitually occurs:

- Willy, age 6, shinnies up a supporting pole and begins traversing the horizontal ladder, hand over hand, his small body twisting under the physical stress of the activity. He goes to the fourth rung and then drops about 7 feet to the ground with a gasp. His father, watching, yells for the world to hear, "What's the matter with you Willy? Your brother can do better than that!"
- Sonia, age 5, is sitting with her parents, waiting for the whale show to begin at the city aquarium. They have been waiting for more than 15 minutes, and Sonia is beginning to be restless. She starts to kick her feet out, in a rhythmic pattern, expressing some of her frustration. Her mother reproaches, "You can't be taken anywhere! Stop that at once. That's the last time I'm taking you to see the whales."
- Adam is reluctant to enter the pool area at the playground. This is his first time here, and he knows none of the children. His father urges, "Don't be a baby. Get in there. There's nothing to be afraid of."
- Arthur requests permission to go to the bathroom, and his teacher admonishes that he *should* have gone during recess, that he can't just go to the bathroom whenever *he* wants.
- Sarah hasn't finished her worksheet in the allotted time and is told by her teacher that she has been wasting her time and not trying her best.

It is easy to forget, as these negative judgments slip from our tongues, the power of such statements to undermine and diminish children's self-respect, to make them unsure of themselves, doubtful, uncertain. It is easy to forget, in our drive to *teach* children our way, that we may, in fact, be disempowering them.

Teachers play a pivotal role in building children's respect for themselves, and for some unhappy children, teachers can play *the* pivotal role. For, even as we must not underestimate children, so we may not underestimate the power of a teacher to breathe new life into children and to empower them for all of their lives. When we think about our own teachers, particularly those who have been powerful forces that shaped us as adults, we inevitably think of those memorable people who empowered us. If we remember what they did and how they did it, and why we remember *them* above all the others, we will recall that they respected us; that they seemed to understand how we felt; that they recognized and appreciated who we were and what we did; that they asked for our ideas and listened to them with serious consideration. They increased, rather than crushed, our choices. They asked for our opinions and used them in making important decisions about what was happening in the class. When such respect is shown for children's persons and their choices, self-respect grows. Children who respect themselves are empowered.

## Providing Active Learning Experiences
## That Genuinely Challenge Thinking

A second condition in empowering young children is active experiences with tasks that are a genuine challenge to their thinking. Such experiences begin at early stages of life, even in the cradle. A mother puts a rattle out and shakes it, and the baby responds by turning toward it and reaching for it. Grabbing the rattle is a challenging task for an infant; she must process some data before she is able to connect hand with rattle. When she has performed the task, the mother makes her acknowledgment and regard explicit. "What a smart girl!" The baby smiles. Though she does not comprehend the language, the tone of voice and the look on Mother's face tell the baby the entire story of delight in the accomplishment.

In toddler years, we give children other active learning tasks that challenge: puzzles to assemble, blocks to build with, balls to throw and catch, beads to string. We also invite them to help with the household chores: putting enough spoons on the table, fetching three potatoes from the bin, finding the matching shoe in the closet, holding the dustpan under the swept-up crumbs. Children seek and need active engagement in activities that challenge them. When we allow for and encourage this, we are building feelings of empowerment, of can-do, of personal satisfaction in their own achievements.

As children grow, we encourage them with more complex and more sophisticated active learning challenges: dialing a telephone, tying shoelaces, finding the can of tomatoes in the pantry. We encourage them to engage in problem-solving situations that require concrete and abstract processing; that call for developing new skill, understanding, and meaning. In these challenges to their problem-solving abilities, a critical dimension is that of active, purposeful engagement. In every task, there is a real need for the task to be done, and the child is aware of this. The cause-and-effect relationship between what is being done and the results is clear and connected to what the child personally sees as important. The challenge must not be contrived if it is to retain its significance as a challenge. It must also be developmentally appropriate — neither too simple nor excessively beyond reach — if it is to be effective in building personal power. In almost every case, such challenges require children's experiential involvement in the task. It is not enough for them simply to watch others do. It is not enough for them simply to listen to explanations of how it should be done. They must do it themselves. Through repeated, everyday experiences with such tasks, children learn habits of thinking and gain confidence in themselves as thinkers, as problem solvers. Such confidence builds feelings of personal power, of "I can do."

When young children come to school, they face other challenges, some of which have very little to do with building feelings of can-do. They may be challenged to sit for long periods of time; to sit in small, confined places without a lot of wriggling; to be silent. They may be challenged to follow a school schedule that is not in harmony with their own organic growing needs; to obey and do as they are told; to eat food that they do not like; to perform bodily functions on schedule, rather than out of physical need. They may be challenged to complete tasks that have little meaning for them; to say they enjoy activities that they in fact despise; to pretend to be interested in books that are substantially dull. None of these challenges, unfortunately, contributes to empowerment, nor does any of them provide any real challenge to young children's higher-order thinking. In fact, the opposite is true: We are training them to be obediently submissive, to do as they are told, to bow to our power over them.

Teachers can do a great deal to empower children as they provide them with opportunities to engage in real activities that challenge their thinking. In Heather Hamilton's kindergarten classroom, students have been grouped for investigative play with science materials. She has gathered the materials to be used and placed them where the children can get to them easily. In one group, the children are carrying on investigations with prisms. An observer sees them designing increasingly sophisticated inquiries that start with, "I wonder what would happen if . . . ?" In another group, they are making observations of three eggs—one that is fresh, one that has been immersed in a vinegar solution for 2 days, and a third that has been immersed in a vinegar solution for 2 weeks. The children decide how their investigations are to be conducted: how and when to break the eggs, how to examine them, and what to look for. These investigations are genuine challenges for them. They learn habits of thinking as they figure out ways to test hypotheses and interpret data, all the while creating new investigations. In each situation, children are actively involved in learning tasks. It is the children who are doing and thinking, rather than sitting and listening to the teacher's thinking.

The teacher is on the periphery of this activity. She has given over control of the learning operations to the children. While she is never far away, psychologically or physically, she does not take direct action in the children's investigations. She is there to answer questions if they arise, or to deal with crises and lend psychological support. Otherwise, she does not intervene to direct what the students are learning. In allowing children control over their decisions of what to do and in allowing them to create and take on these challenges, Heather provides the conditions in which they grow in personal power. In that way she empowers them.

In Brady Kaslo's Grade 1 class, children are routinely challenged by his whole-language program. Their writing and reading skills grow as children exercise choice over what books they read and what stories they write in their journals. They are challenged by working as writers do, in reviewing their stories and in making the corrections they feel necessary. Brady's language arts program is a genuine challenge to children's thinking. As children grow in their capability to take on these challenges, they develop habits of thinking. When thinking capabilities are strengthened, children are empowered.

Active engagement in tasks that challenge students' thinking may not occur simply as occasional "enrichment activities" in the classroom program. They must be part of the normal routine. Unless there is much active involvement and much challenge to higher-order thinking, the habits of thinking that empower children as can-do problem solvers will not have adequate opportunity to grow.

### Ensuring Opportunities for Creative and Investigative Play

In an era of educational accountability where behavioral objectives are spelled out with specificity and a teacher's competence is determined by how well those objectives have been met, I realize that it is courting disaster to come out in favor of the time-worn idea that "play is children's work" and that play experiences are fundamental in the development of children's personal power. No matter how much lip service we may give to the need for play in the developmental experiences of young children, operating conditions in many primary classrooms nevertheless attest to what some teachers, deep in their hearts, believe really counts: seatwork! Seatwork and other pencil-and-paper tasks seem to be the *real* stuff of classroom life. When that work is done, when the jobs have been completed to the teacher's satisfaction, when the *product* is considered acceptable, the child may, if there is some time left over, play.

Our rhetoric may sanction play, but what is seen in classroom practice betrays what is considered to have the greater value. Work and play are not seen as complementary. Work is hard. You have to suffer a bit. What's more, the suffering is good for you. When you are finished working, you may then be permitted to play. We may be considerably liberated in our thinking about many of our own sociocultural mores, but it is the Puritan ethic that drives much of what we require children to do in school.

Teachers who are, by and large, products of their own extensive programming as pupils in the public school system have implicitly come to regard play as suspect. At best, it is frivolous. Time is wasted in play when it could be used more productively *working*! We might have a nice time, but that's not what school is for! A teacher who has allowed the "play period" to carry on for longer than scheduled will doubtless feel guilty. The time has not been used productively. The teacher has not fulfilled the responsibility of bringing the children back from their pleasurable experiences, to work!

Such beliefs about work and play permeate our adult lives as well. The achievement-oriented workaholic is our role model; the dreamer patronizingly tolerated. As professionals, we must give ourselves permission to play, and even then only when we feel we have "earned" the right to do so by having worked productively beforehand. First work, then play. If we reverse the order, we are immediately defensive. These value systems that we hold for work and play are as deeply entrenched as almost any other values we hold.

Yet virtually all of our experience in observing the behavior of young children at play tells us a different story. We see young children at play learning much, and we say, "Yes, this is good. They are learning what is important." We see them designing experiments, exploring, investigating, making decisions, solving problems. We see them generate, create, invent. We see them grow in their risk-taking capabilities, becoming more bold. We see them use language more skillfully and relate to each other more successfully. As we observe young children playing, the boundaries of what is work and what is play evaporate. We know, in fact, that children are working, and in these work-play settings we see what they are learning. We see how play empowers them. Why, then, is it so hard for us to believe and accept this as good, as having validity in our early childhood programs?

The data are unequivocally on the side of play. Bruno Bettelheim, writing in *Atlantic* (1987), reminds us that play is a means for a child to cope with past and present concerns, and that "play is the child's most useful tool for preparing himself for the future and its tasks" (p. 36). Citing the work of Karl Groos and Jean Piaget, Bettelheim points to play's function in developing cognitive and motor abilities, as well as the child's intellectual development:

> Play teaches the child, without his being aware of it, the habits most needed for intellectual growth, such as stick-to-itiveness, which is so important in all learning. Perseverance is easily acquired around enjoyable activities such as chosen play. But if it has not become a habit through what is enjoyable, it is not likely to become one through an endeavor like school work. (p. 36)

He further argues that, through play, children learn that they do not need to give up in despair if things don't work out the first time; that success can be theirs if they persevere. These are attitudes that do not develop when work is geared only to the child's successful performance, or when praise comes only when success is demonstrated.

Jerome Bruner (1985), cognitive psychologist and professor emeritus at Harvard University, has conducted extensive studies of young children at play, and his data should be enough to convince even the most die-hard doubters that what we have observed with our own eyes has been borne out by empirical investigation:

> There is evidence that by getting children to play with materials that they must later use in a problem-solving task, one gets superior performance from them in comparison with those children who spend time familiarizing themselves with the materials in various other ways. . . . The players generate more hypotheses and they reject wrong ones more quickly. They seem to become frustrated less and fixated less. (p. 603)

Players work for feedback, rather than for reward, and "play has the unique character of dissociating means and ends to permit exploration of their relation to each other" (p. 603).

How does play empower children? It encourages flexibility and openness; it asks them to be involved for the sake of the experience, for the sake of the *play*, rather than for any external reward or approval. Play is generative. It is satisfying. Children enjoy play, and they enjoy themselves while doing it. They are encouraged to take risks, within parameters of safety, that extend their learning horizons. Play builds their conceptual awareness. As children grow in flexibility, risk-taking capability, tolerance for dissonance, and inventiveness, they grow in their belief in themselves, in their belief that they can accomplish whatever they set out to do. As a consequence, they grow in personal power (Isenberg & Quisenberry, 1988).

In examining the conditions that improve the quality of children's play, Bruner (1985) and his colleagues found that certain conditions "strikingly increase the richness and length of play" (p. 604). These include

1. *A playmate.* While an individual child rarely plays long at one thing, two children exchange and negotiate meanings and rules, and two children playing together are "the stuff of long and elaborate bouts of interactive play" (p. 604).
2. *Appropriate play materials.* "Puzzles, building blocks, miniaturized versions of life activities, etc., all provoke longer and richer play bouts than, for example, clay and fingerpaint, as these are the materials that provoke more combinatorial exploration" (p. 604).
3. *An adult nearby.* "Play bouts are longer and richer among young children when there is an adult nearby who is buffering the situation, keeping it from getting out of hand, providing occasional comfort and response. The adult is not *in* the action, but a source of stability in the situation" (p. 605).

These data, while sufficiently compelling, still do not cover all the advantages of play. It is, in fact, a many splendored thing. Play is the main source of our creativity. The majestic breakthroughs — the real masterpieces of invention throughout history — have come from the creative thinking of the most fertile, inventive minds, minds that play with ideas as children play with ideas in their experiential play. Only the level of sophistication is different. Such creators behave very much as young children; driven by endless curiosity and not satisfied to accept conventional wisdom, they are given to testing, experimenting, and exploring.

For Richard Feynman, the physicist I mentioned earlier, *play* was the pivotal experience in enabling his thinking to move forward on the physics problem that eventually led to his winning the Nobel Prize. In his provocative and delightful book, *Surely You're Joking, Mr. Feynman* (1985), he writes that, when his work in physics followed a structured pattern, he quickly became disgusted with it, no longer taking any pleasure from the work. So he taught himself to play with physics, doing whatever he felt like doing, because it was "interesting and amusing for me to play with" (p. 173). So, in the cafeteria of Cornell University, much to the chagrin of his colleagues he played with dinner plates, actually tossing them in the air and observing their "wobble rate." As he describes it,

> It was effortless. It was easy to play with those things. It was like uncorking a bottle: Everything flowed out effortlessly. I almost tried to resist it! There was no importance to what I was doing, but ultimately there was. The diagrams and the whole business that I got the Nobel Prize for came from that piddling around with the wobbling plate. (p. 174)

Ashton-Warner (1963) has written that creativity is on the other side of the human coin from destructivity. As she points out, in children are found both creative and destructive impulses, which she depicts as two vents drawn side by side. One vent is enlarged at the expense of constricting the other. We do not need glasses to see that destructive children rarely create. They spend their energies aggressively violating persons and property. Yet this can be turned around, for, as we begin to tap that creative vent, destructive impulses are diminished.

Every teacher who has watched children play knows, too, that play is a "humanizer." In play, young children work through a variety of interpersonal and social problems: "Who will be first?" "Why should I give up my turn?" "When will it be my turn?" "I don't want to share!" "Bobby has my truck." "I don't want to play with him!" "He's not being nice to me." "Sally is spitting!" "She wants my red ball."

To be human is to be a member of a group. We increase our humanness if we are able to behave cooperatively and responsibly in that group, whether it be an office, a class, a bowling league, a professional association, or a line at the bank. The more we are perceived as "cooperative and responsible," the more we are an accepted and acceptable member of that group. The less cooperative and responsible we are, the more we are rejected by the group.

In play, real emotions are expressed. Through play, we learn to tap these emotions and manage them. In these ways, we grow more fully human. Play allows us the full gamut of emotions — joy and pleasure, pain, frustration, anger, exhilaration. It may be the only in-school experience in which emotions may be naturally expressed. Through play, there is genuine, spontaneous laughter. Can we have more laughter in our primary classrooms without the feeling that we are producing a crop of idlers?

We have all seen adults who have lost their spontaneity and consequently their ability to play. Instead of real play, they may engage in directed and controlled "play-type" activities, such as organized sports and games, but what is emphasized in these activities is not so much enjoyment, but competition. "Is this a fun game or a winning game?" asks a 4-year-old, who easily discerns the critical difference.

We have also seen adults who try to legislate play at parties or in other group gatherings. Some of them have to consume quantities of alcohol before they can "let go" of their play inhibitions. Often the resulting behavior is more tragic than joyful, to all parties concerned.

Adults who have lost the joy and spontaneity of play have a missing human dimension. They may be smart, successful, competent; they may have a lot of power-over and many power toys. But they live out their lives bereft of the single human trait that brings the greatest capacity for pleasure into our lives.

If we have cultivated the art of play early in our lives, we are likely to hold onto our self-initiating behaviors, our capacity for risk taking, our inventiveness as adults. We are less likely to have to spend our considerably increased leisure time watching game shows on TV because we have not adequately developed our self-directing resources. Teachers who consistently provide opportunities for play in their early childhood programs contribute substantially to the healthful social, cognitive, and psychological empowering of young children.

☆　☆

Providing young children with learning tasks that challenge their thinking, respecting them and their ideas, allowing them choices and respecting their decisions, and encouraging and validating their creative and investigative play are the essential conditions of empowerment and the main themes of this book. Throughout the following chapters, much attention will be given to how these ideas are put to work in the primary classroom. It should also be stated once again that these are not the only conditions leading to empowerment. There are others; however, these are seen as fundamental to the growth of can-do children and the development of personal power.

# CHAPTER 2

# The Can–Do Classroom

The school is tucked out of sight on a cul de sac, hiding its advanced age and its shabby look from the mainstream downtown traffic. A relic of the time when the town was a small farming village, it now sits within a district populated by newly built tract homes and brand-new schools. While the new schools serve the newly arrived suburbanites, the C. D. Nelson Elementary School enrolls children from a markedly different population: welfare families, single parents, and other groups who live in the downtown core. The personal crises that occur each school day at the Nelson School exceed by tenfold what happens in any of the other schools in the district. The Nelson teachers have more than their share of heartache over the lives and well-being of their children.

This is my visiting day at the school. Bob Sinclair meets me in the staff room before classes begin, and he asks me to spend some time in his class that morning. He has been teaching for 5 years, but this is his first year using the play-debrief-replay approach as a way of organizing instruction for his students (Wassermann & Ivany, 1996). He wants to avail himself of any feedback I might give.

## CLASSROOM SCENE

After chatting with the school principal, I finally get to Bob's Grade 2 class by 9:30. As I walk through the door, the sight dazzles me. Five groups of children are working in investigative play groups with dry cells, buzzers, low-wattage light bulbs, and switches. They are carrying out inquiries with these materials. Bob has used the following activity card to guide them:

> Use the materials in this center to find out what you can about electricity and how it works.
> • What can you observe about the dry cells? The buzzers? The light bulb?
> Talk together about your observations and make some notes about what you did.

I take in the overall scene first and then edge quietly over to the group of five children working near the window, using dry cells and a light bulb. While they have not articulated a hypothesis, I can see that they are implicitly testing the idea that an increase in the number of dry cells strung together will increase the brightness of the light. They try increasing the number of batteries to three, and the light brightens. A shout goes up from the investigators. They begin to rewire with four dry cells. By this time, their enthusiasm has attracted an audience of children from some of the other groups, who come over to observe. The four-cell hypothesis is supported, accompanied by shouts and laughter. "Try six," one observer offers, while others go back to their groups to test the same hypothesis. Meanwhile, the group in the rear is working with a buzzer, testing different ways of wiring and clamping. When the buzzer sounds, they laugh as if watching a clown falling off a stool.

No child is off task. They are either conducting investigations or observing others' inquiries. There is no behavior management necessary. Not once does the teacher have to intervene to tell a child to "settle down" or to "behave" or to "get to work." If there are arguments, they are more about what is likely to work in the next investigation or what should be tried next. I do not observe any other interpersonal conflict. Even though it is almost time for recess, none of the children has lost interest in the investigations. When the recess bell sounds, the children respond in a wail.

"Oh, Mr. Sinclair, do we *have* to go outside today?"

Bob smiles and suggests that the children may choose to go or stay and, for those who wished to stay, he would remain in the classroom. About six children get their jackets and leave. The rest continue "sciencing."

While Bob is very much present in that classroom, he does not intervene to direct the children's investigations. He does not ever say, "Why don't you try it *this* way?" or, "Now do *this*!" His responses to the children are more reflective in nature—for example, "I see that you are now going to repeat the experiment with five dry cells"—or encouraging and supportive—for example, "Hah! I can see that you've got that working just as you hoped you would."

A small girl named Nadya approaches as he and I talk. "Mr. Sinclair, where is the masking tape?"

He tells her that, the last time he saw it, it was over on the shelf, but that she might have to look around, as other children were using it. Bob mentions to me that Nadya is new to the class and that her behavior is more dependent than most of the other children, who have at this stage of the school year (April) grown considerably in their ability to do for themselves. "But," says Bob confidently, "give her time in this program, and she will become much more independent and solve these and other kinds of problems on her own."

When the children return from recess, additional time is allocated for investigative play, with the notice that the teacher intends to "debrief" the play at 11:00. Just before the hour, Bob calls for cleanup. The materials are packed away and stored for easy access for tomorrow's investigations, and the children gather in a large group at the front of the room. Bob begins the debriefing with an invitation:

*Teacher:*   Tell me about some of the observations you made as you investigated with your dry cells.

*Frank:*   We were tryin' to see if the light would get brighter if we put more batteries on.

*Teacher:*   You added more dry cells to see if that would make any difference.

*Frank:*   Yeah.

*Teacher:*   And what did you observe?

*Kuldip:*   When we put four cells, the light got brighter. We wuz goin' to do it with six cells.

*Teacher:*   You have a hypothesis about what might happen with six cells.

*Kuldip:*   It would be very bright. Real bright.

*Teacher:*   The more cells, the brighter the light? Is that your theory?

*Kuldip:*   Yup!

*Teacher:*   Hm! I wonder how that happens. How do you explain it?

*Sarah:*   Well, I think you got more power there. You see there's power in the cells. So if you have more cells, you get more power and that makes the light brighter.

*Teacher:*   The dry cells have power. The more power, the brighter the light?

*Sarah:*   Yeh.

*Teacher:*   Thank you, Sarah, for giving us your theory. Does anyone have any observations that would support Sarah's theory — the theory that dry cells have power and, the more power you add, the more electrical energy you get?

Bob continues the debriefing in this fashion, calling for the students' ideas, listening carefully to what each child is saying, reflecting the statements accurately, building the science vocabulary, and fleshing out important concepts. He does not judge any idea as right or wrong; neither does he praise ("That's a good idea") or condemn ("No, that won't work"). He does not lead students to recite or specify certain pieces of information. Instead, he respectfully hears, attends, and "plays back" the ideas presented, using the students' statements as building blocks to help them reach for the deeper meanings underlying their investigations, the keys to conceptual understanding. In the process, each child feels listened to, respected, important. Every investigation, every idea, every child receives the same courtesy. Bob is likely, too, to raise at least one "puzzler" — a question that might spur new investigations when the children return to "replay" with the same materials in the following days. Some examples might be

- In what ways are the electric light model and the buzzer model alike? How are they different?
- Where do you suppose the "power" in the dry cell comes from? What are your thoughts on this?
- In what ways is the dry-cell–light-bulb model like the electric light system in the room? How is it different?

In the days that follow, children *replay* with the same materials, carrying out new and more sophisticated investigations or replicating investigations already done. Variables are manipulated and results compared. Bob offers some new materials, presenting new challenges: simple electric motors, dead batteries, and different types of switches.

In his classroom, Bob demonstrates how the conditions for growing can-do children are met, through respect for children and their choices, active engagement in tasks that challenge thinking, and involvement in creative and investigative play.

## PLAY-DEBRIEF-REPLAY:
## A WAY OF ORGANIZING FOR INSTRUCTION

The instructional approach called play-debrief-replay was not thought up in a university laboratory. We observed it in hundreds of classroom visits in which teachers of all grade levels found ways to supply basic learning conditions that empower students (Wassermann & Ivany, 1996). As we watched what these teachers did and as we reflected on what we had seen, we created the descriptive labels. If anyone is to be credited with the "invention" of this way of teaching, the prize belongs to classroom teachers.

It has been noted that the play-debrief-replay approach is rooted in the principles of John Dewey (1916), and I will not argue whether he created his conception of experience and reflection out of whole cloth or whether he, too, saw what he liked and liked what he saw in the work of the best classroom teachers of his day and then wrote about it. Nor will I argue that this way of teaching is original or "pure," in the sense that it belongs to a single source. Neither will I take the position that this is the only way in which children may become empowered in a classroom. I will argue, however, that providing opportunities for creative, investigative play, followed by helping children to reflect on their play experiences and then encouraging them to build on earlier experiences through replay, does what it claims: Children who learn under these classroom conditions are empowered. They learn habits of thinking, and they become more self-initiating, responsible, creative, and inventive. They grow in their capacity to understand the concepts or important ideas within the curriculum. Within their play, different learning styles, different learning tempos and different talents are all naturally accommodated. Concepts are learned and understood via the primary route of practical experience, the only way in which learners at any age actually learn to understand. Finally, children enjoy the experience. Whether a child's preferred learning mode is spatial, logical-mathematical, bodily-kinesthetic, interpersonal, intrapersonal, or linguistic (Gardner, 1991), play-debrief-replay seems to provide the learning conditions that allow each one to accommodate to his or her individual learning needs. In Gardner's terms, "intuitive" learners and the "disciplined expert" rise easily to the challenges of independent inquiry, quickly taking giant steps on the pathway of meaning making. Those students whom Gardner terms "traditional,"—those "lesson learners" who are primarily concerned with getting the right answers are, at first, bewildered by expectations that they function as independent, autonomous problem solvers. However, after several weeks of working under these conditions, even "traditional" students become more adventurous, more generative, more resourceful, more flexible.

Our field research, entitled Project-Science-Thinking, provided the initial data we needed to support these claims (Wassermann & Ivany, 1996). It was a 2-year field study carried out with 20 classroom teachers in 12 elementary schools in British Columbia. The objectives of the study were (1) to develop and implement a program for retraining practicing teachers in the principles and instructional strategies of teaching science with an emphasis on higher-order thinking and (2) to observe and assess pupil learning outcomes related to these practices. Since then, this approach has been observed in other contexts, including staff development programs; university-level education courses; professional programs using a case-study approach (e.g., the Harvard Graduate School of Business; see Christensen, 1987); and elementary and secondary school classrooms, in curriculum areas beyond science. Although data from these latter contexts have not been systematically gathered, informal evaluative feedback from hundreds of learners tends to support the claims: Students indicate that they feel respected; skill levels increase, and so does conceptual understanding. Adult learners are particularly eloquent in citing how such learning contexts empower them.[1]

---

1. Play-debrief-replay has been used as a way of organizing instruction in staff development work in the Schools Are for Thinking Projects (Abbotsford, Lake Cowichan, Nelson, and Maple Ridge, British Columbia; St. James-Assiniboine, Winnipeg; Bethel and Tukwila, Washington) and in the Faculty of Education at Simon Fraser University in the following courses: Education 483, Curriculum Studies—Teaching for Thinking; Education 485, Critical Incidents in Teaching—The Teacher as Decision Maker; Education 819, Studies in Teacher-Student Interactions.

The play-debrief-replay approach also provides teachers with a clearly articulated plan for moving teaching for thinking from the level of educational rhetoric into classroom practice; that is,

- Play activities are woven together with higher-order thinking operations, providing students with intellectual and creative challenges.
- Debriefing requires students to reflect and to search out concepts and meanings of substance.
- Replay promotes continued examination and reflection.

Programs in which children's active participation in developing their own conceptual understandings, by using their own ways of learning in a flexible environment, have been long supported in the research of Piaget and Inhelder (1969). In more recent years, constructivist theory—a child-centered orientation to teaching and learning—has evolved from this earlier work. Based on the belief that learners actively create, interpret, and reorganize knowledge in individual ways (Windschitl, 1999), constructivist classrooms operating at all instructional levels utilize pedagogies in which teachers, instead of pushing content at students, aim at in-depth understandings and appreciations.

The options for each teacher who uses a play-debrief-replay program are vast. This approach rests on respect for each teacher as a highly trained professional. There are no formulas to be followed in rote application, but an organizational scheme is suggested that is played out according to individual needs and tastes. The instructional stages may be clearly articulated, but much choice is left to the teacher with respect to the how and the what. It invites teachers to try, to experiment, to generate hypotheses to be tested in the real world of the classroom. As a teacher, can these ideas be made to work for you? Will your students learn the important concepts and skills? Will they feel better about themselves? Will they be empowered? These questions are the stuff of professional life, and this instructional approach calls upon teachers to behave as reflective practitioners with the power to control their own professional actions (Schön, 1983). This is not a program in which teachers blindly follow a set of procedures issued from "on high," from administrative power hierarchies who have subtly finessed the rights of teachers to be in charge of their own professional functioning. If children are empowered through these methods, so are teachers. In the sections that follow, the conditions for creating a play-debrief-replay program are made more explicit.

### The Play's the Thing

A teacher wishing to teach children an important concept begins by designing a play experience. The play allows children to study the concept through active, investigative examination, as was observed in Bob Sinclair's class, described at the beginning of this chapter. Play is generally carried out in cooperative learning groups, in which children contribute substantially to each other's investigations and creative endeavors. The teacher designs the play around a curriculum concept that is important for children to study and learn. The teacher also provides curriculum materials that allow for hands-on and "minds-on" investigations, organizes the learning groups, and sets the stage for the play to proceed. But the children are the players. During the play the teacher observes but does not participate or direct, unless specific behavior management is called for. This may be a new way of looking at the act of teaching, a departure from the "banking" model (Freire, 1983, p. 58) in which the teacher tells, and therefore "deposits" information into the child's head. Rather, this is a "theatrical" model in which the teacher writes the play, gathers the props, sets the stage, and, once the play has begun, assumes the role of stage manager. Stage managers see to it that the play goes on. (Directors, on the other hand, tell the players what to do and how.)

As there are plays like *Macbeth* and other plays like *Ishtar*, so are there differences between the kinds of play opportunities that teachers may design for children. The richer the play, the more potential it has for concept development, creative and investigative opportunities, and the examination of issues of substance. A play calling for observation of a button may not be worth the price of admission, while a play involving observations of many kinds of leaves may lead to substantive and far-reaching understandings.

Productive play activities that yield significant conceptual growth share several criteria in common:

1. Investigative play tasks are open-ended. They do not lead students to "the answers."
2. Play tasks call for the generation of ideas, rather than the recall of specific pieces of information.
3. Play activities challenge students' thinking; indeed, they *require* thinking. Higher-order mental challenges are built into each play task.
4. Play activities are "messy." Children are, in fact, playing around. Learning through play is nonlinear, nonsequential (Wassermann, 1989).
5. Play tasks focus on "big ideas" — the important concepts of the curriculum — rather than on trivial details.
6. Each play task provides opportunities for children to grow in their conceptual understanding. When children carry out investigative play, they grow in their ability to understand larger concepts.
7. The children are the players. They are actively involved in learning.

They are talking to each other, sharing ideas, speculating, laughing, and getting excited about what they have found. They are not sitting quietly, passively listening to the teacher's thinking.
8. The children are working together, in learning groups. Play is enhanced through cooperative investigations. Cooperation, rather than competitive individual work, is stressed.

Teachers may design open-ended play activities or those with some limits, depending on how well the children function independently, how successfully they are able to choose, and how able they are to design investigations on their own. Where children are only just beginning to work in groups and where they are, for the first time, being asked to take the initiative, rather than just following orders or directions from the text, they are likely to benefit more from play activities that allow for fewer options. After they have developed more ability to choose and more confidence in themselves as creators, play tasks that are more open ended may be added. The teacher is the one who appraises the situation and decides.

Primary teachers design investigative play activities as *the* way of teaching curriculum content, not as "extras" or enrichment activities outside the "real work" of the curriculum. Play is the vehicle through which curriculum content is intelligently and thoughtfully learned, and, because the play always involves challenges to pupils' thinking, thinking becomes the method of learning.

In the primary grades, play can and should occur in traditional creative/imaginative play activities using sand and water tables, clay, blocks, Lego or other constructions, paint, "Wendy" houses, arts and crafts, scissors and paste, music, songs, and dance. It can and should occur as well in language learning, the learning of numbering and measuring, and learning about the world in which we live through sociological and scientific inquiries.

Numerous examples of investigative play activities in the content areas of language, social studies, science, and math are given in Part III (Chapters 7–10). In each activity the curriculum concept being studied through play is identified, to demonstrate how the design of the play leads to examination of the concept. The play is presented in the form of a pupil activity card, such as the one Bob prepared for the electricity investigation. When students can read, these activity cards may be placed in the investigative play centers, so that students can use them to guide their investigations. In classes where children are not yet independent readers, teachers may read the directions on the card to the children, leaving the card with the group for reference, or write them on the chalkboard or chart paper. How or where they are written is less important than how they are used to help guide pupils in their investigations. Activity cards should not force pupil play into a lock-step set of procedures; rather, they offer guidelines that suggest action. When pupils seek to extend their play beyond what is written on the activity card, and where this is thoughtfully and experimentally done, these excursions into the beyond should be encouraged.

Designing a play experience requires teachers' awareness of how concepts are taught through pupils' active engagement with selected materials and how higher-order thinking operations are incorporated into the play task. Play activities also reflect the substantive issues of the curriculum, that is, what the teacher thinks is important for pupils to learn. Teachers who design play experiences for children in this "theatrical" model of instruction challenge themselves consistently to provide the richest learning opportunities for children. Perhaps that is why teachers who do this feel exhilarated, energized, and empowered in the process.

## Debriefing: Using Play Experience to Promote Reflection

Experiential play provides introductory learning opportunities during which children carry out explorations, investigations, and dramatic scenarios with the materials that the teacher provides. During play, children manipulate variables; generate hypotheses; design investigations; conduct tests; observe, gather, and classify data; evaluate conditions; make decisions; and learn interpersonal skills. Play experiences provide the arena for the development of conceptual understanding, for values development, and for the development of responsible group behavior.

When the play period is over (the time allocated for play will vary), the teacher uses the play experience as a basis for promoting reflection and increasing children's understanding of the "big ideas." This reflection-on-action stage has been labeled *debriefing*, and an entire chapter (Chapter 13 has been devoted to this procedure.

Teachers who approach play-debrief-replay as if they were making their first bungee jump, have been heard to express unease over the "hands-off" role advocated for the investigative play stage. "But shouldn't I be *teaching*?" they worry. They are concerned that missed opportunities to tell children what to do and why things work will result in some monstrous developmental lag. Vygotsky's work (1978) helps us to understand the concept of the "zone of proximal development" that refers to the difference between children's level of independent problem solving and their potential level of problem solving that can be attained when assisted by the teacher. During investigative play, children are likely to experience disequilibrium when things do not work, hypotheses are not supported, concepts and meanings are elusive. In fact, some play opportunities may deliberately provoke such disequilibrium, or cognitive dissonance. That dissonance, however, provides the motivation that provokes further inquiry.

It is during debriefing that the teacher assumes an active role, providing the assistance that Vygotsky describes. This assistance takes the form of provocative questions and facilitative responses that work to enable children to make sense of discrepancies, shed naive theories for more mature and informed ones, and take the next steps toward new insights and understandings. Ramsey (1998) writes that "to raise children as critical thinkers, we do not want them to achieve and remain in a comfortable state of equilibrium; instead, we want them to learn to continuously question and challenge their information and assumptions about the status quo" (p. 20). In a play-debrief-replay context, children learn not only to live with uncertainty, but to embrace it.

During debriefing, the teacher calls the group members together to discuss aspects of their play. Debriefing may be carried out with the whole class or with smaller groups of pupils, depending on which organization is more suited to the teacher's and/or group's needs. Whatever the size of the group, the teacher uses the reflective questioning strategy demonstrated by Bob Sinclair in the debriefing following the electricity activity. While many examples of debriefing dialogues are presented in Chapter 13, and sample debriefing questions are included for each investigative play activity in Chapters 7–10, some general examples of the kinds of questions and invitations to respond that may be used in debriefing different types of play experiences are provided here.

If the pupils have been engaged in investigative play, the teacher might ask,

> What observations did you make?
> How did you know that?
> How did you figure that out?
> How did you get that to work?

If the play has been with materials of construction, the teacher might say,

> Tell me about what you have built.
> How did that work?
> What did you do to make it work?
> What was that good for?
> Do you have any other ideas for building?

If the play has been dramatic, the teacher might say,

> Tell me about your play.
> What were the parts you liked?
> What were some funny (sad) parts?

If the play was physical-motor, the teacher might say,

> Tell me about your activities.
> What was hard for you to do? What was easy? How do you explain it?
> What do you like best?

If the play was with games, the teacher might say,

> Tell me about your games.
> What did you like?
> What problems did you have? How did you work that out?

These reflective questioning strategies accomplish many things. In the first instance, they require children to reflect upon their experiences, and they call for higher-order cognitive processing. Because the children are asked to respond, they must cognitively frame what they have done and articulate the experience through oral language. The requirement here is that they *think* about the meaning of the experience.

Much has been written about reflection-in-action (Nolan & Huber, 1989; Schön, 1983), which describes the way certain professionals (e.g., town planners, psychiatrists, businesspeople, teachers, social workers, medical practitioners) operate in their respective fields. According to Schön (1983), professional problems are messy, uncertain, complex situations. They do not present themselves in neat formats in which goals or ends are immediately clear and in which methods may be applied according to some predesigned formula. The more sophisticated approaches to dealing with these complex, messy, but critically important professional problems lie in the practitioner's ability to reframe the problems in comprehensible ways, to "make sense of an uncertain situation that initially makes no sense" (p. 40). Implicit in this approach are strategies of "trial and error, intuition, experience and muddling through" (p. 43). These processes yield insights and discoveries that lead to actions aimed at resolving the problem and eventually to understanding and appreciating the problem in a new way.

While Schön refers to this process of experimenting, acting, and reappraising as reflection-*in*-action, it may be immediately seen that debriefing cultivates reflection-*on*-action; that play is, in fact, the reflection-*in*-action stage; and that the whole process of play-debrief-replay promotes the very kind of high-level problem-solving capabilities that Schön describes.

Another requirement of debriefing is that children refine the language skills involved in communicating their ideas. Through these interactions they are called upon to comprehend, to make sense of their experiences. In all of these interactions, higher-order thinking is being engaged and practiced.

It is obvious that such interactive strategies empower children as thinkers. They call for children's assuming responsibility for reporting on and comprehending what they have done. They are also respectful, for they ask children to tell about what has occurred; they invite children's ideas, and their ideas are listened to and given serious consideration. Such questioning strategies are often called *facilitative*. The respect that they convey builds children's esteem and empowers them cognitively.

Debriefing, effectively done, lays the groundwork for carrying out the next day's play. Subsequent play experiences are built upon the kinds of questions that teachers raise, leading to potential new plays or investigations. Subsequent play, or *replay*, forms the third leg of the instructional plan: play-debrief-replay, as children continue to construct knowledge and make sense of the world.

### Replay: Returning to the Scene of the Investigation

Replay follows debriefing and generally occurs over the next few days. It may involve repetition of the investigation, and many young children enjoy and benefit from this, especially when it is their own choice. Replay may involve the addition of new materials, to give the inquiry a new focus. It may move the investigation into another, related area of the curriculum.

Replay has several purposes. It provides additional practice with the concepts and/or skills. Investigations may be replicated, findings verified, and new variables manipulated. The inquiry may be extended into new areas, taking the concepts one step further. More sophisticated, challenging investigations may be called for, based upon concepts developed in earlier play. Replay may show how relationships exist among the disciplines. It builds on previous experience and thus amplifies and provides progression in understanding. Its spiraling path allows children to return to play with the concept at later levels of development. It allows for children to look at experience in retrospect, leaving open the possibility that some point not grasped initially will become simplified when tackled at a later play stage.

The play-debrief-replay process with developing concepts may carry on for as long as the teacher perceives there is benefit to the experience. It is likely that play will continue to be generative and that only pressures of time and the need to go on to other important studies will be the reasons for terminating the cycle. Never mind. There are lots of play opportunities and lots of exciting new contexts to play in.

## DOES PLAY–DEBRIEF–REPLAY WORK?

Will this way of organizing classroom instruction — emphasizing children's play and, through it, the development of personal power, self-respect, and thinking capabilities — be sufficient to insure the growth outcomes that were articulated early in this chapter? It may not be *everything* that we as teachers should do, but the data so far suggest that such conditions do, in fact, contribute substantially to fostering these learning outcomes. How will we know? The behavior of the children will be the telling point. If we are using teaching strategies that are not effective in delivering the learning goals we believe are important, or if we see children's behavior deteriorating rather than improving, then it may well be that what we are doing needs serious rethinking.

If, on the other hand, the way we have organized the curriculum and the teaching strategies we have employed have led to growth in those behaviors we value (increased personal power, a sense of can-do, growing self-respect, responsible group behavior, increased thinking capability), then we may take heart that what we are doing is, in fact, working.

In the chapters that follow, more explicit help is provided in translating the ideas in these two introductory chapters into classroom practices. By making classroom strategies specific and concrete, I hope that teachers may more easily bridge the gap between the ideas and the day-to-day life of the classroom, thus insuring success for every primary teacher.

# CHAPTER 3

# The Teacher Decides

Moira Collins accepted the job as soon as it was offered to her—a first-grade class in a suburban school district 40 miles from the heart of the city where she lived. The school was in a newly developed area with a burgeoning population. The district needed teachers, and the interviewers seemed impressed with her credentials, even though she was fresh out of college, the ink hardly dry on her teacher's certificate. It was going to be a bit of a drive for her to commute from the city every day, but when she learned that this district appreciated innovative and creative teachers and would welcome the new ideas she was bringing with her from college, Rosedale School District seemed the right place for her to begin her teaching career.

When Moira left the district office, her appointment secure, she headed over to the elementary school to meet her new principal. Young, eager, and full of pride, Moira felt that to be a teacher was a wonderful thing. To have a job in which she could do the kind of teaching she had learned about in college and in her fabulous practicum under the mentorship of one of the most creative and exciting primary teachers in the city was nothing short of exhilarating. When Moira entered the principal's office, she could hardly contain her enthusiasm.

A tall, imposing woman in her early fifties greeted her warmly and offered her a seat. Mrs. Marley had been the principal of the Wisdom Lane School for 13 years and was delighted to welcome her to the staff. Now, would Moira talk about how she planned to run her program?

Moira had no difficulty describing her ideal first-grade classroom, patterned upon her excellent practicum experience: children working in groups; emphasis on creative play in music, arts, and crafts activities; a whole-language approach to language arts; and hands-on activities in math, science, and social studies. As she articulated her plans thoughtfully and clearly, she could envision the program in her mind and see it working for her as it did in her practicum school.

Mrs. Marley listened and smiled. She seemed to be enjoying Moira's spirited presentation. When Moira had at last finished with her description, Mrs. Marley spoke, still smiling.

"Oh, my dear, you will quickly learn that these experimental ways of teaching have no place in a real school. These theories are all right in teachers' college, but children need a lot of discipline and a lot of direction if they are to learn. Academic standards are very important at Wisdom Lane. I expect quiet, orderly classrooms, a lot of seatwork and drill on the basic skills, and good classroom control on the part of every teacher. In our school, we use only basal readers and workbooks for beginning reading instruction, to insure that pupils get a solid foundation."

Through all of this response, the smile never left the principal's face. It was as if she were instructing a wayward child who had somehow gotten off the right path and was to be sympathetically but unequivocally corrected.

Moira gulped and marveled at the ease with which Mrs. Marley had reduced her status from teacher to "child." The more she attempted to convince the principal that the child-centered classroom she was proposing could, indeed, support the high academic standards of the Wisdom Lane School, the more Mrs. Marley smiled and held fast to her original position. Such teaching methods were definitely *out* in this school. As Mrs. Marley put it, "We do not experiment here. We stay with the tried and proven methods of teaching." When Moira began to teach here, she would have to conform to the principal's methods. And that was that.

Later that evening, when Moira was having dinner with her friend Hilde, she described her elation over the initial interviews in the district office and her bitter disappointment after the session with the principal.

"I had to give it up, you know," she said, almost in tears. "I couldn't work for an administrator who had no confidence in my professional judgment and who wanted me to teach in a way that would just conform to *her* plans. What is a professional, if not one who has the right to make her own professional decisions, as long as they are educationally sound? How can I keep my self-respect if, on my very first job, I allow myself to be treated as a child—being told what to do, when to do it, and for how long? If teaching means only being allowed to do what your principal wants, then I'd rather sell real estate!"

## THE PROFESSIONAL TEACHER
## AND THE RIGHT TO CHOOSE

The case of Moira Collins has been played out in hundreds of variations in schools throughout the land. Scenes may vary, characters may play out different roles, consequences may have more or less impact, but the nature of the conflict is the same: Who has the right to decide how a teacher teaches? Who is in the best position to choose what is best for the educational growth of the students? Who is to sit in the power position?

It has been a long and hard road for teachers to move from virtually no power over such decisions, to positions of increased power to make choices about what they do in their classrooms (Lortie, 1986). As the status of teaching is elevated from a semiprofession to a full profession, teachers will finally enjoy what all other professionals take for granted in their work: the right to choose. If teaching is to attract and hold the "best and the brightest," those who come to the profession will want considerably more than competitive salaries. They will insist on working conditions that allow them to exercise their prerogatives as professionals. Not only will it *not* be seemly for an administrator or supervisor to call all the shots with respect to how a teacher teaches; it will be intolerable and likely cause for grievance. The signs are very clear that this is the direction in which the profession is heading, albeit at a snail's pace.

Even as the old ways fade, it must be acknowledged that the exercise of a teacher's professional judgment has been and often still is largely a dynamic wherein the teacher's personal power rubs abrasively against certain facts of life in the school: the leadership style of the principal, the setting and ambience of the school, the nature of the parent group and the kind of pressure it exerts, school board mandates, and state departments of education and provincial ministries' directives. Teachers whose sense of personal power is highly evolved find ways to teach true to their own beliefs, in spite of the dictates of the institution. Taking the attitude that "you can close your door and teach as you choose" is one way teachers rebel in the face of pressures to conform. For teachers who choose this path, life in schools is not easy.

In some schools and districts, administrators welcome and appreciate teachers who function at the highest professional levels, and they make great efforts to nurture and support professional individuality. While some teachers who wish to enjoy the power to choose keep looking until they find a "haven" school where they can enjoy academic freedom, others join the quiet revolution of teachers who, despite bureaucratic restrictions on their rights to choose, find ways to circumvent such policies. In many cases, however, where administrators and other school officials believe that the right and responsibility to control classroom teaching behavior belong *only* to them. too many teachers succumb, giving over their power and their right to choose to higher authority. In these cases teachers make some decisions, but not many of professional significance. Decisions of consequence can only be made by the "higher officials." In response, many teachers learn habits of obedience, following what is prescribed, doing as they are told, and perhaps even convincing themselves that giving up their prerogatives to make choices is acceptable. Personal self-respect cannot endure long in a climate where one's professional judgment carries no weight. If teachers are the keystones in the educational arch, their disempowerment threatens the whole of the educational structure.

Whatever forces are breathing new life into the teaching profession these days, let us embrace them with vigor. We need to recruit the very best into the profession and keep them there. But the very best will not long remain in jobs where their personal power is eroded inch by inch and where they are denied their right to exercise their best professional judgment in situations where they themselves have the best data. It is not enough that teachers may choose whether to give the spelling test on Thursday or Friday, or what recreational activity will fill in the time until the 3:00 bell. Professional judgment must include the right to decide *what* (e.g., content, treatment of children), *how* (e.g., teaching style, classroom organization, instructional strategies), and *how much* (e.g., time). This is not to say that there should be unlimited choice. While all decisions must of necessity by circumscribed by some school conditions, professional judgments must remain in the domain of the teacher. The current and very vocal concerns with educational improvements, plus the support and aggressive stance of teachers' unions and professional associations, will help us toward those goals. In the meantime, teachers must not shirk from insisting on their right to decide.

Teachers become empowered when they have the right to exercise professional judgment. We cannot hope that teachers without personal power may effectively empower children.

## THE DILEMMAS OF CHOOSING

A student teacher once complained to her mentor teacher about how hard a job teaching was and how tired she felt at the end of each school day. The mentor teacher quipped, "If you wanted easier work, you should have become a physicist!" While the point is arguable, it is nonetheless true that few outside the profession have a full appreciation of the complexities of teaching and the arduous demands of the job. There are good reasons why teachers are exhausted at the end of each school day, why they are nervously drained each Friday afternoon, why they look to the holiday seasons as oases that replenish body and soul.

Shedding the myth that teaching is nothing more than standing in front of a group of students day after blah-blahing day, and examining the multiple and extensive facets of the teacher's functioning, one may see the true nature of the teacher's work. Teachers are responsible for designing curriculum experiences for their students and for the preparation of original learning materials, selecting those that are particularly appropriate to the needs of individual learners. They are required to understand and deal effectively with the emotional, social, and intellectual problems of students and to give each the individual time and attention needed in order that improved learning may result. Teachers formatively and summatively evaluate students' learning, making diagnoses of performance on specific tasks, making thoughtful judgments about the whole of a student's performance over an interval of time, and reporting all of this in comprehensible ways to anxious parents. Teachers work as competently with large groups as they do with small groups and individuals, even though the approach to each may require altogether different types of skills. They must be masters of the interaction process, knowing when and how to inform and tell, to clarify students' ideas, to challenge students' thinking, to remain neutral, and to offer evaluative opinion.

A teacher must be prepared to deal with students' behavior problems, knowing when and how to be tough and firm without diminishing a student's dignity, and when to overlook the indiscretion. A teacher must know how to organize the classroom for instruction and how to make shifts in the organization so that the learning activity and organizational scheme are in concert. The teacher must be the composer, the orchestrator, and the conductor of the classroom symphony, if the players are to make beautiful music. On top of all of that, teachers must also keep up with their professional development activities, reading what is current, attending meetings and workshops, and making intelligent distinctions about what new ideas are of real value.

It is no wonder that teachers are tired. The job is gargantuan (Raths, 1969). As if the range and complexity of teachers' tasks were not sufficient to make brave souls weep, the job is further compounded by the fact that each task — every function that the teacher carries out — requires that decisions be made. Every day and every minute of the day, teachers make decisions about curriculum: what to teach, how to organize the learning experience, what instructional approaches to use, what to give major emphasis to and what to exclude, how and what to evaluate. Teachers decide how to present material, determining how explicit to make explanations and how much to leave to inference. They decide how to supplement the prescribed curriculum, including selecting which materials to use and assessing what risks they may expose themselves to and whether the educational benefits warrant the risks. They decide how to evaluate learning, which remedies are appropriate for students who have difficulty learning, and what to report to parents. Teachers make decisions, perhaps implicitly through personal style, about classroom climate, group work and interpersonal relationships, discipline, and housekeeping. They decide what professional in-service work to undertake in improving their own competence as teachers, and they make judgments about which new ideas are educationally sound and worth putting into classroom practice.

If this list sounds extensive, it barely scratches the surface. Teachers make hundreds of decisions each day, from the trivial to the very complex. The professional functioning of teachers is riddled with decision-making imperatives that would tax a Solomon. The decisions teachers make are rarely clear-cut. They involve considerable judgment and intuition as well as thoughtful consideration of data. Often the merits of judgments are revealed with time, and teachers need to place trust in their judgments until the results can be seen. Such decision making is not only complex, it is often full of tension, ambiguity, and risk. Most of these decisions are made alone, and it appears, too, that very few teachers are consciously aware of their decision-making processes or of the psychological, physical, and emotional costs of such pervasive decision making in their lives (Manley-Casimir & Wassermann, 1989). Do any of these decision-making dilemmas sound familiar?

> What shall I do here, teacher?
> May I sharpen my pencil?
> Leonard is bothering me.
> I can't find my boots.
> My mother wants me to bring my reader home so she can help me.
> I don't understand this arithmetic.
> Danny won't let me play with the fire truck.
> I want my turn on the swing.
> Can I be first?
> I don't want to go outside for recess.
> I forgot my lunch.
> I lost my bus pass.
> My father says you should give me some homework.
> I didn't finish my work yet.
> How is my son William doing?
> I was absent because I didn't have no clean shirt.
> Hey, Mrs. Gross, Philip wet his pants.
> Do I have to do this work? It's boring.

How does a teacher decide? What are some reasonable and responsible guidelines that teachers might use in charting a course through the many ambiguities of choosing?

There is, of course, no value-free choice. To accept that principle is the starting point from which one eases oneself into increased awareness that each choice represents a tilting toward some value position. Knowing that many choices, if not most, are encumbered by "outside baggage" and that choices come with inevitable consequences guides us in the process of choosing.

Even in schools where teachers' right to choose is sacrosanct, they do not have unlimited choice. Regardless of whether freedom of choice abounds or is to some degree restricted, decision making is facilitated when teachers know that they are choosing; they know the options clearly; they are aware of the pressures (personal, administrative, parental, political, educational) that bear on the choice; they are aware of their beliefs that tilt them in the direction of a decision; they have an idea of the potential consequences of the decision. All of these conditions do not encumber the choosing, but instead facilitate the action of deciding. When teachers are clearer about all of these things, it is easier for them to choose. The following excerpt from a teacher's journal illuminates this process:

> *Wednesday, June 5*
>
> What do I do? This afternoon was a perfect example of "one of those days" when as a teacher I felt overwhelmed and bombarded with circumstances and decisions that pressed a greater and greater weight on the down side of the day. Kids were high, restless, wild. I was tired from the moment I got up this morning. All were conditions contributing to one of those moments when I felt FROZEN, PARALYZED to act effectively in a moment of crisis.
>
> The room is a whirlwind of activity — both productive and aimless, with energy unleashed, when Chelsea comes up to me surrounded by a group of supporters and opponents. She is crying hysterically and two kids start talking to me at once. The problem: a book! Tom says it's his. Chelsea insists it's her brother's. Everyone's talking at the same time, giving their views of whose it is. I sit immobilized, sort of listening but mostly swelling inside with anger and feelings of desperation. What do I do? I hand the book back and ask them to sort it out on their own, stating that I feel uncomfortable and unable to decide because I know nothing about the book. I tell them to try to sort it out in a way that will feel fair to both of them and to let me know what they decide. I feel guilty, at a loss. How should I have handled it? I feel uncertain of my abilities and yet confident the kids will find a solution.
>
> All the emotions and circumstances that lead into and surround a moment when a decision is to be made absolutely boggle my mind. No wonder my exhaustion carries from one day to the next.
>
> But, hey! I made a great, respectful-to-kids decision amid the craziness outside and inside me. Bravo! This situation reinforces my belief that — *in a crisis or critical moment* — you act from deep inside you — your gut! Deep beliefs are the power behind your decisions. I believe in kids' ability to sort through their problems. I respect their individual right to grow no matter what the situation. This is what shows in my decision this afternoon. (L. Muttit, personal journal, 1984)

Linda Muttit, a gifted-classroom teacher and the writer of that journal entry, demonstrates that, in a crunch, in the thick of classroom crisis, what teachers do reflects their deepest beliefs. Somewhere, deep down inside, teachers are able to tune into what is important, to what really *matters* in the situation. Decisions are more easily made when teachers have reflected upon and are clear about what it is they believe about teaching and learning, about children and their life in the classroom, about their own goals, and about what they hope the children will become. When a teacher has a clear perspective and is able to say with assurance, "Yes, this is what I stand for; these are my values," then he or she can in good conscience claim, "I have made a good choice." Such teachers will be less likely to be influenced by pressure to act in ways that are out of harmony with what they believe, less likely to fall for the seductive appeal of "simple answers" to complex problems or to choose impulsively. Such clarity protects teachers from being vulnerable to charges of inconsistency or thoughtlessness about what they have done, or to be caught in a web of consequences that betray hasty and inappropriate judgment.

Always having to think about one's decisions and choosing on the basis of one's well-thought-out educational values may sound like one more onerous burden added to the teacher's formidable job. Yet the opposite is true: Acting out of a clear awareness of what it is that is important, of what is really valued, makes it much easier to choose. When teachers do what they believe, and believe what they do, it is curiously liberating.

Teachers who practice education in ways that are consistent with their values, who are able to say, "That's harmful for kids; I just won't be a party to those procedures," must have more than clarity about their beliefs. They must have the courage to stand for those beliefs and the conviction to present them as educationally sound in a debate about "what is important." Admittedly, this is not easy. Yet these teachers derive personal power from the clarity of their values, and their self-respect is enhanced each time they stand up for what they believe. On the other hand, teachers who are unclear about their educational values are easily influenced by external pressure to choose this way or that. They find themselves vulnerable to others' power over them, causing them to act in ways that make them uncomfortable, disquieted, uneasy. Respect for self cannot grow when others are allowed to decide for us, telling us to do what *they* think is important. When teachers are forced to behave in ways that are truly repugnant to them, ways that are incompatible with what they value, this may be more the cause of burn-out and loss of self-respect than we ever realized.

## PLAY-DEBRIEF-REPLAY:
## IS IT FOR EVERY TEACHER?

Should all teachers choose play-debrief-replay as a way of organizing instruction in their primary classrooms? In a situation where options for
composing, orchestrating, and conducting their own classrooms are relatively open, should all teachers rush, helter-skelter ["with their skelters," as
Arlo, age 5, says] to embrace this way of teaching? As with all educational
practice, choice is a matter of each teacher's beliefs. What do teachers have
to believe about teaching, learning, and children, to choose this way?
What beliefs would be antithetical to such a choice?

Teachers who choose play-debrief-replay have to believe in the importance of children working in groups. This means that the classroom is
perceived not as a place of silence where pupils sit quietly, listening and
watching the teacher doing the work, but as a place where the children do
the work; a place where they talk, discuss ideas, debate and argue, laugh,
move about the room, and find the materials they need. It is a place where
children spill water, knock over paint, break materials, tear the plastic
sheeting, and have all the other "accidents" that occur when people work
actively with materials. These teachers must believe that active participation of children cannot occur without the mess that is a normal by-product
of that participation. A play-debrief-replay program is one in which the
children's busyness and the noise connected with normal, healthy produc-
tivity are the order of the day (Wassermann & Ivany, 1996).

Teachers choosing this instructional approach have to believe, with Bettelheim (1987), that play is children's work and that children learn more—
intellectually, socially, and emotionally—through playing than they do by
sitting alone and filling in worksheets. They must believe that learning
important concepts and skills does not occur through a linear progression
of skill-and-drill worksheets, one building on the other, with the whole
edifice collapsing, like a tower of dominoes, if the child has not "mastered
the third level." Such teachers have to believe in the teacher's role as one of
writing the script, designing the set, gathering the props, and stage managing the players—of facilitating learning, rather than of talking in order
to make "deposits" into children's heads. Teachers who choose this way
must know that building pupils' autonomy and independent functioning is
a key educational goal that results as the teacher relinquishes control over
student learning and provides children with more opportunities to choose
for themselves. They also must believe that the cultivation of pupils' ability
to think is one of the school's *primary* functions and that, without having
developed this ability, it is largely irrelevant that a child has learned to
decode words and add and subtract sums, or "knows the answer" to

the question in the science test about the temperature at which water boils.

If a teacher believes, deeply and truly, in the educational values of a program that is rooted in pupil inquiry, in children working cooperatively in groups, and in the promotion of higher-order thinking, where children are given much control over their learning, the play-debrief-replay instructional program will be very much in tune with those beliefs.

Conversely, it is more than likely that this instructional approach will be an anathema to those teachers whose perception of teaching and learning rests on the beliefs that (1) teachers must be at center stage and in full control of every facet of student learning; (2) pupils must be quiet and orderly, so that they may listen and do as they are told; (3) the teacher's most important job is to cover the content; (4) noisy, messy classrooms are a sure sign that children need to be properly disciplined; (5) silence means the pupils are learning; (6) learning is linear and sequential and must be doled up in a series of worksheet tasks; (7) play is wasting time; and (8) young children are unable to think for themselves.

How do you, as a teacher, determine which beliefs and values you hold? The emotional responses you felt surging in your breast as you read the preceding paragraphs may have already given you advance warning. If you heard silent shouts of "Yeh, yeh, yeh!" as you read one paragraph, that should signal a bias. If you felt repugnance, that should communicate another bias. Tune into those feelings, and let them guide you. Perhaps you can obtain some additional data about where you stand, what you value, and what you hold important by taking the Beliefs Test shown in Figure 3.1. This informal, nonstandardized, not at all empirically valid instrument may serve as one way for you to test the waters of your educational beliefs.

On completion of the test, add up your total score. If it is 60 or higher, play-debrief-replay is likely to be a good choice for you. If your score falls between 40 and 60, reread Chapters 1 and 2, and take the Beliefs Test again. If your score is lower than 40, this kind of instructional program is not likely to fit in with your needs.

## MAINTAINING AND RELINQUISHING CONTROL

In their study of primary and intermediate classrooms, Ann and Harold Berlak (1981) found three domains in which matters of control about classroom life are decided: time, operations, and standards. Maintaining and relinquishing control in these domains is never a "given." It is always "problematical," shifting this way and that in response to the various pulls

## FIGURE 3.1 Beliefs Test

*Rate each statement according to the following scale:*
*1 = if you agree strongly*
*2 = if you tend to agree*
*3 = if you are uncertain*
*4 = if you tend to disagree*
*5 = if you disagree strongly*

1. There is a fixed body of information that must be learned each day in each subject area.
2. Children must master this knowledge before they can go on to the next curriculum tasks.
3. For children to learn anything important, they must be taught the subject matter in a clearly articulated series of sequential tasks.
4. Teachers must adhere to a fixed schedule to insure that the prescribed curriculum content is covered.
5. Children's best learning occurs in a quiet and orderly classroom where the children are sitting still and listening to the teacher.
6. Children can't work cooperatively in groups. They learn to depend on each other too much.
7. Children must learn to compete for that is the way of the adult world.
8. A noisy classroom where children are moving around is a sure sign that the teacher has lost control.
9. The best way to find out what students have learned is to give them short-answer tests to see if they know the right answers.
10. A teacher's most important job is to cover the curriculum of the grade.
11. A teacher must do a lot of explaining, to make sure the children understand.
12. A teacher must instruct each pupil until he or she understands the lesson completely.
13. Primary grade children cannot be expected to behave responsibly in unsupervised group activities.
14. Teaching is primarily concerned with getting children to learn the right answers in each subject.
15. Learning factual information must come before students can learn to think.
16. Children do learn from play, but teachers must be responsive to parents' wishes for skill worksheets if the teacher is going to keep his or her job.

Adapted with permission from *Teaching Elementary Science: Who's Afraid of Spiders?* by Selma Wassermann & J. W. George Ivany (second edition), copyright 1996 by Teachers College Press, p. 40.

of each new situation. So, in fact, the teacher is deciding each time, but the decision always rests upon the framework of the teacher's beliefs.

No teacher with a clear sense of what is important for the health, welfare, and education of children ever gives up total control over classroom functions. Not only would this be foolish, it would be disastrous. The teacher is always the adult in charge, and the extent to which the teacher maintains and relinquishes control, in each of these three domains and for each new situation, is decided by the teacher. It must also be said that, the more the control may be given over to the children, the more children may learn to exercise their own control responsibly. In this way, children are gradually empowered.

There are invisible lines that may not be crossed without creating problems in this already-ambiguous situation. If a teacher relinquishes too much control or lets go too soon, working conditions may quickly deteriorate. If the teacher is afraid or unable to give over any control, children will remain disempowered. Where is that invisible line, and how do teachers find it? It is elusive, but a teacher's eyes and ears are important sources of knowing. Just as the symphony conductor knows, by listening and watching, when the cello is playing off key or when the tympany has missed the cue, and just as that conductor knows how to make the corrections, so does the teacher know when to "reign in" and when to open more options. Naturally, as with most other skills, we learn to do this better with experience.

## Control of Time

When instruction follows a play-debrief-replay organization, two variables of time control — when a task begins and how long the task will take — are largely, but not solely, under student control. Children are not engaged in exactly the same activities at exactly the same time. They are free to talk with each other and even to "mess about" within certain limits that are implicitly a part of the classroom ethic. Different kinds of investigations occur simultaneously, and amounts of time spent on investigations differ. In most classrooms where the program has evolved to sophisticated levels, pupils generate their own investigations, spun out of the given guidelines. Where students are heavily involved and request additional time to conduct further inquiries, this is generally allowed, while other children go on to other activities. The use of time in a play-debrief-replay structure may be characterized as looser or more flexible than in more traditional models, with children having a lot of choice in determining both when and how they begin and how long they will spend at the inquiry.

This is, of course, dramatically contrasted to classrooms where children sit quietly and patiently at their desks, waiting for the lesson to begin or end; where certain tasks are completed at a specified time ("All math worksheets are to be finished and collected at 10:15!"); where learning tasks are tightly prescribed for the entire school day; where decisions about beginning time and duration of task lie almost entirely with the teacher.

How much control over beginning time and duration should a teacher allow to primary students? As with most such questions, the answer is, It depends. The teacher chooses, remembering these important principles:

- The more control teachers can give their students, the better chances the students have for learning to manage their time responsibly; hence, the more they are empowered.
- Too much, too soon may result in a "meltdown" of productive working conditions.
- Teachers should allow only what they are comfortable with, never giving over control to the extent that they feel anxious or uneasy.

## Control of Operations

In a classroom where learning experiences are organized in a play-debrief-replay structure, the control of operations — including sequencing of tasks, monitoring children's mastery of their understanding of concepts, and monitoring children's mastery of procedures (Berlak & Berlak, 1981) — is shared by teacher and students. The teacher designs the investigative play tasks, but there is much tolerance for children to depart from or spin off into self-generated investigations. The extent to which this occurs depends upon the teacher's flexibility. In creating play contexts, such as dress-up, building, arts and crafts, music, and dramatic play, children invent their own scenarios and the teacher intervenes primarily to help arbitrate disputes or to share in the pleasure of children's creations.

The sequencing of learning tasks is also flexible. In science, for example, investigative play tasks may have no relation to the science textbook sequence, so that plants may be studied before or after insects. The teacher controls the sequencing of tasks through the design of the play, and this occurs in response to children's interests or events of current concern, rather than according to some predetermined rule of what should be learned at what time of the year.

In a highly evolved play-debrief-replay classroom, the monitoring of children's mastery of concepts and procedures occurs in a way that almost belies the existence of such monitoring. During investigative play, children may come up with quite extraordinary conclusions, such as this one on the theory of evolution: "The feet of the fish turned into fins and this took about 100 years." While the teacher notes here that the children's conceptual understanding is confused and that more experiential play must occur before the children may grow toward understanding of how mammals evolved from sea life, the teacher does not "correct" the children's ideas at those moments when they are being expressed. Nor does the teacher immediately undertake to provide remedial help.

This is probably the single area that causes the most anxiety for teachers who are considering this approach. Not correct the children? Allow them to maintain their misconceptions? How do teachers do this and still call what they do *teaching*?

The rationale for such a different approach is far from frivolous. As teachers, we all know that children learn concepts (big ideas) from experience. Even very sophisticated adults, with a great deal of experience behind them, who hear or read about an idea in abstraction have difficulty in fully comprehending the vast implications of that concept. We know that, for example, if we want to teach the concept of buoyancy, we are much better off using a water table and a variety of objects that will sink or float. If we merely use telling as a mode of teaching children about buoyancy — that it means "the upward pressure of fluid on an immersed or floating body" — children will neither grasp the concept nor be likely to remember it accurately. Without the prior condition of experience with sinking and floating objects at the water table, children may learn to recite the definition of buoyancy, but they are not likely to know much about what it means. It is experience that promotes conceptual understanding. Experience allows them to know what things mean. Telling, or giving children information, primarily allows them to know the words, but telling cannot substitute for experience or lead to the understanding of meanings.

None of this is new to teachers, and we know this as certainly as we know that Friday is the last day of the school week. Yet, in our anxiety to insure that students "get it right," we often insist on telling them that their conceptual understanding is wrong. We then proceed to "give" them the "right idea."

"No, William. The feet did not turn into fins. You have it backward. The fins turned into feet!"

Bad pedagogy and bad science, too. William may now remember, but if he does, he will likely remember only the words, not the concept. Or, he may not even remember, for words, without the conceptual understanding that gives them meaning, are easily lost or confused. William is also likely to feel "put down" for having gotten it wrong. Pedagogically, the strategy is counterproductive. Scientifically, it is misleading as well as inaccurate. It has been made to sound as if, at some magic moment in time, fish were zapped, fins disappeared, and fish got up on feet to walk out of the sea.

From the point of view of scientific accuracy, fins did not turn into anything. Since this change took millennia, we use the term *evolve* to indicate
an enormously lengthy process. Even that does not adequately explain, for
if fins evolved and feet emerged, how does one explain that there are still a
few fish left in the ocean that have no feet? The concept of evolution is very
large and complex, and we need a lot more experience with the ideas and
data to make real meaning.

Although the idea that students learn to understand complex concepts by
being given information has been repudiated by impressive research findings over the last 50 years, and although "inquiry" teaching and "active
learning" methods have been found to produce better results in promoting
students' thinking and understanding in science and math (Bracey, 1998;
Gorman, Plucker, & Callahan, 1998; Lewin, 1999; Stigler, Gonzales, Kowalsky, Knoll, & Serrano, 1999), teachers continue to "tell" in the sincere hope
that students will understand the concept from hearing the words. "You
would think that we would be further along in teaching and testing for
understanding," argues Bracey (1998). "That we aren't only reveals that we
have profoundly held ideas of how children learn and that these ideas are
also incredibly resistant to change. And wrong." (p. 328).

For teachers who are still uneasy about holding back the tendency to
correct children when their concepts are a little "wonky," it may help to
remember that preschool children who are learning to use language to
communicate their thoughts and feelings are not corrected each time they
use incorrect pronunciation or grammatical construction. Instead, their
teachers and parents go about talking to them naturally, using correct
grammatical construction. These conversations provide them with additional experiences with language. Teachers are not afraid to wait for children to learn language in this way, and eventually, in their own time, they
make the shift from "I ate a little bit all of it" to "I ate only some of it." If
their experiences with language have been rich and extensive, then language usage will flourish.

This understanding of how children learn, if it is applied to all classroom
work, makes it easier to see that the monitoring and correcting of concepts
is more of an evolving process than it is of providing instant feedback.
Teachers do not neglect this responsibility to help children understand
more; they just go about it differently.

The extent to which teachers maintain or relinquish control over operations once again depends upon a variety of factors: the teacher, the individual child, the group of children, and the particular subject area. Teachers
who are in the process of lessening control are urged to do so slowly, so that
they and their children may grow comfortably in the new and less restric-
tive environment. If children are given too much control over operations

too soon, their dis-ease may result in a breakdown of operations, thus causing teacher distress and perhaps the worrisome conviction that children are simply incapable of assuming such control. Teaching strategies for moving students from dependence to greater autonomy are discussed more fully in Chapter 5.

## Control of Standards

Every teacher is concerned with the quality of student performance, and every teacher maintains some control of standards. This involves a process of evaluation, but how it is done may differ greatly from classroom to classroom. In the Berlak and Berlak (1981) study, four areas in which teachers exercise control over standards were identified: (1) children's performance on tasks, (2) how many pages of work were completed in a certain time, (3) children's performance in drawing and painting, and (4) teachers' evaluative statements (e.g., "You can do better, John.").

In a play-debrief-replay program, teachers are more likely to observe from a distance the quality of students' performance in investigative play activities. They may note, but not control, how children are going about their inquiries. No control is exercised over how much investigation is completed in a given period of time, since the replay stage of the instructional feedback loop takes up the slack. Teachers are apt to use procedures that put the burden of evaluation more into the children's court. A common example is the use of probing questions, such as, "How do you feel about that, Sally?" "I wonder if you could explain how that went wrong." "How do you think you could improve that?" That is not to say that teachers never say, "I think you could do that better," but such comments are less frequently heard. The following examples illustrate the preferred mode of exercising control of standards:

- "I liked your painting. I liked very much your use of colors," instead of, "Your painting was very good."
- "Hmmm. I see you used only blacks and blues. I wonder why you chose only those dark colors," instead of, "Blacks and blues make your painting too dark. You should use some bright colors."
- "I see that, when you weighed the rocks, you found they weighed 2.7 kg. Yet when Susan's group weighed them, they recorded their weight as 3.1 kg. How do you explain that?" rather than, "You weighed them incorrectly. Try again."
- "Your group seems to have done a lot of investigating today. I can see how much you have recorded on your chart. That is most impressive," instead of, "Finlay's group did the best investigation today. They accomplished the most."

In summary, when it comes to matters of retaining and relinquishing control over standards, operations, and time, the teacher decides. It is important to keep in mind that no single numerical ratio of teacher/student control (e.g., teachers 20 percent and students 80 percent) that is fixed and remains stable is being suggested. Almost every decision about maintaining or relinquishing control involves ambiguities. Who gets to do what is frequently in flux; that is, it changes in response to events, conditions, moods and other factors that affect one's sense of what should be done. Even in the most sophisticated play-debrief-replay programs, controls shift from tighter to looser to tighter again, not only in the overall scene, but in the separate parts as well. How this occurs and when it occurs comes from the teacher's thoughtful observations of classroom life.

Guiding our decisions as teachers, helping us wade through the swampland of classroom activity to determine what do we do, are our beliefs and values about what is important. When our beliefs and goals have been clearly identified and acknowledged, then it is easier to deal with the difficult task of bringing teaching methods into alignment with educational goals. It is easier to assess whether what we have done measures up to our sincerest expectations. When it has, we can depart for a summer holiday and relax, certain in the knowledge that life in our classrooms has borne the fruit that we hoped. When it has not, we can reexamine, assess, and reconstruct what we must do in the following year to reap better the harvest of our expectations.

## "I LIKE THIS WAY OF TEACHING, BUT . . . "

"I like this model," Charlene announces to her practicum seminar group. "I like it in theory. But I don't see how we can make this work in a real classroom. After all, we have districtwide tests to worry about."

Some of her classmates nod, and a few volunteer other caveats about play-debrief-replay that suggest some of their darkest fears and troublesome doubts: "We believe in a program that encourages student thinking through investigative play, but . . . "

>"How do I give grades?"
>"How will I cover the curriculum?"
>"Won't it be too noisy?"
>"Can I trust young children to work responsibly?"
>"Will submissive children benefit?"
>"What about disruptive behavior?"
>"Will parents accept this method?"
>"How will I know students are learning?"
>"What about my own needs for success?"

These are important questions, and they have no clear-cut easy answers. There is no doubt that the play-debrief-replay classroom is, for many primary teachers, a radically new and different approach. It is likely that a teacher who chooses this way of teaching may be the only one in the school to do so. New methods and innovative programs that aim at empowering children through increasing their options and allowing them greater choices can be very threatening for teachers, administrators, and parents. We all say we *want* children to gain strength and competence as thinkers, but we shrink from providing the means for this to occur.

No important human gains are bought cheaply; there are prices to be paid for everything we want. Teachers have to decide if the empowerment of children is worth the price. The caveats raised by teachers who are contemplating such an approach may, on the surface, be reasonable questions of procedure. At a deeper level, however, they may be more representative of teachers' darkest fears about their confidence in their own professional ability, their needs to be perceived as competent, and their desire to be liked and appreciated. It is far from easy for a professional to stand alone in defense of his or her own strong educational values. To do so in a school where colleagues are, at best, mildly indifferent or, at worst, openly hostile, can be life threatening for even the bravest souls. Perhaps a teacher must believe very deeply, must want children to grow in these ways very much, to take such personal risks. Only the teacher can decide.

Yet, not all schools are hostile to programs that call for children's independent thinking, and the most current wave of educational change finds more and more administrators, and teachers asking for help with implementing programs that emphasize thinking (Cadwell, 1997; Jervis & Montag, 1991; Kohn, 1998; Langley & Wassermann, 1988; Sharon & Sharon, 1992; Wassermann, 1987a, 1987b). The pilgrimage of hundreds of educators to Italy, to study and learn and disseminate the approach to early childhood education found in the preschools of the city of Reggio Emilia, is an ironic example of how we in North America travel to distant lands to find support for what we already know are the best conditions in which young children grow and learn (Cadwell, 1997).

But, if teachers' questions come from their darkest fears about self and competence, no answers, no matter how rational, will wash those fears away. No data, no matter how compelling, will enable teachers to take the steps out of personal fear into implementation. Feelings of fear can only be overcome by recognition of their existence and by addressing the feelings directly. Logic is not a good response to feelings.

On the other hand, many teachers' questions come from a wish to arm themselves with additional data that suggest means for addressing the rational concerns of implementation. It is to these that the following discussion is oriented.

## "How Do I Give Grades?"

A teacher who believes that pencil-and-paper tests that measure students' ability to "get the right answers" are the best way of assessing pupil
learning is not likely to choose play-debrief-replay as an instructional program. Teachers who do choose it, however, find they have many options in
gathering the data they need to assign grades, where grades are demanded.
They will, of course, use that most powerful and important of teacher
assessment tools — their professional observations. In this way, they determine which pupils are showing increased skills in their cognitive and intellectual abilities, which are showing increased personal growth, which are
growing socially, which are growing in their appreciations and attitudes.
In fact, the play-debrief-replay classroom allows for greater opportunity to
observe and make these professional assessments.

There is also no reason why teachers cannot choose to test children, if
that is seen as an important means of gathering additional information
about pupil learning. Tests, however, should aim to measure students' performance in relation to the teacher's articulated learning goals. Watching
students work and watching how they work, plus the option of using tests
that provide data on how pupils think, ought to give teachers substantial
information from which grades, if necessary, may be determined. The
likelihood is great that the play-debrief-replay classroom will yield even
more data about students' performance than may be found through traditional pencil-and-paper, "correct-answer" examinations (see Chapter 13 on
evaluation practices).

## "How Will I Cover the Curriculum?"

There are large numbers of teachers who believe that the curriculum
prescribed for a grade must be covered, in a step-by-step linear progression
of activities, without deviation; that covering the curriculum is what
teaching is; that lapses in covering the curriculum result in pupil lapses,
which make it impossible to put the subsequent curriculum building blocks
in place.

This could be called the "brickbuilders approach" to teaching. The
teachers are the brickbuilders and the pupils are the buildings. The teachers build, brick by brick, "bricking in" the information. Students' knowledge is cemented, brick by brick, with all the informational pieces in place.
With this metaphor of teaching and learning, one can see why there
would be concern that an informational brick be omitted, lest the building be weakened. Yet the data on how children learn tell us otherwise.

Student learning and building with bricks are not the same. If they were, no second-grade teacher would ever accuse the first-grade teacher, "You didn't teach these children anything last year!" Indeed, the first-grade teacher spent long hours putting the curriculum bricks in place, but they were far from cemented in the children's learning. The second-grade teacher must do what he or she always has done during the first 6 weeks of the new school year: *Review*! If covering the curriculum were a sure way of guaranteeing proper placement of all the first-grade learning bricks, there would rarely be this complaint.

There are also large numbers of teachers who see teaching as a way of opening students' minds, so that they may think about and reflect upon the substantive issues in the curriculum. They believe that thinking is not a linear, step-by-step "bricking-in" process, but more frequently a sloppy process in which meaning is finally extracted from a "mess" of data (Wassermann, 1989b). These teachers are more satisfied with knowing that their students have demonstrated ability to understand complex concepts, to see issues from many perspectives, to make sense out of complicated situations, and to process data intelligently. Teachers who work for these learning goals know that teaching strategies must not emphasize the *giving* of tidbits of information to build up students' storehouse of knowledge. Instead, the emphasis is on the extracting of meaning, the "working with students' ideas" so that their ability to comprehend intelligently is expanded.

In the one scenario, student learning is concerned with the accumulation of information bytes; in the second, it is on students' ability to process information intelligently. Covering the curriculum is a nonissue for teachers who believe that learning to think about curriculum is what education is for.

## "Won't It Be Too Noisy?"

Noise is a normal by-product of children's working and playing together. When children discuss, argue, and try to decide how and what, their exchanges are bound to make noise. Several groups of children working and playing together means a noisy classroom.

There is noise and there is *noise*, and teachers will want to insure that the noise level doesn't reach decibels that are stressful and counterproductive to a safe and healthy learning environment. They can develop their own management strategies to remind children to "settle down." This may take the form of a prearranged signal: switching lights on and off, playing a chord on the piano, making a hands-up signal — whatever reminder serves the purpose. Primary teachers will already know that classroom noise in moderation is evidence of healthy children engaged in generative learning activities and that a classroom in which 25 children sit and work in utter silence is unhealthy on both emotional and physical levels. Silence imprisons children, and that is not what education is about. If classroom noise in moderation is disturbing for prospective primary teachers, they might wish to reconsider teaching as a profession.

## "Can I Trust Young Children to Work Responsibly?"

The question of whether children are too young to work without adult supervision is only raised by adults who have not seen preschool children at play with their friends. While adults may be within calling distance, children do play with playmates in the back yard, at the playground, at the beach, or at day-care centers, without the requirement of adult direction. Observing preschool-age children together, one can see that their play is generative and rich with imagery. They do not need or want adult intervention. This does not mean that adults are not nearby, available for the emergencies or crises that invariably occur. In the absence of crisis, however, even very young children play and "work" together admirably. This is true largely because children's play is of their own making. It is only when children are required to do what they do not want to do that adults must monitor and supervise, to see that the children stay on task. This is very much like the office supervisor whose job it is to monitor the behavior of the office staff, to insure that they are "working" and not "playing." When they are engaged in activities they enjoy, activities that are personally meaningful for them, neither children nor adults need behavior management.

The key to the question is the learning task. If a task is created that calls for children's imaginative, generative play, teachers will observe behavior similar to that seen at the beach, where a group of young children set about, with no adult direction, to play in the sand and water. Adults *should* be available to watch and insure that children are safe in their group work and to help in the resolution of conflict as needed. Otherwise (unless there is a child in acute emotional distress) children will carry on investigative play quite productively on their own and grow in their sophistication to do so.

## "Will Submissive Children Benefit?"

It is in the nature of the human organism to seek personal power. "Please, Mother, I'd rather do it myself," urges a healthy child who wants to experience that he or she can do. Healthy and well-integrated children enjoy purposeful self-directedness, which is their means for attaining personal power, and they resent rather than appreciate adult "help" that gets in the way of such growth. This is true as well for healthy, well-integrated adults.

There are, of course, children as well as adults whose sense of can-do has been seriously undermined, as discussed in Chapter 1. Such people may have come to believe that they have to be told what to do. It is important for teachers to remember that, when they see the dependency behaviors manifest in children who "prefer to be told," these are a warning that the children are in danger of becoming even more submissively obedient and that corrective measures to restore their independent, autonomous functioning and the development of their personal power are urgently needed. For such children, play-debrief-replay seems imperative.

### "What About Disruptive Behavior?"

What about the child who hurts other children? Who has a short attention span? Who cannot get down to work? Who breaks materials? Who gets into fights? There is no trouble-free classroom. Every teacher will face at least one child who manifests some manner of problem, and some teachers, to their anguish, have groups of such children in one class. Children who are hurting on the inside often resort to hurting others, and, even in the very best of circumstances, the problems that create their distress are not easily solved, nor do they go away. A child who is suffering the pain of parental separation, or whose parent is an alcoholic, or who cannot ever meet parental expectations, or who is left in his or her own care, or who is overburdened with adult responsibilities, or who does not have enough to eat, or whose parent has left home — all of these children take their troubles to school. They do not make life easy for the teacher who cares. Teachers want to help these children, yet they cannot fix what is broken in these lives, nor can they cause the pain and suffering to end. They can, however, give the children moments of comfort, reassurance, and love. This teachers give gladly, but the behavior, like the pain and longing, does not go away. Teachers who work with children in distress know that they must always provide them with extra measures of help and that they require more, much more than the "emotionally stable" ones. Although teachers would like to think that extra attention and thoughtful care might cause the distressed behavior to diminish, that is often not the case. The best they can do is to keep these children from slipping further.

Distressed children will be a source of distress for teachers no matter what instructional model is chosen. These children are, however, more likely to find acceptance and nurturing conditions for positive growth in a classroom where they are respected and they can develop a sense of person-

al power, than they are in one where they are merely managed. But nobody said it was easy!

## "Will Parents Accept This Approach?"

Most parents want what's best for their children. They want their children's schools to be places where the children are learning, where they feel
accepted, where they are happy. Teachers have the professional responsibility to provide the conditions for bringing this about, which can be done
in several different ways. There is no single route, no single set of classroom
methods that produce these results.

It is no secret to the profession that parent education is an important
part of a teacher's job. Teachers call parents in for conferences, hold open
house, and have PTA meetings. All of these are ways in which they "show
and tell" parents that what is being done by way of curriculum and instruction will help their children to become responsible citizens. Even
teachers who choose conventional instructional tools must accept the responsibility of "showing and telling."

The play-debrief-replay classroom reveals many important facets of children's learning, and this too may be demonstrated to parents. The teacher
can discuss the children's developing conceptual understanding, increased
knowledge and skills, problem-solving capability, higher-order thinking,
ability to work productively in groups, creativity, and ability to reason
logically from data. Children's learning in these domains is repeatedly
revealed in the play-debrief-replay program, and reporting such learning is
likely to assure most parents that their children are benefitting from these
experiences. These parents will be allies and strong supporters. Some parents will be uncertain but will, nevertheless, be open to the teacher's ideas.
If teachers believe in what they are doing, they will find ways to alleviate
parental anxiety and help them understand how play-debrief-replay promotes quality learning. Parents can be helped to understand that skill-and-
drill worksheets, in and of themselves, are inadequate to develop children
into responsible, thoughtful citizens and intelligent problem solvers.

Teachers who wish to exercise the option of providing supporting data
on child-centered programs to doubting parents might find the film *Why
Do These Children Love School?* of particular value (Fadiman, 1992). Available in video form, the film documents the 70-year-old inquiry-based program at the Peninsula School, in Palo Alto, California as a place of "improved test scores and classrooms of students with the capacity for self-
directed learning." Convincing arguments are provided by parents who describe the impact of this program on the later high school performance of
their children.

There may be a parent who is not convinced, who believes that children should be pressured to perform and that, the more seatwork and home-work a child gets, the better off he or she is for it. There may be a parent who is adamant that "playing in the first grade will not get my son or daughter into Harvard." Here again — no matter what program is chosen, no matter what curriculum, no matter what teaching style — there will invariably be parents who want something radically different from what the teacher is doing. They are sources of much heartache for teachers. Yet, right or wrong, parents will call the shots about their child's education, for the raising of their own children is considered to be the ultimate responsi-bility of parents. In these cases, wherever possible, parents who want otherwise for their children and are adamant about it should have the option of transfer to other classes.

### "How Will I Know What Students Are Learning?"

More teachers need to ask this question, not only those who are operat-ing a play-debrief-replay classroom. They also need to take seriously the ways that are used to make such determinations. In making the assess-ments, means (measures) must be consistent with ends (questions to be answered about student learning).

If adults want to measure how much taller a child has grown since his or her last birthday, they are not likely to use a pencil-and-paper test to make that assessment. They choose a means (measuring stick) that will allow them to determine, to some level of confidence, the ends they seek (the gain in height). In educational assessment, school personnel have often chosen the means (tests) before they have adequately reflected on the ends (ques-tions to be answered about growth). Consequently, students are subjected to tests and testing up to their armpits, but few instruments provide teach-ers with critical information about the questions they want answered about pupil growth. I realize it's a novel idea in education to begin with the questions instead of the tests, but that is what I am proposing for teachers who want to know what students are learning, no matter what the program.

What *do* teachers want to know about children's learning? If the ques-tions can be clearly articulated, the means for making the assessments — for finding the answers — will be as easily revealed as using a measuring stick to determine growth in height. Because this function of the teacher is so important, Chapter 14 is entirely devoted to a discussion on the how and what of evaluation practice.

### "What About My Own Needs for Success?"

Other authors have written extensively about the loneliness of the teach-er's work (Cuban, 1986; Jersild, 1955; Lortie, 1975). When things "go right" in the classroom, teachers have no one to share these successful moments with, other than the children, who may or may not appreciate the brilliance of what was done. Even those children who notice hardly have the insight to appreciate on the mature level of colleagues. When things "go wrong," teachers have limited opportunity to talk this out with a colleague, unlike, say, scientists in a laboratory, who can look at the problems and brainstorm ideas for diagnosis and possible corrective interventions. Perhaps that is why education is so slow to change (Cuban, 1982; Jennings & Nathan, 1977). Teachers rarely enjoy the chance for acclaim for the risk taking they do that leads to more creative teaching, and rarely do they enjoy the professional and emotional support of colleagues for their innovative efforts. Perhaps this is one reason that the Reggio Emilia approach has such appeal, not only for the learning rooted in meaningful connected experiences where rich projects based on children's explorations are seen in day-to-day practice, but for the opportunity of teachers to work in pedagogical teams, collaboratively, rather than in isolation (Cadwell, 1997).

The need for success is present in all of us, and this is no less so for teachers who are waiting to see the results of their efforts to build a play-debrief-replay program. Teachers need to feel that what they are doing is benefitting children in important ways, and they need to see evidence of that success. It's not the salary that keeps us teaching; it's knowing that we are doing something worthwhile for children.

One very fine teacher I know, Neil McAllister, says that he keeps anecdotal records for all his children in his play-debrief-replay program. He sits at his desk every afternoon after school and jots down notes about each child. This helps him to remember where each child started from and gives him a detailed record of month-to-month growth. When he *feels* he has not accomplished very much, when he is feeling "down on himself," a look at his records confirms his many successes with children. Sometimes it's hard to notice the growing when you are too close to it. The anecdotal notes help Neil to see the growth gains clearly. His written notes reflect what he sees in the children's behavior, and they are keyed to the growth outcomes he aims for.

He also finds support and nurturance for himself and his work from respected colleagues. These he chooses carefully with an eye to those who share his educational values, who are vigorous problem solvers, who are empathic. Dialogues with such colleagues are integral to his teaching life. He cannot envision teaching without such collegial interchange and support. With them, he also takes pleasure in sharing the successes of his program. For Neil, teaching is a shared experience. It takes more time and more effort to do this, but, as he says, "It beats the hell out of teaching in isolation, where the institutional press causes me to lose my perspective too easily" (N. McAllister, personal communication, April 1989).

## Part II

# BEFORE PLAY

# CHAPTER 4

# Organizing the Can–Do Classroom

It's one of those mean, rainy January mornings, when the chilly dampness sticks to your clothes and your feet think they will never get warm again. As I walk through a now-deserted schoolyard toward an ancient wooden four-story building, I see rooms cheerfully lit and gay colors of children's work adorning the walls. It is a striking contrast to the bleakness of the day.

Hastings Street School is in the heart of the inner city. While the children who attend represent the ethnic diversity found in a large urban area, they share a single common characteristic: their poverty. Many are from families of recently arrived immigrants unable to speak English, unfamiliar with the customs and the surroundings of their adopted land. Many are children of the streets, who bring to school the emotional baggage of lives in turmoil: children of single parents on Welfare; children abandoned to grandparents' and foster-parents' care; "latchkey" children who must, even in the primary years, look after themselves. The obstacles in the way of these children creating can-do spirits seem formidable.

## BREATHING OUT AND BREATHING IN

Entering the school I wind my way through the high-ceilinged corridors, with timeless school smells that somehow never change, and find Maureen Cumino's room at the very top level. I think it odd that the youngest children Grades K–2 combined, are on the highest floor. But then, why shouldn't the littlest children have the advantage of the spectacular view of the city?

Maureen's classroom is a very large, open room where two teachers share the load of working with a single group of 45 children in kindergarten through second grade. The environment that the teachers have created makes the room seem like a children's garden, an anomaly in this ancient wooden structure. Obviously a lot of care has gone into its creation, and it speaks of the values these teachers hold about the importance of physical space. The teachers' emphasis on play is also made explicit by what is seen: centers or stations for sand and water play; for building with blocks and Lego; for paint, clay, and paste; for dress-up and housekeeping; for making music, singing, and dancing; for puppets and a stage; for other crafts. There are investigative play centers that operate later in the day: a science center featuring play with magnets; a reading center where children may find a book they love and read it by themselves, look at the pictures, or read it to someone else; and a writing center with a computer and printer, pencils, paper, chalk, and lap blackboards. Each center is arranged so that it beckons invitingly, and centers are continually "refreshed" with new materials to replace what has been worn out or broken, or to give students' investigations a new and different focus. For example, mirrors will soon replace magnets as the emphasis for investigative play in science.

Near the entranceway to the classroom, the teachers have placed a choosing board that pictorially indicates what center options are available and how many spaces are available (i.e., how many children may be accommodated) in each. The painting center has space only for four children at a time, since there are only two double easels. The blocks center allows as many as six children to play at a time. After hanging up their outer garments, children go immediately to the choosing board, pick up their own nametags, and place them on a hook that allows them to occupy a "space" in the center of their choice (see Figure 4.1).

Children may choose to remain at one center's activity for the entire 90-minute session, or they may split their time among several centers. The choice is theirs and is always a free choice. To change from one activity to another, they need neither the advice nor the permission of a teacher; they merely return to the choosing board and place their names in the spaces alongside their alternate selections. The children call this play period "choosing time." Maureen and her co-teacher refer to it as "Breathing-Out" time, a period that allows children to "exhale," to "unpack their suitcases" and unload some of the emotional baggage of their burdened lives. Breathing-Out time is rooted in the work of Sylvia Ashton-Warner (1963), who sees this critical period as forming a bridge from a child's destructive impulses to increased creativity. In this classroom, all children, K–2, work together, and it's hard to tell who is at what level, except for Keith, a kindergartner who's been stuck to the blocks since early September, giving Maureen pause to wonder when and if he is ever going to be ready to move out to other creative experiences.

As I observe the children at their play activities, they appear deeply immersed in what they are doing. For the first 15 minutes of the Breathing-Out period, the teachers watch from the sidelines, making sure that the centers' activities are functioning smoothly, that children are productively

**FIGURE 4.1**   A Choosing Board

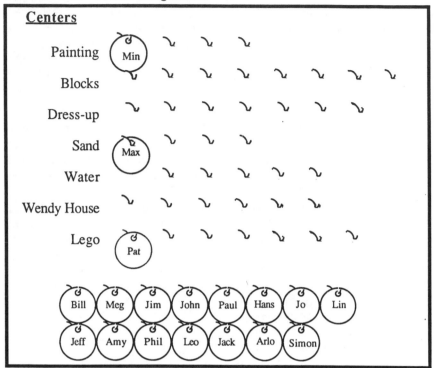

engaged. When they are satisfied that this is so, they proceed to their instructional tasks, calling individual children away from their centers on a "temporary assignment." This may mean taking some children's key vocabulary — those words of significance in a child's personal experience that are tapped by the teacher and form the bridge into reading (Ashton-Warner, 1963). It may also include listening to original stories; giving instruction in spelling, handwriting, or phonics; and listening to stories read from a chosen library book. The work is tailored to each individual learner by the artistry of these master teachers.

All is not perfect in the way children work together. There is invariably argument, dissension, sometimes open warfare. None of these interpersonal difficulties goes unnoticed by the teachers; however, if the level of argument is moderate, teachers do not intervene. They allow the children to work out the problem in their own fashion. If hostilities escalate, a teacher's intervention will require the children to sort the problem out for themselves, arriving at a truce. While teacher may mediate, she will rarely direct the solution ("Now this is what you should do."), nor will she accuse, make harsh critical judgments, or invoke guilt. These types of interactions are just never heard in this classroom. (For insightful and fascinating scenes of how teachers work with children wrestling with interpersonal and moral dilemmas, see Paley, 1992.)

The classroom is, of course, noisy; yet a visitor may be surprised by the absence of rowdy behavior, of aimless wandering, of mischief making. The noise level hovers around decibels that are quite bearable. When it sometimes becomes too noisy, a signal is given (a chord or two on the piano) to remind children to "lighten up." No words are spoken, and all return to activities with a renewed calmness. While the noise is an indicator of children playfully working together at various interest centers, it is *never* the noise of children out of control.

About 10 minutes before the recess bell, the cleanup signal (another series of piano chords) is given and the children go to work washing paint brushes, storing blocks on shelves, returning equipment and materials neatly to their appointed places. This done, all 45 assemble on the carpet near the piano for a song. As the melody is discerned, a chorus of very young voices is heard in varying applications of the English language:

> Oh, ha' you see d' Muffin Men,
> D' Muffin Men, d' Muffin Men,
> Oh, ha' you see d' Muffin Men,
> Who libs across d' way?

In spite of the chilly, rainy day, children climb the three flights down and join friends from other classes for an outdoor recess. In this weather-side city, no activity is canceled because of the rain. If it were, no one would ever get to do any of the outside things they like.

If the beginning of the morning until recess is characterized as Breathing Out, the session from recess to lunch is designated as "Breathing In," and much emphasis is given during this time to whole-language activities. While each teacher will work with a single instructional group at a time, other children work cooperatively in language activity groups with a focus designated by the teacher. In these groups there may be sharing of words or stories, story writing (on lap chalkboards or in scribblers), story telling, silent reading, or writing words in personal dictionaries. The groups may be as large as six or as small as two, and their formation and the instructional tasks are a reflection of the teachers' professional judgment of children's instructional needs. Groups therefore are modular and flexible; that is, their composition and activities shift according to perceptions of instructional need. These activities follow the play-debrief-replay format, with play centering on language activities and debriefing occurring when an instructional group is called to work with a teacher.

Instead of sitting in with the teachers' groups, I choose to sit on the

periphery of one of the unsupervised children's work groups. Six first graders are sitting in a circle on the carpet, sharing their key vocabulary words.
Each has a word on a card, face up on the floor. Wu Lei has been chosen by
the others as group leader. He calls on children whose hands are raised.

*Wu Lei:*   I choose William.
*William:*   My word is *egg*. (He holds it up so all can see.) Any questions?
    (A child raises her hand.) Amy.
*Amy:*   Do you mean a egg for breakfast?
*William:*   No, I mean a egg from a bird.
*Wu Lei:*   I choose Bruce.
*Bruce:*   My word is *knife*. (He holds it up.) Any questions?
*Daljit:*   My fodder gotta knife. He say you gotta be careful.
*Bruce:*   I know. I hope to get it for my birthday.
*Wu Lei:*   I choose . . . hmmmmm, Amy.

As the words are shared in this fashion, each child gets an opportunity to
read his or her own word and all the children in the group are exposed to
the others' words in their growing use of English as a spoken, read, and
written language. Thus, when Amy later sees the word *knife*, she says, "Oh
*knife*. That's Bruce's word."

When the group finishes sharing, they go off on their own or in pairs to
practice writing their new words, to reread to each other the words in their
growing key-vocabulary collection, to read, or to write stories. Breathing
In, in this classroom, is largely oriented to the language arts. It doesn't
have to be so; this is a matter of these teachers' choice, based upon their
professional judgment that enriched language experience is critical for
these children's educational development. These group activities are quite
sophisticated applications of investigative play with language.

The afternoon session has fewer children. The 12 kindergartners who
attend only the morning session have left for home, and the remaining 33
first and second graders seem lost in the large space. During afternoon
sessions, hands-on investigative play in numbering and measuring (math),
in sciencing, in explorations of the community (social studies) follow more
closely the play-debrief-replay pattern. The teachers design investigative
play tasks to insure children's growth in concepts and skills that reflect
school district curriculum guidelines. Interwoven also are activities such as
field trips, cooking, playing music, singing and dancing, storytime, and
arts and crafts projects such as making puppets or masks or sculpting.

Thus each day's shape unfolds: In the morning, there is Breathing Out
followed by Breathing In, in which play-debrief-replay is implicit in the
creative play and language activities of the children. In the afternoon,
play-debrief-replay provides the structure for curriculum activities in
math, science, and social studies. While all the activities in all parts of the

program are flexible, the shape of the day reveals how instructional plans accommodate the important learning goals. Within that shape, the key conditions of empowering children are also seen: opportunities for choosing and respect for individual choice; opportunities for hands-on, experiential play as a means for conceptual, intellectual, emotional, and social development; and opportunities to reflect on experiences, through specially designed tasks and teachers' facilitative interactions. The entire program offers challenges to primary children that require them to stretch their abilities within margins of comfort and safety. But, does it work? Do children learn? Are they empowered?

I leave Hastings Street School at the end of the day and walk back outside to the cold and wet schoolyard, with scenes from Maureen's classroom resonating in my mind. What evidence do we need to assure us that children are empowered? That they are self-sufficient in their functioning? That they are respectful of one another? That they are able and willing to solve problems of their own? That their ability to use language in increasingly sophisticated ways is growing? (Many of the children come in September with no English at all.) How do we know that they are interested and enthusiastic about the work they are doing? That they have increased their conceptual understanding, as seen in their articulation of how things work? I've seen all of that with my own eyes, in Maureen's classroom. But there is more—the more subtle evidence of what was *not* seen in this classroom. There is a marked absence of children's dependency on the teacher to "tell us what to do," and of persistent arrogance and rudeness to each other or a lack of respect for others and for classroom materials. Boredom and disinterest in the work are not in evidence, and there is no need for teachers to motivate the children to perform. The need for teachers to exercise control and maintain classroom discipline to keep the children "in line" and "on task" is also lacking.

One classroom's success may not necessarily sell soap, but I have presented Maureen's classroom as an example only because the conditions she faced made her job that much more difficult. There are, of course, dozens of other examples in other classrooms that might have been described. But, more to the point is your own classroom. How could you organize such a classroom? What steps could you take at the beginning of the school year to bring about such a smoothly functioning, child-centered, can-do classroom?

## DECIDING ON THE SHAPE OF THE DAY

There is no rule that insists on a single shape to a day in the can-do primary classroom. There are many shapes, each accommodating different learning needs. Shapes may change, reflecting the teacher's concern that what is important for that particular time of year be given major emphasis. No matter what the shape, the bedrock conditions for learning include respect for children, providing opportunities for children to choose, and personal challenges to children's intellectual growth.

No matter what the shape, Breathing Out is a preferred starting point. This may sound shocking to teachers who have heard for years that the first hours of the morning are the times when children are the freshest and that consequently we must make the most of them by scheduling our more important instructional tasks at that time — usually the "basic skills" of reading, writing, or numbering. Ashton-Warner (1963) advises us otherwise, and her ideas about this juxtaposition of "output" and "intake" have been put to the test in a study carried out in 10 primary classrooms where this approach was used over a 2-year period (Wassermann, 1976). The data from that study support Ashton-Warner's position: Children did learn to read, write, and number. They grew in their ability to work cooperatively with each other, to function autonomously. There were significant gains in their creative capabilities in arts and crafts work and in writing. At the end of 2 years, the children in the experimental classes tested as well on the Gates McGinitie Reading Test as those in the control-group classes, in spite of the fact that control groups were not randomly selected and were biased in favor of high-achieving students. Significant beyond the .01 level of confidence was the enthusiasm for school and for school activities expressed by the experimental-group children. The data show that not only did Breathing Out as a starting activity not diminish children's levels of achievement, but that the very opposite was true.

There are other data besides statistics to support this approach. Classroom observations of what and how the children are doing, plus systematic and cumulative records of performance provide "records of achievement," an important means of "assessing and recording pupils' personal qualities and achievement, along with the role of the pupil in that process" (Hargreaves, 1988–1989, p. 2). In the reality of classroom life, Breathing Out is an emotionally, socially, and intellectually responsible way of beginning the school day.

Breathing In follows, usually just after morning recess. It includes those activities that the teacher wishes to give emphasis to at this time. Maureen chooses whole-language activities because she is sensitive to the limited English-language experiences of her students and wants to insure that this area gets adequate attention. In other classes with other instructional needs or interests, teachers may choose a mathematics or science emphasis. Once a shape has been decided, it does not have to stay that way forever. The changes that are made, however, should always reflect the teacher's considered judgment of what is important and what the best shape is for helping students learn what is important.

The following are several examples of different shapes of the day.

### Class A, Grade 1

8:45   Opening exercises: greetings, choosing time

9:00   Breathing Out: conversation, finger painting, clay, sand, water, key vocabulary, blocks, dress-up, crafts, paste, paint, dramatic play, sculpting

10:15   Cleanup and singing

10:30   Recess

10:45   Language experiences: sharing key words and sentences, practicing key words, discussions, spelling, phonics, writing stories, vocabulary, reading stories

11:45   Singing and dancing

12:00   Lunch

1:00   Play-debrief-replay: children's investigative play with a focus in either sciencing, numbering and measuring, social studies, crafts, cooking, or making music, followed by debriefing

2:30   Storytime and reflections on the day

### Class B, Grade 2

8:15   Choosing time

8:30   Breathing Out: sand and water play, painting, crafts, blocks, reading corner, creative writing, dramatic play

10:00   Cleanup

10:15   Class meeting

10:30   Recess

10:45   Play-debrief-replay in science

12:00   Lunch

1:00   Language experiences: reading, creative writing, vocabulary, phonics, spelling, journal writing

2:00   Play-debrief-replay in mathematics

2:45   Cleanup, singing, dramatic play

### Class C, Grades 2 and 3 (two teachers in an open area)

8:45   Children meet in "home base" groups for attendance, announcements, special assignments, choosing

9:00   Breathing Out: a choice of creative activities, including painting, clay, carving, drawing, constructing, music-making, dramatic play, writing stories

10:00   Play-debrief-replay in mathematics: hands-on, experiential group work in math projects emphasizing concepts and understandings, followed by debriefing and replay, individual skills work

10:45   Recess

11:00   Play-debrief-replay in selected curriculum units in science (motors, sounds, mirrors, shadows, growing plants, small animals, personally designed investigations, etc.), followed by debriefing and replay

12:00   Lunch

1:00   Play-debrief-replay on selected projects in social studies (community surveys, comparison shopping, making maps, building houses, writing and performing plays, health and fitness projects), followed by debriefing and replay; alternates on Tuesdays and Thursdays with assigned physical education activities

2:00   Language experiences: individualized reading, writing stories or journals, special assignments, small group work, reading to comprehend meaning

2:45   Cleanup

3:00   Debriefing the day


*Class D, Grades 1 and 2 (one teacher)*

9:00   Breathing Out: blocks, paints, books, water table, drawing and coloring, construction, dress-up, writing stories

10:00   Cleanup, singing and dancing

10:30   Recess

10:45   Numbering and measuring: play-debrief-replay in cooperative learning groups, with tasks emphasizing taking measurements of lengths of different objects and recording the measurements

12:00   Lunch

1:00   Language activities: reading, writing stories, spelling, phonics work, vocabulary, storytelling, dramatic play

2:00   Sciencing: play-debrief-replay with selected materials in cooperative learning groups, on tasks that call for examination of air pressure and air weight, with subsequent debriefing and replay

3:00   Closing activities: clean-up, singing and dancing, reflections on the day


The shape of the day is the teacher's choice. As noted already, it should reflect what is important to the teacher. Observations of what is happening within that shape should serve as indicators of whether or not the shape the teacher has chosen is useful in meeting his or her instructional goals.

## GATHERING THE MATERIALS

The can-do classroom is organized around the principle of children's play as the central learning experience. Play can be investigative or creative, although such distinctions collapse in the playing out of the activities, and either kind generally demands hands-on experiences with materials, tools, and equipment. Children's manipulation of these materials is the basis for their growing and learning. Therefore, what teachers gather and put into the hands of children should meet certain standards of what is educationally sound. Since not all materials are entirely appropriate, some guidelines for choosing are presented here:

1. *Please don't taste the detergent!* Materials, tools, and equipment should, of course, be *safe*. Materials that are toxic or otherwise dangerous (e.g., matches, very sharp tools) should not be included for play. The teacher's own judgment is the best source for determining whether the children in *that* class, at *this* stage of their development, will be able to handle more sophisticated materials and equipment.
2. *Please don't break the porcelain vase!* Materials, tools, and equipment must be *expendable*. In the normal course of work and play, even adults are known to break things. This is likely to happen more frequently with children, who have less physical coordination, less experience with caretaking, and less appreciation for the consequences of breakage. Simply saying, "Teacher, it got wrecked" generally results in a magical replacement of the item as needed. The principle here is not to include materials that are too valuable or too precious to be used up. Materials that are especially sturdy and durable, made for children's play, abound in school equipment catalogues, and there's likely to be considerably more available than the classroom has room for. Nothing should ever be put into a play center that, if lost, would cause heartbreak.
3. *Please don't aim that machine gun at me!* While materials should be expendable, we should not be persuaded to include those articles that are offensive to personal taste or aesthetics. My personal values dissuade me from including any of the "junk" toys found in department stores and supermarkets — toys that promise much on the wrapper but deliver little of any lasting value. Similarly, I would shy away from toys of violence and destruction, such as plastic hand grenades, machine guns, and "laser" weapons. I cannot find worth in these items. I believe that, as a general rule, "junk" pervades children's lives, in the TV they see, in the food they eat, in the toys that they are pressed to buy. I would not want to add to that depository. While I recognize that children do need some healthful and acceptable ways of venting built-up anger, I am intractable about the inclusion of toys of violence and destruction in a classroom.

These are matters of personal taste and values, but I hold fast to the belief that a classroom should include materials that raise aesthetic appreciation and offer peaceful alternatives to mayhem and killing.

When the materials, tools, and equipment meet at least these three criteria, teachers are less likely to have to intervene to manage behavior in order to protect children's safety and/or thwart breakage or put a stop to open warfare. If the objective is to encourage children to evolve as thoughtful, responsible, collaborative group players, it helps enormously when the materials work as allies, rather than adversaries.

Materials will always reflect the kinds of investigative/generative activities the teacher has in mind. They should be selected with a view toward availability and storage. The school can be used as a primary resource. In almost every school there are abandoned materials that are stored for long periods of time, in locked cupboards, walk-in closets, and basements. Perhaps other primary teachers have no need of some materials and equipment stored in their classrooms and would welcome unloading them. Whatever else is needed that cannot be found in the school may also be requisitioned from the district office. These are starting points.

In some schools, parents may be willing and eager to donate materials from attics and basements that would greatly enhance a dress-up center or science center. The school custodian may have some ideas on materials acquisition. Beyond the walls of the school lie other potential resource areas for materials acquisition, such as second-hand stores, flea markets, garage sales, and junk stores (junk is *not* the same as junky toys). If your school funds for equipment purchase are short, involving parents in a fund-raising effort can help. These are only a few ideas for teachers to think about in questing for classroom materials.

The scope of what could be put into a can-do classroom is vast, so it is not essential to gather everything at once, lest there be no room for the children! Serious players can operate productively with carefully selected materials, and teachers can add to what is there on the basis of how the program evolves. Appendix A provides a partial list of suggested materials for a can-do classroom.

## SETTING UP THE CLASSROOM

As a primary-grade teacher I was never able to accommodate successfully, within the narrow confines of the classroom walls, all the materials and equipment I wanted for my program. As my teaching plans grew more ambitious and sophisticated, my need for space grew. When I remember back to those days, it seems now that I was perpetually moving furniture around, in the hope that *this* time would be the last time, that this time I would have finally solved the space problem.

Later on I learned that other primary-grade teachers with expanding and developing programs also spent countless hours after class rearranging furniture. It seems to be an occupational hazard when our plans for what we want in the classroom far exceed the square footage of our rooms. Given my own history, perhaps I should be the last person in the world to give advice to anyone else about interior arrangements, but I shall, nonetheless. In retrospect, I can see that room arrangements that never change may signal static, never-changing programs, while arrangements that are transient may reflect programs that continually evolve and grow. It is clear that I tend toward the latter. Those primary teachers who lean in this direction will always be assured of exercise!

## Guiding Principles

In room arrangement, as in other educational practice, there are principles to guide the teacher, and here, too, you may take comfort from the fact that you are not just shifting chairs and tables for benefit of change alone. For example, a principle of good architecture—that form follows function—applies equally to classroom arrangement. Your program needs are the starting point for interior design. What Breathing-Out activities are to be included? What space requirements are necessary for those activities? What storage space is needed? What other activities are contained in the shape of your day? What is the best way to "locate" these activities in the space provided? As you reflect on these questions, think about some of the following features:

1. *Working surfaces.* Large tables with easy-to-clean tops are imperative, so include as many as you have space for. If you are stuck with individual child-sized tables and chairs, these can be arranged together to form a larger work area. In some schools, though, they can be shipped out to storage and traded for larger worktables. Some teachers prefer that each child have his or her own desk and argue that these may be arranged in working-group order. Other teachers insist on larger tables. Individual desks consume more space, but they provide each child with his or her own space, and children at this age are territorial and possessive. Worktables are more space conserving, and they implicitly call for students working together. Worktables on casters may be moved out of the way when activities are concluded, to make space for other centers. If you choose worktables, you will have to make alternate arrangements for children to keep and store their personal belongings as well as confront the larger issue of territoriality.

2. *Display tables.* While some children's creative work and teacher displays can be mounted on walls and bulletin boards, some will require display tables. You will want to be circumspect, however, about how many are included, since with a finite amount of room, display tables and working surface always compete for the same space.

3. *Reading "corner."* Not necessarily set in a corner, the reading area ought to seem like a mini-library, with easy access to shelves of books, some larger floor cushions, a small display table, and some soft furniture. If possible, the reading area should be as far removed from noisier activities as possible.

4. *Private areas.* The can-do primary classroom is usually a beehive of activity, yet not every child works comfortably in a beehive, nor is every learning task effectively carried out in a beehive. Making space available for some children to work quietly and undisturbed may forestall potential problems as well as provide for individual learning needs.

5. *Storage.* Most modern primary classrooms have ample storage areas that will adequately contain blocks, paints, construction materials, manipulatives, and books. You will also want to store math and science manipulatives, crafts materials, dress-up clothing, junk materials, musical instruments, and supplies. A can-do classroom requires that children have access to and responsibility for materials, so storage areas ought to allow for this in so far as possible. For efficiency and simple expediency, materials for activities should be near enough for you to reach out and get what you need without the hassle of having to make a trip or carry out an extended search. The easiest access should be to supplies that are in constant use — water, paper towels, newspapers, scissors, paper of all kinds, crayons, pencils, felt-tip pens, paste, tape, string, chalk, and the like.

With very few exceptions, consider each of the activity centers as transitory. Children's interests will wax and wane in response to activity centers, so plan for the eventual collapse of an activity center and its replacement with a new one. Being prepared for change will allow your program to evolve and grow.

Very few primary classrooms are large enough to include all the activity centers that we might desire. In school, as in life, we can't have everything we want; we've got to make choices and trade-offs. As you set up your room, choose the activity centers first that are imperative for your program, based upon the shape of your day. Put "on hold" those centers that cannot, at this first stage, be accommodated comfortably. Balance what you want with the amount of space available. Too much may be as unhealthy as too little. Just as too little results in inadequate programs, too much may cause visual clutter, crowding, and feelings of claustrophobia.

It may not be possible or advisable to have both sand *and* water tables *and* blocks *and* construction all at the same time. Select what you want, based on thoughtful consideration of what you need, remembering that change is refreshing.

A little creative thinking applied to storage needs may open up new possibilities. Plastic bins that can be slid out and in easily and/or large cardboard boxes from the supermarket, painted and decorated by the children, can be used to store your more lightweight equipment. The advantage is that these can be moved as needed. Large plastic garbage bags may be used to line cardboard boxes in which damp materials are stored. Smaller pieces of equipment may be stored in shoeboxes, in cottage cheese containers, plastic 5-gallon ice-cream buckets, and other plastic food containers.

Shelves in many classrooms have become repositories for out-of-date textbooks that are difficult to get rid of, although never used. If your classroom is one of these, then dispatch materials, equipment, and books that are not presently being used to long-term storage areas, preferably outside of the classroom. Be absolutely merciless in unloading the unwanted and unneeded detritus of school programs past. I recognize that this is a formidable task for primary teachers who share the pack-rat mentality, clinging to every book, every toy, every piece of equipment, just in case it is ever needed. Should you overcome that attitude, I predict that you will be ever so pleased with the space you have gained and will hardly spend a sleepless night on what has been discarded.

Nowhere it is writ that classrooms have to be dull, lifeless places that are about as appealing as shoeboxes. Since physical space has a considerable effect on our mental and emotional states of being, I believe classrooms should be attractive, comfortable, inviting places where children prefer to spend time, given the choice. Many teachers invest a lot of care and energy in making their classrooms attractive, and I believe that this time is more than well spent. Not only is it nicer for children and teachers to spend their school hours in such classrooms, it also teaches, implicitly, about aesthetic standards. Choosing pictures of quality for the walls (Degas rather than Disney), displaying a large collection of children's creative work, and bringing in fresh flowers are all ways of making rooms colorful, warm, and hospitable, offering silent invitations to children to come and play. Rooms that are too tidy show that not enough play is going on, while excessive messiness means that not enough responsibility is taken for cleanup. Somewhere in the middle is the "right" balance.

Since the classroom is, first and foremost, the children's workplace, they ought to have some voice in its set-up. They must also play responsible roles in its care and upkeep. Helping children to learn responsibility for the care and keeping of materials, equipment, and tools is an important feature of the can-do classroom. To teach children to behave responsibly—to share, to treat materials respectfully, to wash paintbrushes carefully, to store materials where they belong—is a task more formidable than teaching children to read and number. Yet teachers must not shirk their own responsibility to do this, no matter how difficult it is. If it's the children's classroom, they must play active roles in its maintenance. (See particularly Chapter 5, "Preparing Children for the Can-Do Classroom.") To the extent that children are free to choose and find the materials and supplies they need, without teacher assistance, their autonomy has been increased. When children are still asking, every step of the way, "Where is the red paint?" and "Where is the wastepaper basket?" and "I'm finished; what shall I do now?" these are indicators that much more work needs to be done in promoting self-sufficient functioning.

### Designing the Space

Since organizing space is a reflection of the shape of your day, it's best to begin by studying the shape you have created, to determine which activities require special space arrangements. For example, which ones need a larger area? Which need to be separated because of the noise spillover? Which are "wet" activities? Which will occupy space that is built-in and nonflexible? Which need floor space? Which need large project tables? Which need to be close to cupboards where materials are stored? Which activities require "permanent" space arrangements? Which are "transitory," in that they may be opened up for work and closed up and stored away when the work is over?

It's helpful to begin with a pencil-and-paper plan, giving a bird's-eye view of how the space may be arranged, before the actual task of moving furniture is undertaken. Figure 4.2 shows how flexible use of classroom space may accommodate the changing activities throughout the day.

☆    ☆

Organizing your can-do classroom means confronting a variety of choices with respect to how your day is to be shaped and how the room is to be comfortably and attractively arranged. Once again, examining your beliefs and determining for yourself what is important are the keys to helping you through the maze of options.

## FIGURE 4.2 Flexible Use of Classroom Space

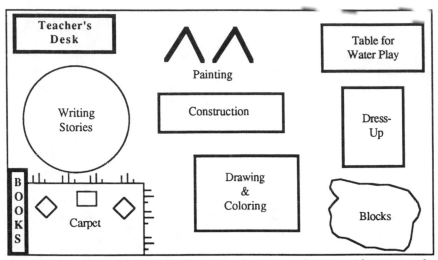

**Breathing Out, 9:00–10:15.** The room is arranged to provide centers for block play, looking at and/or reading books, playing with water, drawing and coloring, painting at easels, construction, dressing up, and writing stories. **After 10:15**, blocks, construction materials, dress-up materials, easels, and water play buckets are stored away. The table for water play converts to other uses in later activities.

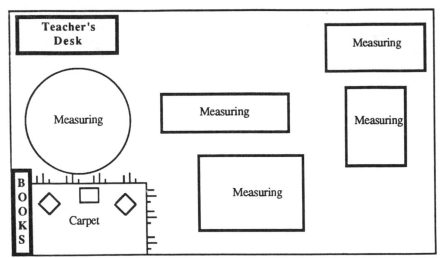

**Measuring and numbering, 10:45–12:00.** These tables form measuring centers. Manipulative materials for measuring tasks are taken out of storage bins and placed in the centers.

FIGURE 4.2 *(continued)*

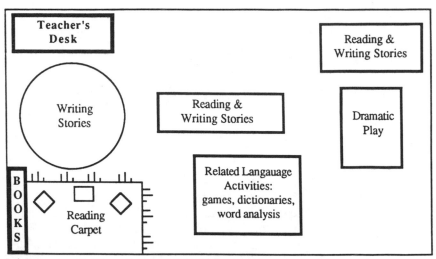

**Language activities, 1:00–2:00.** The room is arranged for reading, writing stories, related language activities, and dramatic play.

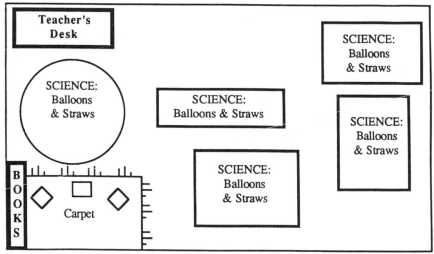

**Sciencing, 2:00–3:00.** The tables become sciencing centers. Manipulative materials for science investigations into air pressure and weight are taken from storage areas and placed in centers.

# CHAPTER 5

# Preparing Children for the Can–Do Classroom

It would be wonderful if children came to school fully prepared to take on the burdens of self-sufficient functioning. It would be wonderful if children were born with responsible behaviors and we didn't have to work so hard at developing them. It would be wonderful, if, by age 5, children had already mastered the art of cleaning up their messes, of looking after materials, of taking turns and sharing, of being reasonable, of making intelligent decisions. It would be wonderful if 5- and 6-year-old children were cooperative in their dealings with other children; if, when given choices, their decisions were thoughtful and responsible and with an eye toward consequences. It would also be wonderful if no child came to school hungry, or ill, or battered, or full of fear or rage. And it would be truly wonderful if each child was sent to school by "perfect" parents who had only that child's health and well-being uppermost in their minds. Ah, if teachers' wishes were butterflies, we should always see the sky through multicolored hues.

The facts of children's lives tell a different story. However, while we teachers may not have many options with respect to "fixing" what happens in a child's home, we do have many options with respect to what we do in our classrooms.

All children can and should learn to develop a sense of their own autonomy, a spirit of can-do, and feelings of increased personal power. Primary classrooms are places where such growth can flourish or wither. There is no secret to doing this, only great effort on the part of the teacher and a willingness to commit time and energy to providing opportunities for children to practice responsible behavior, again and again and again, until such behaviors have been well-integrated into personal functioning. Of course, the more children learn to behave in these thoughtfully responsible ways, the more they grow in personal power. Thoughtful and responsible behavior is one of the keys to the successful functioning of a can-do classroom, and that is why particular emphasis is given to preparing children for learning to choose and for working cooperatively in groups.

As one does not learn to ski by listening to a teacher give a lecture on the how and what of skiing, so children do not learn responsible behavior by adult commands for them to behave responsibly. The paths to skiing competence and responsible actions are similar. In both instances, the learning is achieved through both the doing and the thoughtful examination of what has been done. With practice and reflection-on-practice, there is improvement and finally even mastery. As there are no shortcuts to learning to ski masterfully, so are there no shortcuts to learning responsible behaviors. Teachers must be prepared to teach these critical life skills and to wait out the time it takes for students to master them. This does not happen in a week or two of practice. From September to January would be a more reasonable expectation.

Before pressing on to the "how" of the practice, a few last words need to be said about responsible behavior. While some teachers might take this to mean obedient behavior, as evidenced by children doing just as they are told, this is not the definition that is intended here. In a can-do classroom, responsible behavior includes the ability to make thoughtful decisions about work and play, to take a self-initiating part in all the activities of the program, to work cooperatively and productively on learning tasks, and to maintain an appropriate level of self-discipline. Furthermore, it means doing all of these things without having to be told, persuaded, encouraged, led, bribed with promise of reward, or given the benefit of close supervision to monitor performance. These responsible behaviors become a way of being in the world. They are difficult to master not only because they require a sophisticated level of cognitive and social functioning, but also because they depend on embracing attitudes of responsibility as worthwhile. Where attitudinal development is involved, there is bound to be a long haul. The rewards, however, are more than worth the effort.

## LEARNING TO WORK IN GROUPS

In most new growth experiences, learning is enhanced when at least three steps are taken in the process: orienting the students, providing opportunities to practice, and providing opportunities to reflect on practice. These steps are equally applicable to learning to work in groups.

### Orientation

Orientation precedes the experience. It begins with the teacher's explaining and describing what is involved. It includes reference to the kind of behavior that will be expected and to how the routines are to be carried out. Procedures for handling difficulties that may arise are identified, and directions for materials' use, storage, and cleanup are made clear. Children's questions are invited, and any source of potential difficulty is given full examination. At the end of the orientation, children should be much clearer about the ideas behind working in groups. In orienting the children, consider the following guidelines:

1. In the very beginning, talk to the children about how they are to work in groups, about what group work means, and about the materials they will be using. Invite opportunities for them to raise questions about their concerns.
2. Talk about the choosing board, about the options, and about how choices can be made. A demonstration of how this is done is helpful.
3. Communicate your enthusiasm for group work, and talk about why you believe this is a good way for children to learn.
4. Communicate your confidence in their ability to work cooperatively.
5. Discuss with them what you believe to be the requirements for effective group work: taking turns, sharing, telling (instead of hitting), being polite and respectful to others, and being careful about materials.
6. Make explicit the procedures for handling problems that arise; for example, "If the paint gets spilled, this is what needs to be done." Make sure they understand the signal you use to say, "Whew! Too much noise. Please settle down."
7. Be explicit about the way materials are to be cared for; for example, "When you are in the dress-up center, I hope you will be very careful about putting on and taking off the clothes. I hope you can do this without tearing them. It wouldn't be very nice to have to play dress-up with torn clothes."
8. Be explicit about your cleanup procedures and about how and where materials are to be stored; for example: "When you hear these notes on the piano (da-da-da-DUM; da-da-da-DUM) that means it's cleanup time. Even if you are playing an important game, and even if it's hard to stop, you will have to help with the cleanup. I want to show you where the materials belong and how they are put away. Everybody must take a part in cleaning up and putting away all the materials. This may be hard for you to do at first, but I know you will be able to do this very well."
9. Invite children's ideas and suggestions for making the working procedures more effective. Allow them opportunities to take ownership of the way the classroom groups are running.

## Opportunities to Practice

When the initial orientation session has concluded, a practice session should follow soon afterward, either immediately, later in the day, or the following day, but not later than that, lest the message of the orientation be forgotten in the interval. Practice may be a "dry run," but it's probably a better idea to allow a practice session that includes all the key components of investigative play in cooperative groups.

Set up at least eight play centers. These should be centers of your own choosing, ones you think will capture the interest of the students and that are likely to sustain interest for at least several weeks. Have the choosing board ready for your first trial run, and stay close at hand to supervise and monitor the process.

1. Introduce the choosing board, show the play centers to the children, and explain how many "spaces" there are for children in each center. Describe how children use the board and what can be done if the center of first choice is filled. Invite questions to insure that children understand this process.
2. Call on two or three children at a time to choose. At least in the early stages of choosing, a small number of children at the board at one time is preferable to a mob.
3. When children have chosen, they may proceed directly to the play center and begin.
4. Children should know the procedure for changing a choice, if or when they wish to make that change.
5. Be a visible but nonintrusive presence during investigative and creative playtimes. At first supervise closely, but taper this off as you observe children's increased ability to work on their own.
6. Observe children's behavior, making mental notes about children with special needs or children who require specific interventions. Children who need special help and adult assistance should get it.
7. Take an overview of children's work in the play centers. What play activities are flourishing? What seems to be less than inspirational? Which children enjoy which activities? Which children shun which activities? What activities allow for the best, most productive play? Which never seem to get off the ground? Which centers are the most popular? Least popular?
8. Be available to monitor procedures when breakage or spillage occur. Be supportive and encourage children to take ownership of the cleanup.

9. Be available to settle disputes about sharing and about taking turns. When battles occur, be on the scene to prevent bloodshed. Wherever possible, however, avoid dictating the settlement of the dispute and taking control of the behavior management. Whenever possible, involve the adversaries in settling their own arguments. Responses such as, "Hmmm. Let's see what's happening here. Tamara wanted to be the mother, but Arlene wanted to be the mother, too. Both of you want to be the mother. I wonder how we are going to settle this one?" (The more you allow yourself to fall into the trap of taking control over children's actions, the longer they will depend on you to exercise that control and the longer will it take them to assume the controls for themselves.)

10. When you sound the cleanup signal, supervise closely the procedures and intervene with advice as necessary. When cleanup has fallen short of your standards, request a better job, without invoking guilt.

11. When the trial run has been concluded, congratulate the children on all the good work they did and give examples of things you liked (without singling out some children for praise and not others). For example, you might say, "I liked very much how the painting group washed the brushes and picked up the newspapers and put them in the trash. My, that was hard work, and now the painting area is sparkling clean."

## Opportunities to Reflect on Action

Essential to improvement of practice is the opportunity to reflect on practice. Without it, one tends to repeat bad practice until it becomes ingrained and far too difficult to change. At the end of the first several dozen opportunities for practice, children and teacher engage in a critical examination of the experience. What was good about it? What went wrong? How might that have been avoided? What could be done better tomorrow?

Inviting children's evaluative comments and respecting their ideas not only helps to improve the practice, but also gives them ownership of the process and pride in their ability to be discriminating and critical. Reflection-on-action as an evaluative process is a partnership effort of teacher and children in which standards are examined and maintained and levels of performance continue to evolve. Of course, in all of this, it is a given that no child is singled out for praise at the expense of any other child, nor is a child condemned for poor performance. In the reflection-on-action process, there are neither stars nor villains; neither awards nor public hangings.

1. After cleanup, ask children to tell what was good about the play session. Ask them to talk about what went wrong.
2. Help them to focus their responses on process and procedures, rather than on individual children.
3. Ask for their ideas about what might be done tomorrow to help improve the process. Be accepting of all viable ideas. Where ideas are not feasible, help the children to understand why that is so; for example, "Marilyn suggests that we try to remember where the different-shaped blocks go, and maybe we could have a sign to help us remember that. Well, I think I could do that for you, and thank you, Marilyn, for your helpful idea." And, "Patsy, you are suggesting that we get another water table so that more children can have a chance to play at that center. It would be nice if more children could play. But we have a real problem. If we move one more water table in here—whew! It would be very crowded, and then we would not have enough room for the other activities. I know that you would have liked to have had a chance to play at the water table center today, and I know you are disappointed."

In spite of the most careful and well-prepared orientations to learning to work in groups, it is best to remember, once again, that the development of these complex social skills takes time. Sometimes teachers feel a great urgency to see children master them, if not today, then certainly by tomorrow. It is hard to wait for children to grow into these habits of sophisticated social functioning, yet teachers must not abandon the process because they are impatient with how long it takes or because there are too many mishaps along the way. Bringing children back into line, removing their options, and placing them under our authority may give the appearance of things running smoothly, but, under such strictures, opportunities for the most important aspects of children's growth as cooperative and responsible citizens are greatly diminished.

## LEARNING TO CHOOSE

Knowing how to choose wisely distinguishes mature adults from immature ones. Immaturity is associated with indecisiveness, with the inability to make up one's mind, with the inability to take action; or, on the other hand, with making impulsive choices, with choosing without thinking about options or about consequences. Immaturity is also associated with the need to turn to others to make decisions for us. Adults who ask, "What shall I do?" are in danger of giving over their personal power to others.

Personal power is very much a reflection of choosing thoughtfully for oneself.

Choosing is one of the most pervasive acts of living. Almost every action requires choices to be made. The decisions may be explicit or implicit, and they may involve trivialities or matters of life and death. Even choosing *not* to choose is a choice.

Knowing how to choose wisely (and sometimes courageously) is not a trait a person is born with. It has to be learned through years of practice and reflection on that practice. Yet, even as adults, we sometimes still make "foolish" choices. And some adults tend to repeat foolish choices over and over again. Somehow, they have missed opportunities to learn to choose wisely.

While choosing plays a major role in life, learning to choose wisely does not appear on any list of educational objectives that schools have listed as worthwhile. Perhaps it is assumed that learning to choose is a by-product of other learning. If so, it is a bad assumption. Learning to choose wisely comes with repeated opportunity to do so, followed by a critical and nondefensive examination of how and why the choice was made. In other words, it takes practice and reflection-on-action.

When we teachers do all the choosing for students, we hold the power and students learn habits of obedience. When we offer opportunities for children to choose, gradually increasing both the number and significance of the choices, students grow in their ability to choose wisely, as well as in their personal power. We cannot have it both ways. We cannot hold all the cards with respect to choosing and still hope that children will grow as independent thinkers. Growing independent, reasoned, and reasonable adults begins with allowing even very young children many opportunities to choose.

The use of a choosing board is an explicit way to communicate to children, "This is a time for you to make some choices about what you want to do." If choices are offered, they should be offered freely, without encumbrances that persuade children to choose "our way." If we want children to choose X over Y, we'd best not offer a choice. We'd best simply tell them that X is required.

Some children may have difficulty choosing at first, as it may be a new experience for them. The choosing board will set the parameters and allow them to consider and reflect on the alternatives. It is a safe and effective procedure for initiating both the concept of choice, as well as practice in choosing.

Children's choices should be observed over the short and long term, for how and what children choose tells us much. How are choices being made? Is a child choosing the same activity again and again? Does a child flit from choice to choice several times a day? Helping children to reflect on their actions in neutral ways is likely to lead to greater insights about choosing and eventually to more thoughtful choices. *Choosing*, however, means just that; it does *not* mean manipulating children to make the choice we think is right.

When children have learned habits of choosing, more choices can be offered. If choosing is seen to operate successfully for Breathing-Out activities, it may be time to open out choices and begin using play-debrief-replay in other areas of the curriculum.

## STUDENTS WITH SPECIAL NEEDS

In every heterogeneous classroom, we teachers will find a spectrum of talents, abilities, and special needs, which can be easily observed in the behavior of the children. We may feel that such variability taxes our teaching skills to the limits, and we may wish that individual differences might disappear so that we wouldn't always have to be thinking, "Now, how am I going to handle *this*?" But there is no escaping the fact that children are all different. Some of them come to us happy, secure, and ready to learn, while others come damaged and full of pain. We are expected to find ways to teach them all.

Happy and secure children give us lots of pleasure in the teaching. They smile at us when we give them tasks that challenge them. They rarely get into the kind of mischief that requires a reprimand. They like us and tell us so. They make us feel good and provide us with the satisfaction of knowing that we are performing competently.

Troubled children cause us anguish and pain. We worry about them all the time, always wondering, "Am I doing enough?" Their behavior is a source of concern for us and for their classmates. They may reveal their own unhappiness by making others unhappy, through acts of aggression and violence. They may be so full of their own troubles that they are unable to be interested in anything the school has to offer. They may be withdrawn, shunning contact with other children and even helpful adults. They may lack the most simple courtesies; they may curse and swear; and they may not have good hygiene habits. They may be disabled, seriously ill with a terminal disease, or labeled "emotionally disturbed." They may be tense and anxious all the time, reflecting the lives of children in the "fast lane" (Stevens & Price, 1992).

In some primary classrooms there may be several such troubled children, and it is the teacher's job to find ways to reach and teach them. They seem to take up an unequal amount of our time, since they require more attention. Whatever we give them or do for them, it does not seem to be enough. Sometimes our efforts to help seem like pouring water into a sieve. The troublesome behaviors do not go away. These children creep into our dreams, and they cause us to doubt our teaching effectiveness and ourselves.

Will a can-do classroom be a good placement for children with special needs? Will the freedom to choose and the relinquishing of tightly held teacher controls be too much freedom for troubled children to cope with? Will it cause an increase rather than a decrease in their distress?

I would not want to promise you a rose garden, but the data are convincing: A classroom environment that is respectful to all children, that challenges them at their level of ability, and that encourages them to express themselves through creative play is therapeutic and educationally sound for all children, not only the emotionally and physically healthy ones (Arnoud & Curry, 1971; Aspy & Roebuck, 1977; Bredecamp & Copple, 1997; Bruner, 1966; Jones & Reynolds, 1992; Purkey, 1978; Saltz & Saltz, 1986; Wassermann, 1976). In fact, the can-do classroom may be the very best environment for children "in trouble."

It may be tempting to think of placing children with special needs in classrooms where their excessive behaviors are controlled by coercion, force, or tough disciplinary measures. But we know in our hearts that such means are not only *not* helpful, but actually psycho-noxious for these children's well-being. Behavior controlled by strict discipline and force may give a classroom the appearance of an orderly learning environment, but one need only to look to the playground at recess, or to the streets after school, to see what we all know: Repression breeds violence. When the repressive controls are not in place, the behavior erupts in full force. It is a very big price to pay for an orderly classroom.

The means for helping—truly helping—children with special needs lies in the way we treat them in our schools. Treating them with respect, caring for them, recognizing their pain, and providing them with creative outlets to channel their aggressive drives is the hard, high road. But it is the primary route to helping these children grow and learn.

They will tax us to the limits of our endurance, yet we will know by our observations of their interpersonal behaviors that we are planting the seeds that have a far better chance of taking root for their healthful development. Nobody said it would be easy.

## FINDING A COMFORTABLE "WAY IN"

The thought of designing and organizing a can-do classroom may be very appealing. It may also be very intimidating to think about classrooms where students are active, noisy, and highly involved in making decisions that matter. Such a classroom presents many challenges to teachers who believe that these learning environments are right and good for students, and it's conceivable that, in the evolvement of a can-do classroom, even the most intrepid teachers may pause to wonder, "Egad! What have I done?"

The word *evolve* offers a good description of what to expect. It suggests that can-do classrooms do not happen overnight; that children do not learn independent, cooperative functioning easily; that helping children grow from positions of dependence and lack of responsibility for their actions, to thoughtful decision making, are hard-won gains. During the process of can-do classroom evolvement, the teacher's sense of comfort about what he or she is doing is the key. If teachers become afraid that they have gone too far, too fast, they may abandon the program because they feel too stressed, tired, and anxious. If teachers are too ill at ease with what they are doing, they cannot feel content, secure, and confident about their work. Therefore, teachers attempting to create can-do classrooms must find and follow an evolutionary pace that is comfortable for them. This will be an individual matter, and while 10 years is far too long for making these adjustments, 10 days is just as unrealistic. I am recommending that teachers tune into their inner voices when reading the following guidelines and select an approach that is likely to represent a comfortable "way in" to can-do classroom evolvement.

## Approaches

### A. Toe-In

1. Begin by choosing a play activity that feels safe to you, one that creates a minimum of mess and involves a minimum of higher-order decision making for the children. This may include arts and crafts, language, social studies, science, or math. Activities suggested in Chapters 7 through 11 may provide a good starting point. Let's say that you have chosen Linear Measurement (Chapter 9, Activity 5).

2. Get ready for the activity by gathering the materials and preparing the suggested activity card. (See Chapter 6 for information on preparing activity cards.) Have one activity card for each working group.

3. Schedule a time of the day and allow about 1 hour for this activity to be carried out.

4. Arrange the children into groups of two or, at the most, three. Set up the groups, based on your ideas of who may work well together. Working with a partner in duos may be the smoothest initiation into group work for many primary children, and you can decide whether to begin with pairs, trios, or a combination of pairs and trios.

5. Give explicit instructions to pupils about carrying out these investigative or creative play activities. Remind them about behavioral expectations for group work, care of materials, and cleanup. Instruct the groups about how to work together and, when appropriate, to record their measurements.

6. Allow 10 to 15 minutes for investigative play. Move about the room, observing what the children are doing and responding as needed. Otherwise, do not direct the children's inquiries.

7. At the end of the play period, signal cleanup. Then call the children together and ask them to tell about their investigations. Make it safe for children to share their observations, by avoiding directive and/or judgmental responses. Use responses that call for students' reflection on their ideas. (See Chapter 9, Activity 5 for sample questions, and Chapter 13 for specific help with these interactive skills.) Limit this debriefing session to about 10 minutes.

8. At the end of debriefing, ask the children to tell you what they enjoyed about this investigative play activity. What was good? What did they not like? What went wrong? What might be helpful to do the next time, to make it work better?

9. The next day, follow up with a replay, as suggested in Chapter 9, Activity 5 (put out new items to be measured and/or include other measuring tools). After replay, follow procedures 7 and 8 again. Consider regrouping some children as you see necessary.

## B. Foot-In

Using the guidelines in Approach A as a basic set, extend the options in *one* of the following ways:

- Choose an activity that invites children to work outside of the confines of their own desks. In this, you would be increasing the "moving-around" option.
- Choose an activity that allows for a wider scope of investigative play or one that is messier. In this, you increase investigative opportunities.
- Provide more time for the investigative play, perhaps 15 to 20 minutes.

## C. Leg-In

Using the guidelines in Approach A as a basic set, extend the options in *two or more* of the following ways:

- Choose two or more investigative or creative play activities. Organize the session so that all groups get to work at both activities in that session.

- Choose investigative or creative play activities that are of higher risk for you, that is, activities that involve more movement, are messier, or extend investigative/creative opportunities.
- Provide at least 40 minutes for the play session.
- Allow the students to choose their own work/play-group mates.

### D. Waltz-In

Use the following guidelines to initiate a Breathing-Out program, as described in Chapter 4:

1. Create six centers for play activities.
2. Design a choosing board. (See Chapter 4 for help with this.)
3. Prepare the children for choosing.
4. Prepare the children for cooperative play.
5. When you are satisfied that all preparations have been made, let the play begin.
6. Move about the room, observing what the children are doing and responding as needed. Otherwise, do not direct their play.
7. Allow at least 1 hour for Breathing-Out activities.
8. At the end of the Breathing-Out period, call for cleanup. Be a high-profile presence during cleanup, but avoid directing, if possible.
9. Call the children together and reflect on the Breathing-Out experience. Involve the children in a critical examination of the process and their responses. Invite suggestions for the next day's activity.
10. Build Breathing Out into your teaching plan as a regular beginning-of-the-day activity. Extend and expand play-center choices to the limits of your comfort margin.

Within at least a week of children's initiation into Breathing Out, follow Approach A and initiate at least one investigative play activity into your teaching plan, to be built into a later part of the day.

### E. Dive-In

1. Begin with your Breathing-Out program, following the guidelines in Approach D.
2. Plan for at least an additional hour in the morning and another in the afternoon, in which play-debrief-replay is carried out in one or more curriculum areas. (Refer to the guidelines in Approach A.)
3. Extend your play-debrief-replay program to the limits of your margin of comfort.

### F. Fly-In

Use a combination of Approaches A to E, or create your own set of strategies that enable you to take comfortable steps to make your program "fly."

## Ground Rules

Whichever approach you choose, consider the following ground rules in planning what you will do:

- Begin with a clear notion of your comfort level with respect to each of these approaches. Choose an approach that feels safe yet also allows you to take on some new challenges.
- Take the time you need to prepare the children for whatever approach you have chosen. Preparing them may well involve more time than you initially expect.
- Remember that grouping the children for cooperative learning may be more difficult than it sounds. You may have to group and regroup several times, before working together is a successful operation. Even so, problems will inevitably arise from time to time, and it's helpful to be ready to deal with them when they do. Smaller groups are generally a better idea, and some children may need to begin group work in pairs.
- Make sure you have the materials you need to make investigative work in each center inviting. Investigations depend on good materials, and inquiries may fail if preparation of materials is not carefully done.
- Make yourself a high-profile presence, especially during the first weeks of the program's initiation. This will communicate to the children that you are there and aware, as they are evolving through their first stages of independent work. It will also allow you to attend to trouble immediately, if difficulties arise.
- Involve children frequently in evaluating the program, so that they assume ownership for the health of the program, for their roles in it, and for its overall effectiveness. Invite their suggestions for improvement.
- Communicate frequently your confidence in the children and in their ability to work responsibly. Recognize their accomplishments and their gains as independent, cooperative workers.
- Observe your own interactive style. Try to avoid telling the children what to do. Avoid praising children for their investigations. Be consistent in your use of responses that require children to be reflective about what they are doing.
- Be a reflective practitioner/teacher. Observe what is happening in your classroom in a diagnostic way, and use these data to keep building and improving the program. The most creative and sensitive profes-

sionals use the reflection-in-action process as a means for examining existing situations, diagnosing weaknesses and strengths, and creating strategies that lead to improved practice (Schön, 1987). Reflection-in-action allows teachers to keep the classroom dynamic and to be consistently responsive to instructional improvement.

Part III

# SERIOUS PLAY

Ballet dancer

# CHAPTER 6

# Curriculum for Serious Players

Children learn in many ways. They learn by watching, and even the youngest children are keen observers who take in data and process them without adult intervention. Simon, age 5, looks at the digital clock and says, pointing to the numbers, "It's eight-oh-oh and that means it's time for Papa to hear his news program." No one has "taught" him this. He has, however, learned it from many observations, making the connections for himself that the numbers eight-zero-zero signal the time for Papa to turn on the news broadcast. He does not yet know what 8:00 *means* and still counts days by counting "sleeps"; yet, by observing, he learns an important relationship between a certain time and a certain event. Children learn by observing far more than we even realize.

Children also learn by listening and by example. "Look, sweetie, this is how you hold the scissors." Aunt Claudia places the scissors with points down, into her closed hand, and shows Katie the way. "That's so the pointy parts can never hurt you. Just hold them down, like this." Katie takes the scissors and holds them as she has been shown. Listening to adults and seeing examples are also important ways in which young children learn.

Play is another arena that provides fertile ground for children's learning. While observing, listening, and example teach children many things, it is only play that allows active, experiential involvement: testing and trying, manipulating variables, gathering data in many different contexts, and interpreting data to develop meaningful concepts. Good teaching includes all of these learning opportunities. The teacher who chooses a play-de-brief-replay program will also wish to give a lesson, instruct in certain academic and/or interpersonal skills, tell children what to do and how. In every highly evolved play-debrief-replay classroom, teachers use a variety of pedagogies and choose among them those that are more appropriate for particular learning situations. Such flexibility is the hallmark of the professional teacher—a person who is not a technician, stuck to a single method, whatever the situation, but a wise, thoughtful, informed, flexible, and reflective practitioner who sizes up an instructional need and uses methods that are appropriate to that need, recognizing that children learn as much if not more from the context in which the learning occurs. Whatever pedagogy is chosen, sound educational principles guide teachers toward more effective practice.

## DEVELOPING CURRICULUM TASKS
## FOR PLAY-DEBRIEF-REPLAY

### What's the Big Idea?

A teacher who wishes to develop curriculum experiences for play-debrief-replay opportunities must first come to terms with the a priori question, What's the "big idea"; what are the concepts worth studying that are embedded in this learning experience? Big ideas are the more important issues and concepts; for example, machines work for us, time and speed can be measured mathematically, living things grow and change, language is a means of communicating ideas, sound can be created and manipulated in a variety of ways, and certain sounds in certain words provide clues to decoding those words. "Small ideas," on the other hand, reflect content that is considerably less substantive, or content that deals with the acquisition of specific facts; for example, buttons come in different shapes and sizes, bottles are used to hold liquid, mittens keep your hands warm in winter, ducks quack and lions roar, some houses are made of wood, and 3 + 4 and 4 + 3 both equal 7. This is not to say that curriculum must always deal with big ideas and never emphasize fact acquisition. What is being suggested is that curriculum that reflects big ideas will enrich classroom life and promote deeper and more sophisticated understanding of the world we live in. What's more, it is of critical importance that teachers know the difference between curriculum that addresses big ideas and that which concentrates on matters of minor consequence.

When play-debrief-replay experiences reflect big ideas, and when teachers are clear about these, this not only gives shape to the curriculum experience, but it also gives direction to what is being taught and what is being learned. When teachers are clear about the issues of substance that they want students to study, they are in a better position to develop investigative play experiences that lead to increased and sophisticated understanding.

There are, of course, big ideas, and then there are *very* big ideas. Some are so large and so complex that they are necessarily too general to act as a clear focus for investigative play. While criteria for what is big, what is very big, and what is small often lie in the eye of the beholder, these three examples are nevertheless offered:

1. *There are many ways in which humans pollute the environment, and our environment now is at serious risk.* This very big idea, very present in human consciousness, is so vast that it defies providing a clear focus for shaping investigative play. Teachers who want children to examine issues related to the pollution of the environment are better served by breaking down this very big idea into smaller units that allow for more sharply focused inquiry. The following example shows how this may be done.

2. *Oil spills are very difficult to clean up. Oil spills kill marine life, as well as damage property.* This big idea represents a "piece" of the very big idea in item 1, and it gives a sharp focus to the creation of an investigative play session. With this big idea in mind, an investigative play task may be designed in which children create an oil spill. One quart of used automobile oil will go a long way to "pollute" a basin of clear water, in which selected materials are used to simulate marine life and property, for example, feathers (birds), grasses and leaves (plant life), pieces of wood and plastic (boats), and sand (shoreline). Children are then asked to carry out investigative play, making observations of what happens to the materials in the basin and experimenting with ways to clean the oil from the materials and from the water.

3. *Buttons come in many shapes and colors.* This small idea may lead to a classification exercise in which children sort buttons, but because of the trivial nature of the idea, the children have limited opportunity to examine issues of consequence. A play activity derived from this idea may be fun, but it is unlikely to lead to deep conceptual understandings.

In attempting to formulate big ideas — those issues of consequence that illuminate our understanding — it is helpful to ask in each case, Why is this worth knowing? If teachers answer this to their own satisfaction, big ideas are likely to emerge. When a first draft of an idea is written, it is helpful then to ask, Is this sufficiently focused to give clear shape to the investigative play? Or is it so vast that it is too general to shape the play? The more teachers are able to teach to the big ideas, the more they may be assured that children's school experiences address issues of substance — ones that are truly worth knowing.

Where do big ideas come from? One important source is the district's curriculum guide, which presents learning goals for each grade. Big ideas are embedded in these learning goals, and investigative play activities may easily reflect district-articulated educational values. Big ideas also come from each teacher's perceptions of children's educational needs and from issues of current concern. Teachers make observations about the educational needs of their classes and develop curriculum activities accordingly.

Deborah Dunn, an experienced primary teacher, wrestled with the big-idea concept for several weeks before she was able to understand its implications for her classroom curriculum. In her reflections, she noted, "Choosing *one focus*, and carefully planning a sequence of activities that will teach *one* concept thoroughly, is the goal. Picking one concept that is worthwhile and staying focused on that concept is my main problem." She compared this approach with how she had been organizing her curriculum activities:

> I used to develop what I called "themes." We used to brainstorm a topic — let's say it was "apples" — and then barrage the children with countless activities, all relating to the same theme. I realize now that most of these activities were busywork. They were fun; the kids enjoyed them (and so did the teachers), but none of them really went anywhere. Just because they measured, cooked, drew, and papier machéd apples, after doing apple poems, didn't mean that they had a strong knowledge base that they could build upon. Our "higher-level thinking skills" were not always higher, [and did not necessarily involve] any thinking. I feel that we were all caught up in the showmanship, more than we were providing significant learning opportunities. Our rooms were dazzling, the atmosphere was fun, but it was shallow. That sounds quite harsh. I shouldn't throw out several years of work, for after all the kids did learn. It's just that, when I look back at the units I planned then, I realize that what was missing was a focus on the "big ideas" — on concepts of substance and value that we could all build on. I tended to introduce too much, spend too little time on it, and give too much time to teaching "little skills" — those that could have been taught more effectively in another way. I'd spend a month on one theme and cover every aspect I could think of, until the topic was bled dry. I wonder now if many of these children still enjoy "apples" or "rainbows" or even "teddy bears." We were so busy flitting through related activities that we never had time to really stop and "taste the apples." (D. Dunn, personal journal, April 1987)

In Deborah's notes we find that her curriculum plans, while on the surface appearing "dazzling," tended to focus on activities that reflected a very narrow range of ideas. Apples, however much fun, are not a big idea. Nor are teddy bears. There are big ideas that could be generated out of the theme of apples, if a teacher wished to do so. Here are some examples:

- Apples are self-generating foods. They contain the seeds from which other apples grow.
- Apples are a variety of fruit. Fruits are foods that share certain common characteristics.

- Apples contain certain substances, such as cellulose, fructose, and water.
- Apples are the fruits of living, growing plants. They have a life cycle that follows a predictable pattern.
- Apples decompose when they are attacked by microorganisms.
- Apples that are "returned to the soil" nurture the soil for more growing.
- Apple trees are sprayed with pesticides to keep the bugs from attacking and destroying the plants. Some of these pesticides, besides killing the bugs, are harmful for humans and other creatures.

It is easy to see that, when big ideas are clear, they give direction to the kinds of investigative play tasks that allow for the ideas to be studied. Even more important, teaching to the big idea calls for pupils to study ideas of significance, value, and power—ideas that have important larger meanings. Teaching to the big ideas means that children's studies emphasize concept development, rather than details or specific bytes of information. Conceptual understanding grows when learning tasks are provided in which children play around with the ideas, and are actively involved in investigations that allow concepts to develop.

In generating curriculum experiences for a play-debrief-replay program, a first step is to identify some of the big ideas in the curriculum for your grade. Start with one curriculum area—math, for example. Study the math curriculum guides for your grade, together with a very good teacher's guide or math text. Some examples of big ideas in primary mathematics follow:

- A set is a group or collection of things that are related. A set of things belongs together in some way.
- Sets can be compared to discover how they are similar to or different from other sets.
- Math is the study of relationships.
- Geometry is the study of shapes, sizes, and place.
- Mathematics allows us to measure things. We measure in order to help us build, which we do all the time.
- Linear dimensions of objects can be measured.
- Weight of objects can be measured.
- Volume of containers can be measured.
- Time can be measured.
- Estimation is one form of measurement.

## Creating the Play Activity

A second step in designing the curriculum experience is to create an investigative play activity that will guide the children's inquiries. The play activity should stimulate children's thinking about possible investigations. It should not set narrow parameters that limit the play, nor should it lead pupils to "correct answers." The play activity also encourages children to inquire beyond what is asked on the activity card. The big idea always gives shape to the activity, and play activities always incorporate several higher-order thinking operations in their design.

Activity 5, "Jobs and Work," in Chapter 8, is an example of how the big idea gives shape to the activity. This activity is based on the big idea, "People work at different kinds of jobs and have different ways of earning income." Each group of students is given a large collection of photographs showing women and men at work in a variety of occupations, along with the following activity card:

> Use the photos to make some observations of the kind of work that people do. Talk to each other about what these jobs are like.
> - What do you think it's like to work as an artist? A baker? A farmer? A pilot? A taxi driver?
> - What's good about those kinds of jobs? What might you not like about them?
> Think of a way to classify these job pictures. Set up some groups, and put each picture in the group where you think it belongs.

This play might carry on for several sessions. Much discussion about individual pictures may occur before classifications are attempted. Different classifications may also lead to examinations of different aspects of jobs, for example, status of some jobs, jobs and income, dangers in jobs, excitement or boredom of some jobs, value of some jobs to society, and reasons why people work.

A good indicator of the effectiveness of the play activity is the extent to which it stimulates children's investigations. Observing this and what happens when children are guided by the play activity will yield valuable data for use in refining one's play-activity-design skills.

## Insuring the "Goodness of Fit" Between Big Ideas and Play

A well-designed investigative play activity should lead to children's investigations of the big idea. If this is to occur, there must be a "goodness of fit" between the big idea and the play task. This is, of course, an exercise in means–ends consistency. The task (means) should serve the learning goals (ends).

A student teacher who was just beginning her training with play-debrief-replay strategies identified, as her big idea, "The development of an awareness of pollution and its effects on the environment." (A quite big idea in the first place!) For the play activity, she gathered the following materials: face mask, cigarette butts, aerosol can, bottle of suntan lotion, oil can, dead fish. These she put into the play center, with the following activity card:

> Pick two items from the group, and make some observations of them. Compare them.
> • How are they alike?
> • How are they different?
> Talk together about your observations and your comparisons.

The children's play yielded some observations and comparisons of the objects, but came nowhere near an examination of pollution. Some adults may perceive a relationship between a face mask and pollution, but to most children the connection is remote. A face mask may be used by a person with pollen allergies or by a dentist or physician for avoiding contact with germs. If one compares a face mask with a bottle of suntan lotion, the results will hardly lead to increased awareness of problems of pollution.

A play activity that would better fit the big idea of increased awareness of pollution would be the oil-spill activity described earlier. Another play activity might include an examination of biodegradable and nonbiodegradable garbage. Both of these inquiries would attend to the "goodness of fit" criterion, and both are likely to result in deeper understandings of how pollution affects our world.

### Incorporating Higher-Order Thinking Operations

Another step in designing curriculum experiences is to insure the incorporation of higher-order thinking operations. This requires familiarity with those mental processes that call for higher-order cognitive involvement: comparing, observing, classifying, summarizing, interpreting data, examining assumptions, suggesting hypotheses, applying principles to new situations, designing projects and investigations, making decisions, evaluating and judging, creating and inventing (see Raths, Wassermann, Jonas, & Rothstein, 1986). Investigative play experiences incorporate several higher-order operations so students who work through these tasks are required to *think*.

Looking again at the "Jobs and Work" activity presented here and in Chapter 8, it can be seen that the play activity itself calls for observing and classifying. During debriefing, the teacher is likely also to raise questions that call for comparisons to be made, for hypotheses to be generated, for assumptions to be examined. These operations create a "thinking lens" through which knowledge is filtered, so that students are cognitively processing information, instead of merely receiving it. When higher-order thinking operations are threaded through investigative play-debrief-replay experiences, students' thinking is promoted and increased understanding of concepts results.

The activities presented in Chapters 7 through 10 are examples of how teachers may develop their own play-debrief-replay learning experiences for their students. Each activity involves learning about a big idea in a particular curriculum area and demonstrates the "goodness of fit" between the big idea and the investigative play task. Each activity incorporates several higher-order thinking operations and involves children working in cooperative learning groups, actively involved in hands-on/"minds-on" investigative play with the concepts. For each activity, potential debriefing questions are provided, demonstrating how the connection is made between investigative play and debriefing and how debriefing is used to further reflection on the big ideas. Chapter 11 provides examples of more spontaneous, open-ended play activities in drama, music, and arts and crafts, that depart from the need for activity cards. Chapter 12 offers examples of how play-debrief-replay is applied to classroom discussions in which children play with ideas to examine and reflect on moral/ethical issues. The examples are, of course, more than guides to teachers' own creation of curriculum activities. They are also suitable for classroom use.


## THE TEACHER'S ROLE


The act of teaching in a play-debrief-replay program has a different appearance from that of other forms of teaching. Teachers need not be at center stage for teaching to occur. They may be working individually with a student, supervising and monitoring group work, developing curriculum, or modeling certain behaviors. *Profiles of Teaching Competency* (Wassermann & Eggert, 1989) identifies 20 different functions of a teacher's job. Other lists of what teachers do are even more extensive. In *Profiles*, different functions of teaching fall into two categories: active and reflective. While these are not mutually exclusive (one hopes that teachers are also reflective when they are active), the surface appearance of what the teacher is seen doing in each category is markedly different.

When the teacher is functioning in an active way, these behaviors are more clearly visible to the observer's eye. Active teaching may involve interactions with students, instructing or telling, evaluating, or organizing the class for instruction. Some active teaching occurs "behind the scenes," for example, when teachers read and examine students' work and provide evaluative feedback; when they plan and organize learning tasks, set up the classroom, and consult collegially with other teachers or specialists.

Other teaching acts are more reflective. They are less visible to the untrained eye, but they are occurring nevertheless. For example, when teachers observe children's behavior in order to gather data about their learning difficulties, and then use that data to make informed diagnoses about how best to help those children, that aspect of teaching may not be easily discerned by the untrained observer. When teachers conceptualize how to take a new idea and weave it into classroom practice, that more reflective function is hardly discernible. When teachers operate as reflective practitioners, "watching themselves and the impact of their actions on the classroom situation, with an open attitude that allows for assessing the effect of their actions on a classroom situation" (Wassermann & Eggert, 1989, p. 12), they are performing professionally at the very highest levels of competence (Nolan & Huber, 1989). Yet even the most well-trained observer may not see this reflection-in-action actually occurring.

It may not be easy for teachers to learn to believe in the idea that observing children while they are actively engaged in cooperative group work is also teaching. Many of us have been programmed by other schools of thought. For those who have been trained to believe in teaching as "direct instruction" only, the idea of teaching as reflection-on-action may be hard to swallow; yet, it is a significant aspect of a teacher's professional functioning. It is the level at which experts operate in all professions (Schön, 1983).

Teachers who operate play-debrief-replay programs are called upon to teach as reflective practitioners as much as they are to engage in more "active" or observable acts of teaching. This means that they are sometimes involved in active teaching or telling, while at other times they are interacting with individual children and with small and large groups, such as seen in debriefing. Sometimes they are planning and inventing new strategies, testing them to see if they work. Other times they are reflecting on action—observing from the sidelines as the children are actively engaged in learning tasks and mentally gathering data about what is happening and what next steps to take. All of these functions are part of the teaching act, and not only should teachers not apologize if they are "caught" while reflecting on action, they might even learn to point with pride at their ability to function in this highly professional role.

Shifting gears from teaching that is consistently active, where the teacher is always at center stage, to reflection-on-action may take some doing. Certainly some self-training is required. Standing on the sidelines "merely" observing may be very hard to teach oneself to do. One feels so unproductive, so—useless! As teachers, we want to help! So, while watching from the sidelines, we may be tempted to move in on a group, to direct their investigative play, or raise challenging questions, just to feel that we are "doing our jobs." Yet, observe the consequences on the children when you do intervene to direct their play. They "play to you" rather than following their own leads. Their behaviors are aimed more at pleasing you than themselves. We lose, through our own needs to intervene, much more than we gain. Training ourselves in the art of reflective teaching during children's investigations may be one of the more difficult challenges in developing the can-do classroom. Yet, with practice and increased self-awareness of our own needs and behaviors, this role, too, may be mastered.

## GUIDE TO THE CURRICULUM ACTIVITIES

The curriculum activities included in Chapters 7 through 10 follow a format that should be helpful to you in choosing what may be useful in your classroom applications of play-debrief-replay. The sections included under each activity are explained below.

**Concept(s):**  The big idea or ideas in a particular curriculum area that are examined in the investigative play task and in the debriefing are identified.

**Learning Goals:**  The outcomes toward which the curriculum experience is directed—that is, what the teacher hopes will occur as a consequence of children's engagement in these experiences—are outlined.

**Thinking Operations:**  A list is given of those higher-order mental functions included in the curriculum activity that require children to process data through a "thinking lens." These thinking operations, as identified by Raths et al. (1986), include comparing, observing, classifying, hypothesizing, examining assumptions, evaluating and judging, designing projects and investigations, imagining, making decisions, summarizing, interpreting data, applying principles to new situations, creating, and inventing.

**Materials:**  Equipment and supplies appropriate for use in the original play activity are noted. In those instances where additional materials are required to replay tasks, these are specified in the replay section.

**Activity Cards:**    Provided to give direction to the children's investigations, these cards suggest potential investigations, but do so in open-ended ways. While setting some guidelines for children's inquiries, the cards do not constrain investigations. Investigative play activities always invite examination, never leading to predetermined answers. When children begin to play, they use the initial activity card. During replay, children may continue their investigations with the original activity card. After investigative play with these concepts is exhausted, it is time to add a new activity card to guide further replay, and examples of these are found in the replay section. Each investigative play group should have its own activity card. Where pupils are able to read, they will find it a helpful reference. Where pupils are still unable to read, the teacher reads the guidelines on the card to them and also leaves the card in the center for reference. Many activity cards ask children to record their observations, and even those with the most rudimentary language skills should be encouraged to do so.

**Sample Debriefing Questions:**    These questions are presented in two groups. In the first group — Asking Children to Reflect on Their Observations — the questions require students to articulate their observations and describe some of the investigations tried and some comparisons made. These questions address the children's actual investigative play experiences. They are relatively nonthreatening and give children initially safe experiences in expressing their own ideas. The second set of questions — Challenging Children Beyond Their Observations — contains those questions that pose greater challenges to children's thinking. They go beyond children's firsthand experiences with the materials and ask students to generate new ideas. These kinds of questions should typically be raised during later debriefings, with perhaps only one and never more than two used during a single session. The art of questioning skillfully to promote reflection in a climate of safety is discussed in Chapter 13.

**Suggestions for Replay:**    Students returning to play with the same big idea may wish to spend several sessions with the very same materials. At a point that the teacher determines, new life is breathed into the play by introducing new (additional) materials and/or new activity cards. These additions are designed to extend the play to new levels.

**Suggestions for Creative Play:**    While children's investigative play is creative and generative, this section emphasizes particularly those activities that are rooted in the more nonacademic areas of music, art, cooking, crafts, and dancing. These suggestions are provided for those teachers who wish to treat examination of the big ideas in more integrated and holistic ways. It should also be noted that Chapter 11 is devoted entirely to creative play opportunities and presents further examples for play in drama, music, and arts and crafts.

☆   ☆

All the activities in the chapters that follow may be implemented as presented or modified as you feel appropriate. Thoughtfully implemented, either as is or in modified form, these activities have considerable potential for realizing the goal of the can-do classroom — that of empowering children as thoughtful, responsible, conceptually aware, and independent learners. The activities should also serve as examples of how you can develop an extensive range of play-debrief-replay learning opportunities that become especially tailored to your students' needs and the curricular demands of your classroom and school.

# CHAPTER 7

# Serious Play in Science

Science is everywhere around us, from the early morning fog that immobilizes the airport to the burned toast, from the flooded carburetor to the first robin of spring, from your personal home computer to the 5 pounds you gained on your summer vacation. Whether it's pearls, or butterflies or popcorn, it's science. Whether it's the weather, toxic waste, or the moon, it's science. Whether it's gravity or oil spills, it's still science. What can children do to increase their understanding of science? Everything! The options are virtually unlimited. (Wassermann & Ivany, 1996, p. 121)

The activities included in this chapter provide children with opportunities to carry on scientific investigations leading to concept development. None of them direct children to find the "right" answers, nor do they stress the acquisition of specific information. Instead, pupils are encouraged to inquire; to exercise their higher-order thinking skills; to compare and observe; to imagine, invent, and design experiments; and to decide. Through these investigative experiences, scientific thinking grows, as does scientific awareness and understanding. These activities are not concerned with teaching children that water boils at a temperature of 212° F; rather, they are concerned with teaching children how to find out the boiling temperature of water and, further, why it might vary in different contexts. Learning science is learning to question, not to accept given information as fact or truth.

Even at the primary level, selecting some big ideas in science on which to base investigative play activities is a daunting task. The ones I have chosen for inclusion here are certainly not more imperative than some others, and a good case could be made for other big ideas. Yet, these seemed the ones that appear in many science texts as suitable and appropriate for primary children's learning. Two fully fleshed-out play-debrief-replay opportunities are presented for each of the following big ideas:

Living things grow and change.
Plants and animals are living things.
Machines and tools help us do work.
Our senses are used to discover the properties of objects.

## ACTIVITY 1.  SEEDS AND PLANTS

**Concept:**   Living things grow and change.

**Learning Goals:**   To promote understanding of the ways in which plants grow and change; to increase skill in learning to make thoughtful observations from data and in learning to classify data

**Thinking Operations:**   Observing, comparing, and classifying data; suggesting hypotheses; creating and inventing; making decisions; applying principles to new situations; designing investigations

**Materials:**   A variety of seeds (flower, fruit, and vegetable seeds; birdseed; seeds from trees, e.g., fir cones, acorns, chestnuts); an assortment of fresh flowers and leaves; an assortment of dried flowers and leaves; photographs of flowers, plants, and trees budding, in full bloom, and dormant; magnifying lenses; scissors, measuring tools, knives

### Activity Card

> Use the materials in this center to find out what you can about how plants grow and change.
> - What observations can you make about how flowers (plants, trees) grow?
> - What observations can you make about how flowers (plants, trees) change as they grow?
>
> Make some observations and then decide how these things might be classified.

### Sample Debriefing Questions

*Asking Children to Reflect on Their Observations*
What observations did you make about how plants grow?
What observations did you make about how plants change?
How is the growth of flowers different from trees? How is it similar?
In what ways did you classify these things? Tell your reasons for making
    those groups.

*Challenging Children Beyond Their Observations*
What are some differences among flower, fruit, and vegetable seeds? What
    are some similarities?
What makes seeds grow? What hypotheses can you suggest to explain
    this?
Where do you suppose seeds come from? What are your ideas?
How come some trees lose all their leaves in the winter and grow again in
    the spring? How do you explain this? How does it happen?

## Suggestions for Replay

The children may replay with the same materials and the original activity card.

New seeds (nuts in shells — peanuts, sunflower seeds, almonds, pecans; dried beans — lima beans, mung beans, lentils) may be added, along with the following new activity card:

Use the materials in the center to make some observations about these seeds.
• What observations can you make about the nut seeds?
• How are they like flower seeds?
• How are they different?

Fresh fruits and vegetables (cucumber, apple, pear, cherries, green pepper, string beans, squash, pumpkin) may be added, along with the following new activity card:

Use the materials in the center to make some observations about fruit and vegetable seeds.
• What observations did you make about fruit and vegetable seeds?
• How are they like nut seeds? How are they different?
• How do seeds get into the vegetables and fruits? How do you explain it? What are your ideas?

Some longer-term investigations might also be carried out, such as growing plants from seeds, caring for classroom plants, planting and caring for a garden, and adopting a neighborhood tree and looking after its care.

## Suggestions for Creative Play

Making crepe-paper flowers, jewelry from seeds, or mosaics by painting seeds and gluing them on paper
Drawing and painting flowers, plants, and trees
Cooking with fruits, vegetables, and nuts
Making dyes from vegetables, fruits, and nuts

## ACTIVITY 2. EGGS

**Concept:** Living things grow and change.
**Learning Goals:** To promote awareness of the ways in which animals

grow and change; to increase skill in learning to make thoughtful observations from data

**Thinking Operations:**    Observing, comparing, and classifying data; suggesting hypotheses; examining assumptions; designing projects and investigations; making decisions

**Materials:**    Several hens' eggs, preferably brown and white (one egg for each pair of students); photos of chicks, full-grown chickens, and roosters; plastic or aluminum-foil plates; newspapers; paper towels; probing sticks; magnifying lenses; balance scales; tape measure

### Activity Card

Use the materials in the center and make some observations about the eggs and the photos.
- What observations can be made of the outsides of the eggs?
- What observations can be made of the insides?
- What observations can be made of the size? Of the weight? Of the colors?
- What observations can be made of the differences in the "yellow" and "white" parts of the egg?

Talk together about your observations. Then talk about where you think eggs come from.

### Sample Debriefing Questions

*Asking Children to Reflect on Their Observations*
What observations did you make about the eggs?
What observations did you make about the shells? The insides?
What were some differences between the yellow and white parts of an egg?
What observations did you make about the photos of the chicks? The full-grown chickens?

*Challenging Children Beyond Their Observations*
How do you suppose chickens grow? What are your thoughts on it?
Where do you suppose eggs come from?
What are some differences between eggs and chickens?
What do you suppose chickens need to grow? What are your ideas?
What other animals grow from eggs? What do you think? How did you figure that out?

## Suggestions for Replay

The children may replay with more eggs, provided funds are available to keep them in supply.

Other types of eggs (fish, turkey, insect) may be gathered and added to the center for use with the following new activity card. (Under no circumstances, however, should pupils be encouraged to gather wild bird eggs.)

Use the materials in the center to make some observations of these eggs.
- What observations can you make of the fish (insect) eggs?
- How are these like hens' eggs? How are they different?
- How do fish (insects) hatch from eggs? How do you explain it? What are your ideas?

Photographs of a variety of young and fully grown animals (fish, insects, mammals, birds, human infants) may be added to the center, along with the following new activity card:

Use the materials in the center to make some observations about these animals.
- What observations can be made about these animal young?
- How are these animal young alike? How do you know?
- What animals are born without hatching from an egg? How do you know?
- What are some differences about these two kinds of birthing?

Other types of replay activities include having the children hatch baby chicks (definitely a production!); examining the bones of chickens, turkeys, ducks, and fish; comparing sets of animal photos, for example, dinosaurs and ducks, elephants and whales, seals and rabbits, vultures and penguins, snakes and bees; classifying photographs of animals; studying insects in their natural habitats or in glass observation cases.

## Suggestions for Creative Play

Dramatizing, in which children create their own scenarios and/or in which topics are offered for freely invented playlets, such as Nik Nik the

Rooster (the life and times of the King of the Barnyard from egg to full-grown bird)

Drawing and painting pictures of eggs, of egg hatching, and of animal young

Writing or telling stories with specific topics for children to choose from (When I was a baby; My dog [cat] is very old; Ally the alligator; I'm scared of snakes; My dog had six puppies) or with more general topics about animals (An animal that I loved; An animal that scares me)

## ACTIVITY 3.  LIVING AND NONLIVING THINGS

**Concept:**   Plants are living things.

**Learning Goals:**   To promote understanding of the concept "living things"; to further awareness that living things need certain conditions in which to grow; to increase skill in learning to make thoughtful observations from data; to develop skill in suggesting hypotheses based on logical interpretations of data

**Thinking Operations:**   Observing, comparing, and classifying data; suggesting hypotheses; making decisions; applying principles; interpreting; imagining; designing projects and investigations

**Materials:**   A variety of "started" vegetable sprouts (lima bean, mung bean, alfalfa, potato, sweet potato, onion, radish, carrot top); cuttings from several house plants (ivy, philodendron); several inanimate objects (rocks and stones, pieces of plastic, marbles, balls, rubber bands); dissecting knives; magnifying lenses; paper towels; growing dishes

### Activity Card

Use the materials in the center and make some observations about living and nonliving things.
- What observations can you make?
- What are some important differences between living and nonliving things?

### Sample Debriefing Questions

*Asking Children to Reflect on Their Observations*
What observations did you make about what is alive?
In what ways are these living things alike? What are some common characteristics?

How are living things different from nonliving things? How did you determine this?

*Challenging Children Beyond Their Observations*
How do living things grow? What are your ideas on this? What observations did you make that allow you to make those statements?
In what ways do living things change? What observations did you make about this?
How can you tell if something is living or nonliving? What do you look for? What are your ideas?
In what ways are living plants like living animals? How are they different?
Where do you suppose nonliving things come from? What are your ideas?

## Suggestions for Replay

Replay may occur with the same materials and the original activity card. New examples of living and nonliving materials (flower seeds, growing flower plants, leaf cuttings and branches from larger trees; soil, sand, milk, water, plates, cups, utensils) may be added to the center for use with the original activity card.

The children may be given the opportunity to observe live animals (white mice, gerbils, hamsters, guinea pigs, snakes, rabbits, insects), with the use of either of the following new activity cards:

Make some observations of the mice (gerbils, hamsters).
- What can you observe about how these animals grow?
- What makes them grow better? How do you know this?
- What hurts their growth? How do you know this?

Make some observations of the mice (gerbils, hamsters).
- How are living animals like living plants?
- What similarities do you observe? What differences?

The children may be given seeds for planting (grapefruit, orange, lima bean, mung bean, squash, or flower seeds) with the following new activity card:

Plant some seeds, and make some observations about how living things grow.
- What makes them grow better?
- What observations can you make about this?

- What hurts their growth?
- What observations can you make about this?

For another type of planting and growing activity, root vegetables (potato, sweet potato, carrot, turnip) may be added for use with an activity card similar to that just given.

Pictures of living things (plants, trees, flowers, fruits, vegetables, different species of animals) may be gathered for children to classify and/or compare.

For more long-term investigations, children may grow seeds under different experimental conditions: no water versus adequate water; no sunlight versus adequate sunlight versus too much sunlight; poor soil versus good soil; too hot/cold versus proper temperature.

### Suggestions for Creative Play

Writing or telling stories with a "life" focus (Once I was a baby, but now I am a big boy [girl]; The day my dog had puppies; The day my dog died)

Growing a garden, with children planning together and gathering the necessary materials; in schools in urban centers, plans may include planting in large-size window boxes

Participating in arts and crafts projects such as painting and drawing of plants, flowers, and animals; making dyes from plants; using colors from vegetables (beets, carrots, onions)

Cooking and tasting foods made from things that grow from seeds, such as popping corn, making orange juice, making peanut butter

## ACTIVITY 4.  LIVE-ANIMAL STUDY

**Concept:**   Living things grow and change.

**Learning Goals:**   To promote understanding of the ways in which living animals grow and change; to promote attitudes of respect for living creatures; to increase skill in learning to make thoughtful observations from data; to increase observational skills

**Thinking Operations:**   Observing, comparing, classifying, gathering, and interpreting data; making decisions; evaluating and judging; designing projects and investigations

**Materials:**   One or more animals that can easily be housed in the classroom (hamster, white mice, rabbit, snake, lizard, gerbil, guinea pig, bird, tropical fish); appropriate "home" for the class pet, one that provides the most natural environment; adequate food and water supply; timer, watch, or clock

## Activity Card

Study the animal for a long time.
* What observations can you make?
* What can you observe about its shape? Color? Skin or fur? Tail?
* What can you observe about how it moves? How it hears? How it sees? How it makes sounds? How and what it eats?
* What observations can you make about how the animal behaves when it thinks it's in danger?

## Sample Debriefing Questions

*Asking Children to Reflect on Their Observations*
What observations did you make about this animal?
What observations did you make about what it eats? How it eats? How often it eats?
What observations did you make about what it drinks? How it drinks? How often it drinks?
What observations did you make about how it sleeps? How long it sleeps?
What observations did you make about how it protects itself from danger?
What observations did you make about how it moves? How it uses its tail? How it breathes? How it sees? How it hears? How it makes sounds?

*Challenging Children Beyond Their Observations*
In what ways is the animal like other animals in this species? How is it different?
What ideas do you have about how to keep this animal healthy? What are your thoughts on it? Where do your ideas come from?
What observations have you made about how this animal grows?
What hypotheses can you suggest about how this animal cares for its young? Where do your ideas come from?
How do you suppose this animal communicates with its young? What are your ideas?
How do you suppose this animal feels about being in this classroom? What are your ideas? Where do your ideas come from?

## Suggestions for Replay

The children may repeat and replicate live-animal studies using the original activity card.

Another animal of a different species (insect, turtle, chick, earthworm) may be introduced for study and comparisons, along with either of the following new activity cards:

> Study the turtle (spider, earthworm). Make some observations about this animal.
> - What do you observe about the way it moves? Gets its food? Eats?
> - What do you observe about its shape? Color? Eyes? Ears?
> - What do you observe about how it behaves when it thinks it's in danger?
> - How is this animal like _____ ? How is it different?

> Study the turtle (snake, rabbit).
> - What do you think its life is like?
> - How would you describe a day in the life of this animal?

Photos of animals from sources like *National Geographic* and *Wildlife* magazines may be gathered for children to classify. In addition, children may compare photos of pairs of animals (chimpanzees and dogs, dinosaurs and snakes, dolphins and octopus, kangaroos and camels).

Animal bones (chicken, beef, fish) may be added for children to study. These can be obtained from washing and drying out the bones left from meals. Children may also do dissections of, for example, squid, beef hearts, kidneys, or fish. Such materials can be obtained easily from local butcher shops or fish stores.

## Suggestions for Creative Play

Participating in arts and crafts projects, such as making animals from clay and/or papier maché; drawing and painting pictures of animals

Writing original poetry or stories about animals

Writing and/or telling stories that speculate about the disappearance of dinosaurs, animals in zoos versus animals in the wild, fears of animals

Engaging in dramatic play on suggested animal themes (We are the animals in the zoo; Me and my pet rhinoceros; We are the gorillas living in the jungle; I'm a very shy koala and I live in a eucalyptus tree), as well as inventing original scenarios about animals

## ACTIVITY 5.  WHEELS AND GEARS

**Concept:**   Machines and tools help us do work.

**Learning Goals:**   To promote understanding of how machines extend human capabilities to "do work"; to appreciate the effectiveness of machines to perform certain functions; to increase awareness that the motion of a machine requires energy; to increase skills in learning to observe critically and analytically; to make intelligent comparisons; to suggest reasonable hypotheses that are borne out by data

**Thinking Operations:**   Observing and comparing, suggesting hypotheses, designing investigations, evaluating and judging, making decisions

**Materials:**   A supply of wheels and gears of various sizes and constructions (rubber wheels, plastic wheels, metal wheels and axles, bicycle wheels, old automobile tires, wagon wheels, roller skates, wheels from children's toys, gear assemblies from such household appliances as a manual pencil sharpener, an egg beater, and a wind-up clock); heavy objects to move (bricks, cinder blocks, large pieces of wood, large plastic or wooden tubs, bucket, pails of sand and water, flat wooden boards)

### Activity Card

Use the materials in this center to make some studies of wheels and gears.
- What observations can you make about how wheels work? How gears work?
- What observations can you make about how wheels are built? How gears are built?
- What observations can you make about how wheels are used to move things? How gears are used to move things?

### Sample Debriefing Questions

*Asking Children to Reflect on Their Observations*
What observations have you made about wheels? Gears?
What observations have you made about how wheels are made to turn? How gears are made to turn?
What observations have you made about how wheels make our work easier? How gears make our work easier?

*Challenging Children Beyond Their Observations*
How do you suppose wheels and gears help us to move things? What are your ideas?

What makes a wheel or gear move more easily? What are your ideas?
What kinds of machines need wheels? Gears? How do these tools help the
    machines move? What are your ideas?
How are gears different from wheels? How are they alike?
What are the differences between ice skates and roller skates?
What are the differences between bicycles and wagons?
If we didn't have wheels to help us move these cinder blocks, what might
    we do instead? What are your ideas?

## Suggestions for Replay

The children may productively replay with the same materials and the
original activity card. New materials (pulley with rope and hook, bicycle,
toy trucks and cars) may be added to the center, for use with the original
activity card.

New materials may be added for making comparisons (egg beater and a
wire whisk, sled and wagon, toy truck and flat-bottom container).

New activity cards may be designed that call for investigating ways to
move heavy equipment across the room; to study differences between
wheeled/geared and nonwheeled/nongeared vehicles or tools; to study how
wheels and gears are used in toys.

New activity cards may be designed that call for making lists of machines and equipment around the school that are wheel- and/or gear-
driven and the setting up of a classification system for the items on the
list.

## Suggestions for Creative Play

Writing or telling stories about tools and machines on suggested topics (My
    brother thinks he is a big wheel; My friend got stuck on the ferris
    wheel; There are 100 wheels in a merry-go-round; She always gives
    me the gears) or on their own topics
Designing and building an exercise wheel for a class pet or a wagon to
    carry blocks
Drawing pictures of things with big wheels or gears (ferris wheel, merry-
    go-round)

## ACTIVITY 6.  SIMPLE TOOLS

**Concept:**    Tools extend the reach and capacity of the human hand.
**Learning Goals:**    To promote understanding of the varieties and na-

ture of tools that have been designed to help us work; to appreciate human inventiveness in the creation of tools; to increase awareness that tools are energy driven; to increase skill in making thoughtful, intelligent observations based on data; to increase ability to make thoughtful comparisons that discern significant differences; to increase skill in suggesting reasoned hypotheses; to increase skill in raising intelligent questions that lead to information gathering

**Thinking Operations:** Observing and comparing, classifying, suggesting hypotheses, imagining, examining assumptions, designing investigations, evaluating and judging

**Materials:** An assortment of many different kinds of tools (hammer, saw, pliers, screwdriver, nails, scissors, paper punch, stapler, egg beater, ruler, thermometer, scale, flashlight, mousetrap, needle, eraser, paper cups, air pump, magnet, gears)

## Activity Card

Use the materials in this center to make some studies of tools.
- How do these tools work?
- How do we use tools to work for us?

What observations can you make?

## Sample Debriefing Questions

*Asking Children to Reflect on Their Observations*
What observations did you make about these tools?
What observations did you make about how the tools work?
What observations did you make about how the tools help us do work?
What observations did you make about how tools make our work easier?
    What are your ideas?

*Challenging Children Beyond Their Observations*
How come it's easier to dig a hole with a shovel than it is with your hands?
    What are your ideas?
How come it's easier to drive a nail into a piece of wood with a hammer
    than with a pair of scissors? What are your thoughts on it?
How are hammers like shovels? How are they different?
How do you suppose hammers (saws, scissors) got invented? What are your
    ideas?
How are rulers and clocks alike? How are they different?
What are tools? What are your ideas?

## Suggestions for Replay

The children may replay productively with the same materials and the original activity card for several additional sessions.

New tools (microscope, candles, thread, wire, ballpoint pens, hooks, plastic tubing, buckets, ice pick, barometer, telescope, magnifying lens, stethoscope, telephone, atomizer, pocket calculator) may be added to the center for use with the following types of new activity cards:

> Conduct some studies to see how plastic tubing works.
> - What observations did you make?
> - What, do you suppose, are some good uses for plastic tubing?
>
> Classify all the tools in the center.
> - Put each tool in a group.
> - Tell why you think each tool belongs in that group.

The children may carry on investigations in which they compare tools such as a knife and a saw, a clock and a liquid measuring container. They may also take tools apart and study their working parts. As an additional activity, they may gather data about all the tools used in class, in the school, at home, or at a workplace.

## Suggestions for Creative Play

Writing poems or stories about the invention of particular tools, about life without certain tools, about how we depend on tools, or about topics of their own choosing that are related to tools

Participating in arts and crafts projects such as designing and building tools, drawing pictures of tools and parts of tools, inventing tools that have never been heard of before

Dramatizing the discovery of a new tool that could, for example, transport you back in time, turn you invisible, or clean up your room

## ACTIVITY 7.  EYES, EARS, NOSE, AND TONGUE

**Concept:**   Our senses are used to discover the properties of objects around us.

**Learning Goals:**   To promote awareness of specific sense organs, their distinguishing characteristics and how they work; to further appreciation of individual differences; to increase skills in making thoughtful observations about how our senses work for us, in raising intelligent questions, in making comparisons of significant attributes, in formulating reasonable hypotheses

**Thinking Operations:**   Observing and comparing, classifying, imagining and inventing, suggesting hypotheses, designing investigations, making decisions, evaluating and judging

**Materials:**   Small hand and shaving mirrors, ceramic or plastic models of eyes and/or ears, tongue depressors, large magnifying glasses, flashlights

## Activity Card

Use the materials in this center to find out what you can about your eyes, ears, nose, and tongue.
- Make some observations of your eyes. Study your own eyes. Then compare them with the eyes of others in your group.
- Make some observations of your ears. Study your own ears. Then compare them with the ears of others in your group.
- Make some observations of your nose. Study your own nose. Then compare it with the noses of others in your group.
- Make some observations of your tongue. Study your tongue. Then compare it with the tongues of others in your group.

## Sample Debriefing Questions

*Asking Children to Reflect on Their Observations*
What observations did you make about your eyes? How are eyes alike? How are they different? What did you observe about how eyes work?
What observations did you make about your ears? How are ears alike? How are they different? What did you observe about how ears work?
What observations did you make about your nose? How are noses alike? How are they different? What did you observe about how noses work?
What observations did you make about your tongue? How are tongues alike? How are they different? What do you suppose is the work of the tongue? What are your ideas?

*Challenging Children Beyond Their Observations*
How come some eyes see better than others? How do you explain it?
How come some ears hear better than others? How do you explain it?
How come some noses are very sensitive to smell? How do you explain it?
Why do you suppose the sense of smell is important to us? What are your ideas about it?
What do you suppose impairs our vision (hearing, sense of smell)? What are your ideas on it?
How do these senses help us to know our world better? How do they protect us? What are your ideas?
How does the tongue help us taste? What do you think?
How come some people prefer foods with different tastes? How do you explain it?
How come cats and dogs can hear and smell better than humans? How do you explain it?

## Suggestions for Replay

Children may continue with investigations from the original activity card for several sessions. The replication of these investigations is enhanced further if the make-up of working groups changes.

Other activity cards, such as the following, may be added that shift the investigations onto new planes:

- What are some things that eyes can do?
Conduct some investigations and see what you can find out.

- What are some things that ears can do?
Conduct some investigations and see what you can find out.

- What are some things that noses can do?
Conduct some investigations and see what you can find out.

- What are some things that tongues can do?
Conduct some investigations and see what you can find out.

Children may classify the eyes of all the children in the class. They may carry on investigations in which they compare the eyes, ears, noses, and tongues of humans to those of animals.

Children may be asked to design investigations to see whose sense of smell (sight, hearing, taste) is more acute.

## Suggestions for Creative Play

Writing poems or stories and telling stories that relate to sensory experience on suggested topics (The boy or girl who could hear everything; The boy or girl who could not hear), or other topics of the children's own choosing

Making pictures or building models of eyes, ears, noses, or tongues

Participating in musical projects that involve studying sounds that are pleasurable and sounds that are harsh, listening for differences in pitch, singing in harmony

## ACTIVITY 8. HUMAN SKIN: A SENSE ORGAN

**Concept:**   Our skin is a sense organ through which we take in information and which protects us.

**Learning Goals:**   To promote awareness of and appreciation for the function of the skin as an outer protective covering and as a means through which we experience sensation; to promote awareness of how and what we learn from the sense of touch

**Thinking Operations:**   Observing and comparing, interpreting, suggesting hypotheses, examining assumptions, imagining and inventing, evaluating and judging, designing investigations, making decisions

**Materials:**   Magnifying lenses, small hand mirrors, thermometers, ice cubes, soft fabrics (velvet, silk, cotton), rough-textured fabrics (corduroy, brocade, and velcro), an assortment of objects that lend themselves to different tactile sensations (steel wool, metal, felt, sandpaper, chalk, clay, fingerpaint, wooden and metal objects of rough and smooth textures, paper), cloths for blindfolds

## Activity Card

Use the materials in this center to find out what you can about what can be felt with your skin.
- Make some observations of what your skin can feel when your eyes are closed.
- Talk to each other about the messages your skin sends to your brain.
- How are your "touching" experiences similar? How are they different?

- What parts of your skin can feel things better than other
  parts? How do you know?

Conduct some investigations to discover how and what you
learn through the sense of touch.

## Sample Debriefing Questions

*Asking Children to Reflect on Their Observations*

What observations did you make about your skin? About its texture? Its
  color? Its hair? Its temperature? About what your skin feels?

When your eyes are closed, how does touching an object give you information? What are your ideas on this?

What information can you gather by touching? What are your ideas? How
  do you know this?

*Challenging Children Beyond Their Observations*

How does skin tell the difference between hot and cold? How can you
  explain this?

Why do you suppose we have skin? What are your thoughts on it?

How is our skin different from dog skin? Snake skin? What do you think?

How come some parts of our skin have hair? What's the hair for? What
  hypotheses can you suggest to explain why we have hair?

How come skins come in different colors? How do you explain it? How
  come some skins have freckles? How do you explain it?

How come some skin areas are ticklish?

## Suggestions for Replay

The original activity card will provide for many sessions of productive
replay, and children should be encouraged to repeat and carry out new
investigations with the original materials.

New materials may be added for more challenging observations and
investigations: a variety of other skins, such as fruit skins (apple, banana,
orange, coconut, melon), vegetable skins (onion, potato, carrot, eggplant,
squash), nut skins (peanut and almond shells, sunflower seeds hulls), animal skins (pieces of leather, pieces of fur, molted reptile skins); as well as
small knives, microscopes. These materials should be used in conjunction
with the following new activity card:

Conduct some investigations and make some observations
about fruit (vegetable, animal) skins.
- How are fruit (vegetable, animal) skins different from human skins? How are they alike?

Find as many similarities and differences as you can.

The children may be asked to design experiments with the use of the following new activity card:

Design an investigation that would show how your skin can change its temperature.

**Suggestions for Creative Play**

Drawing pictures of different skins (snake skins, alligator skins)
Finger painting
Making fingerprints and comparing them
Writing poems about skin
Writing stories about the way we use the word *skin* idiomatically (He gets
    under my skin; She's got a thin/thick skin; It made my skin crawl; A
    skin as smooth as glass)

☆   ☆

While there are potentially dozens of other kinds of play-debrief-replay experiences that could be added to this group, the eight that have been included in this chapter will doubtless give teachers and children much to work with and many enjoyable hours of learning in the content area of science.

# CHAPTER 8

# Serious Play in Social Studies

The examples of curriculum activities for primary social studies flow from the larger topics, "The Clothes We Wear" and "Jobs and Work." While other social studies topics might have been chosen as well, these topics seemed both generic, in terms of wide applicability, and appropriate, in terms of addressing some important social studies concerns.

## ACTIVITY 1. THE CLOTHES WE WEAR

**Concepts:**   The clothes we wear are manufactured. They have different functions.

**Learning Goals:**   To promote awareness of how clothes are made and how different clothes are appropriate to different situations

**Thinking Operations:**   Observing, comparing, and classifying data; suggesting hypotheses; imagining and inventing; evaluating and judging; designing investigations; making decisions

**Materials:**   A selected sampling of children's and adults' articles of clothing (tie, belt, suspenders, jacket, gloves, hat, sweater, jeans, T-shirt, socks, coat, rainwear, winter and summer clothing — heavy coat, bathing suit, shorts); pictures of clothes. More "exotic" clothes (robes, headdresses, tuxedos, clothes from yesteryear) should be included if possible. Children may be asked to make contributions to this collection, or clothes may be scrounged from other sources such as rummage sales or thrift stores.

### Activity Card

Use the materials in the center to find out what you can about clothes.
- Make some observations about how clothes are made. What kinds of fabrics are used? How are clothes put together? What kinds of differences can be observed?
- Make some observations about the purposes for which some of the clothes are worn.

126

Then, talk together and think of a good way to classify
these articles of clothing.
- Which belong together?
- Why do you think so?

## Sample Debriefing Questions

*Asking Children to Reflect on Their Observations*
What observations did you make about these articles of clothing?
What observations did you make about how they are made? About what
    they are made of? About what they are worn for? About how styles
    change?
How are certain articles of clothing alike? How are they different?

*Challenging Children Beyond Their Observations*
Which articles of clothing did you like better? Less? What determines this?
Where do you suppose these clothes are made? How do you know? How
    can you tell?
Which would you like better, a shirt of cotton or a shirt of polyester?
    What's the difference? How do you know?
Why do some men wear ties? What are they good for? How do you know?
Why do you suppose we "dress up" for special occasions? What does *dress
up* mean?
Why do you suppose "old fashioned" clothes look silly to us now? What are
    your thoughts?
Where do the fabrics come from? How are they colored? How do they get
    these designs? What are your ideas?
How come certain designer-label clothes are so popular?

## Suggestions for Replay

The students may replay with the same articles of clothing and the
original activity card. New articles of clothing (knitted garments, woven
garments, scarves or shawls, fur pieces, a muff, costumes, gym clothes)
may be added for use with the original activity card.
New activity cards may be added; for example:

Go around the classroom and observe the label in everyone's shirt or sweater or jeans.
- Make a list of all the countries in which these articles of
clothing are manufactured.
- Then, design a chart to show this information.

Work together and figure out a way to make a pattern for a T-shirt.
• Make the pattern.

Work together and make some observations of the different kinds of fabric used in the manufacture of clothing.
• Make a list of all the fabrics.
• Then, classify your list.

Design a dress or jacket in a "new" style.
• Talk together and make some drawings of your design.
• Decide what kinds of fabrics, colors, and adornments your jacket or dress will have.

Pictures cut from the latest fashion magazine may be added, along with the following new activity card:

Make some observations of these pictures of "latest-fashion" clothes.
• Talk together and put them into groups.
• Which did you like? Which did you dislike?
• What makes clothes attractive?
• Which designer-label clothes are more popular? How do you explain it?

**Suggestions for Creative Play**

Growing a cotton plant
Dying fabric with natural dyes
Textile printing
Weaving, knitting, or sewing
Engaging in dramatic play with dress-up costumes
Designing costumes

## ACTIVITY 2. THE SHOES WE WEAR

**Concept:** Shoes appear in different styles. Different forms of shoes have different functions.

**Learning Goals:** To promote awareness of different styles, fabrics, and functions of certain articles of clothing, specifically shoes

**Thinking Operations:** Observing and comparing; suggesting hypotheses; classifying; imagining and inventing; evaluating and judging

**Materials:** A collection of shoes (rain boots, sneakers, running shoes, sandals, sports shoes, workboots, shoes with laces, shoes with straps, shoes with high heels, snowshoes, slippers, moccasins, booties, snow boots, platform shoes, high-button shoes); photos of "old-timer" shoes. Children may be asked to bring in old or discarded shoes from home; thrift stores and rummage sales may yield a large supply as well.

## Activity Card

Use the materials in this center to make some observations of shoes.
- How are these shoes different from each other? How are they alike? What similarities and differences can you find?
- Talk together and think of a good way to classify these shoes. Which ones belong together? How come?

## Sample Debriefing Questions

*Asking Children to Reflect on Their Observations*
What observations did you make about shoes? About styles? About the fabric? About how they are made? About what we wear them for?
What differences did you observe about the shoes? What similarities?
Why do you suppose some women wear shoes with high heels? What are your ideas on this?

*Challenging Children Beyond Their Observations*
Which shoes, do you suppose, are "old fashioned?" How can you tell? What do you suppose "old fashioned" means?
How do shoe styles change? What observations did you make about this?
Why do you suppose there is such a big difference in shoe styles? Why do you suppose shoe styles change over the years?
How do you suppose shoes are made?
What do you think shoes will look like in 100 years? Try to imagine it.

## Suggestions for Replay

The children may replay with the same materials and the original activity card until interest in these materials is exhausted.

For later replays with the original activity card, the children may be given new shoes and pictures of shoes (high-style shoes; baby shoes; shoes from other cultures such as wooden shoes and clogs, mukluks, thongs, and Japanese wooden sandals; military boots; ballet slippers; designer-label running shoes).

New activity cards that focus on different aspects of shoes may be introduced; for example:

Make some observations of how shoes are made.
- What kinds of materials are needed?
- How are the materials put together?

Make some observations of how different shoes feel to wear.
- Which shoes feel good? Which hurt your feet?
- Which are easy to walk in? Hard to walk in?
- Which look beautiful? Ugly?
- Which keep your feet warm?
- Which are good to wear for working? Playing soccer? Riding a bike?

Make some observations about the shapes of shoes. Make some observations about the shapes of feet.
- How are shapes of shoes and shapes of feet alike?
Talk together and share your ideas.

### Suggestions for Creative Play

Drawing pictures of shoes
Imagining what the first pair of shoes in the world looked like and drawing pictures of those shoes
Designing shoes for the twenty-first century and for space travel
Making shoes out of fabric and heavy-duty cardboard
Dramatizing stories about shoes (*The Shoemaker and the Elves*) and/or creating original plays about shoes

## ACTIVITY 3.  FABRIC

**Concepts:**   Fabrics are woven cloths. A variety of fabric is used in the manufacture of clothing. Natural and humanmade fabrics are used to make clothing.

**Learning Goals:**   To promote understanding of the kinds of fabrics that go into the making of the clothes we wear; to develop awareness of how fabric is made

**Thinking Operations:**   Observing, comparing, and classifying; examining assumptions; suggesting hypotheses; evaluating and judging; making decisions

**Materials:**   An assortment of scraps of fabric (velvet, cotton, felt, terry cloth, silk, rayon, polyester, velour, corduroy, brocade, chiffon); fabrics with different textures, thicknesses, and prints; needles, thread, and scissors

## Activity Card

Use the materials in this center to find out what you can about fabric.
- What observations can you make about these fabrics? How are they alike?
- What differences can you observe about texture? Softness? Thickness? Print? Weave?
- What other differences can you see?
- How might these fabrics be classified? What kinds of groups could be set up?

## Sample Debriefing Questions

*Asking Children to Reflect on Their Observations*
What observations did you make about these fabrics? About texture? Thickness? Softness? Weave? Design?
What similarities did you find? What differences?
How did you classify the pieces? In what other ways could the fabrics be grouped?

*Challenging Children Beyond Their Observations*
How do you suppose a fabric is made? What are your ideas about it?
Where do you suppose silk (cotton, leather) comes from? What are your ideas about it?
Where do you suppose velvet (felt, polyester) comes from? What are your ideas about it?
How do you suppose they get the designs and colors onto the fabric? What are your ideas about it?
What fabrics are good for making jackets (trousers, dresses, shirts)? What are your ideas? What makes you think that is true?

## Suggestions for Replay

The students may replay with the same materials and the original activity card until interest in these materials is exhausted. Then the original activity card may be used with new fabrics (fur, leather, knitted fabrics).

Raw materials (balls of wool, spools of textile threads, weaving cards) may be added, along with photographs of the spinning of thread and the manufacture of textiles and clothing. The following new activity cards may be introduced in conjunction with these new materials:

> Work together and use the materials in the center to make an article of clothing.

> Make some observations about how cloth is woven. Use the materials in the center to weave some cloth.

### Suggestions for Creative Play

Designing patterns for clothing
Sewing or knitting
Making patchwork quilts
Making puppets
Making fabric mobiles and fabric collages

## ACTIVITY 4.   CLOTHING STYLES

**Concepts:**   Clothes change in style. What was stylish years ago looks silly to us today. Sometimes people are judged by the clothes they wear.

**Learning Goals:**   To promote awareness of the idea of "style" in clothing as a reflection of cultural standards and values

**Thinking Operations:**   Observing and comparing; evaluating and judging; suggesting hypotheses; examining assumptions; imagining and creating; making decisions

**Materials:**   Photographs and illustrations of "fashionable" apparel dating back at least 1,000 years. Such photos and illustrations of clothing worn in earlier decades of this century can be obtained from old magazines, easily found in used book shops. Illustrations of clothing worn in earlier centuries can be found in old textbooks. These could be cut out and mounted so that they may be examined closely and manipulated. Examples of men's, women's, and children's clothing should be included.

### Activity Card

> Make some observations of the photos in this center.
> - What observations can you make about the styles of clothing that were worn long ago?
> - What observations can you make about how the styles of men's (women's, children's) clothing have changed over the years?

Talk together about what you have observed.

- What are some important differences about the fabrics used in making the clothes? The shapes of the trousers? The shoes? The length of the dresses? The colors? The shapes of the dresses? Of the jackets?

## Sample Debriefing Questions

*Asking Children to Reflect on Their Observations*
What observations did you make about the kinds of clothes that were worn long ago?
How were these clothes (of a particular time) different from ours?
What are some important differences about fabrics? Styles? Shoes? Dress length? Colors?

*Challenging Children Beyond Their Observations*
Why do these clothes of long ago look so funny to us today? How do you explain it? What are your ideas?
What do you suppose our clothes will look like in the future? Can you imagine it? What are your ideas?
How do clothes get designed? Who makes up the idea for the design of clothing? How does this work?
What can we tell about people from looking at their clothes? What are your ideas about this? How do you know that is true?
In the early days of this country, the clothes of the Pilgrims were very "plain," while the clothes of some wealthy landholders were very "fancy." How do you explain the differences? Why do you suppose some people wore plain clothes and others wore fancy clothes?
What makes clothes plain? What makes them fancy? What are your ideas?
How does the way people dress influence the way we think about them?

## Suggestions for Replay

Children's interest in the original activity is likely to be sustained over several replay sessions with the same photos and illustrations and the original activity card. If possible, articles of clothing representing styles of yesteryear may be included.

New photos and illustrations may be added for use with the original activity card or with new activity cards; for example:

- How might these photos of clothes be classified?
Talk together and decide. Then put the clothing photos into groups.
- What are some other ways to classify the photos?

Compare the pictures of clothes worn 100 years ago with
the pictures of clothes worn 500 years ago.
• How did the clothing change?
• What are some important differences?
• How many is 500? (Count out 500 paper clips or toothpicks, so you will have an idea of how many years have
passed.)
Talk together and make a list of all the differences you can
see.

Observe the photos of clothes.
• What can you tell about the people who are wearing
these clothes?
Talk together and see what you can tell about them.

**Suggestions for Creative Play**

Dressing up in costumes of yesteryear
Engaging in dramatic play in old-fashioned clothes
Dramatizing stories about clothes (*The Emperor's New Clothes* or *Cinder-
ella*) or creating original plays about clothes
Imagining and inventing clothes for space travel
Drawing and illustrating clothes of long ago
Writing stories and poems on suggested topics (I wanted a new dress for the
party; They laughed at my funny clothes; I hated my new shoes)
Making and dressing puppets and then putting on a puppet show

## ACTIVITY 5.  JOBS AND WORK

**Concepts:**  People work at different kinds of jobs. Different jobs require different talents, skills, and abilities. Certain kinds of work bring
certain satisfactions or dissatisfactions.

**Learning Goals:**  To promote awareness of the different kinds of jobs
and occupations that provide income; to promote appreciation for the
variety and complexity of work and job opportunities

**Thinking Operations:**  Observing, comparing, classifying, and interpreting data; evaluating and judging; suggesting hypotheses; examining
assumptions; imagining and inventing

**Materials:**  A collection of photos of men and women at work at a
large variety of jobs (dentist, sailor, taxi driver, salesperson, coal miner,
construction worker, baker, farmer, auto mechanic, secretary, teacher, pi-

lot, member of clergy, painter, sculptor, musician, fisher, football player, technician, electrician, plumber, astronaut, tailor, telephone repairperson, hotel clerk, barker, doctor, railroad engineer, office worker, film star, fire-fighter, police officer, carpenter, photographer, nurse, bus driver, clown). Photos for this task may be found in old picture magazines, such as *Life*. Try your local used bookstore for copies of old photo magazines. Try to insure that photos used are nonsexist in their references to who holds what jobs.

## Activity Card

> Use the photos in this center to make some observations about the kind of work that people do. Talk to each other about what these jobs are like.
> - What do you think it's like to work as an artist? A baker? A farmer? A pilot? A taxi driver?
> - What's good about those kinds of jobs? What might you not like about them?
> Think of a way to classify these job pictures. Set up some groups, and put each picture in the group where you think it belongs.

## Sample Debriefing Questions

*Asking Children to Reflect on Their Observations*

What observations did you make about the kinds of work these people were doing?

What do you suppose it's like to work as a farmer (baker, plumber, con-struction worker, railroad engineer)?

What's good about that job? What are some things you might not like?

Why do you suppose people work at jobs? What are your ideas?

Why do you suppose people choose the jobs they do? What are your ideas?

*Challenging Children Beyond Their Observations*

What kinds of groups did you make for those job photos? What other kinds of groupings might have been made?

Why do you suppose people choose dangerous jobs, like construction on bridges or tall buildings, or coal mining? What are your ideas?

What happens when people cannot find jobs? What are some of your ideas about this?

What kind of a job would you like to do when you grow up? Tell why you think you might like that work.

What do you think you have to do in order to become a pilot (or any other job for which extensive training is required)? What are your ideas? How do you know that is true? How is that different from working at a fast-food restaurant? What are your ideas?

How come some jobs have lots of men working at them (like pilots), while others have mostly women (like nurses)? How do you explain it? What are your ideas?

## Suggestions for Replay

The children may replay with the same photos, setting up other classification systems.

New photos of people at work (veterinarian, forest ranger, lighthouse keeper, oil-rig worker, zoo attendant, lion tamer, ship's captain, pharmacist, lab technician, chemist, astronomer) may be added for use with the original activity card or with new activity cards that reflect the additions; for example:

> Compare the job of veterinarian to the job of zookeeper.
> • How are these jobs alike?
> • How are they different?
> Talk about all the similarities and differences you can think of.

> Compare the job of carpenter with working as an actor.
> • How are these alike?
> • How are they different?
> Talk about all the similarities and differences you can think of.

The children may participate in a role-playing activity in which each child in the group chooses a part to play in one of the following types of scenarios: a visit to the dentist's office, working hard in the supermarket, working together to build a house, a flight crew on an airplane going to Alaska, a staff of newspaper workers trying to get the newspaper out on time.

## Suggestions for Creative Play

Drawing or painting pictures about people at work at different jobs
Writing stories or poems about working at different jobs

Acting out scenarios such as those in the role-play activity mentioned above
Singing and dancing to folksongs with a job or work theme ("I've Been
    Working on the Railroad"; "I Owe My Soul to the Company Store";
    "Come Mr. Tally Man, Tally Me Banana"; "Sweet Molly Malone")

## ACTIVITY 6.  WORK AND PAY

**Concepts:**  Some jobs are highly paid. Others are poorly paid. Some
jobs carry higher status.

**Learning Goals:**  To promote awareness of the range of incomes connected to certain jobs; to promote understanding of the relationship between income and status

**Thinking Operations:**  Observing, comparing, classifying, and interpreting data; examining assumptions; evaluating and judging; suggesting
hypotheses; imagining and inventing; making decisions

**Materials:**  The same collection of jobs and work photographs used for
Activity 5 is used for this task, but the photos should be classified into two
groups: higher-income jobs and lower-income jobs. Choose about six photos for each group.

### Activity Card

> The photographs in this center have been grouped into two
> categories. In Group 1 you see people working at jobs
> where they earn higher incomes. In Group 2 you see people
> working at jobs where they earn lower incomes. Study the
> photos in these two groups.
> * What observations can you make about higher-paying
>   and lower-paying jobs?
> Talk together about what you observe about these jobs.
> * What can you tell from your observations about why peo-
>   ple working at jobs in Group 1 are making much more
>   money than the people working at the jobs in Group 2?

### Sample Debriefing Questions

*Asking Children to Reflect on Their Observations*
What observations did you make about the jobs in Group 1?
What observations did you make about the jobs in Group 2?
What are some important differences about these two groups of jobs?

*Challenging Children Beyond Their Observations*
Why do you suppose a famous football player earns much more money
    than a teacher? What are your ideas? How do you explain it?
Is it better to earn lots of money? What are your ideas about this?
Should movie stars earn more money than house painters? What do you
    think? What are your ideas?
What kinds of jobs should be the highest paid? What do you think?
What might be some advantages to having a higher-paying job? What
    might be some disadvantages?

## Suggestions for Replay

Two new sets of photos may be used that are grouped once again into
higher-paying jobs and lower-paying jobs, along with the original activity
card.

The children may be given other photos showing homes, neighborhoods,
cars, and recreational activities, along with new activity cards that ask for
observations, comparisons, hypotheses, and interpretations, to establish
the relationships among jobs, income, and standard of living. This, however, should be done with great sensitivity to the feelings of children regard-
ing the standard of living of their parents or the kinds of jobs they hold.

Role-playing activities may be added, with each child in the group
choosing a part to play in one or more of the following scenarios: a movie
star comes to visit your house; a maid wants a job in a fancy house; the son
in a family wants to take a dangerous job; your friend has a boring job as a
dishwasher; a friend doesn't earn enough money at her job as a newspaper
delivery person; people think a friend's job walking dogs is silly.

## Suggestions for Creative Play

Drawing or painting men, women, and children at work
Writing stories or poems about jobs and work
Engaging in dramatic play and role play about jobs and work
Pantomiming to express certain job functions (this could be turned into a
    form of charades)

☆    ☆

These six activities do not represent a total social studies curriculum for
primary graders. They do, however, provide for rich investigative experiences on topics of substance, as well as point in the direction of how other
investigative opportunities may be created.

# CHAPTER 9

# Serious Play
# in Mathematics

The curriculum area of mathematics is a "natural" for play-debrief-replay, since the learning of mathematical concepts is most successfully done with manipulative materials and through hands-on, experiential play. Virtually all beginning mathematical concepts lend themselves to such investigations: volume and capacity; shapes and sizes; symmetry; area; estimation and measurement of length, time, speed, and temperature; balancing; angles; and two-dimensional space. Examples for a teaching-for-thinking approach to primary mathematics, following the play-debrief-replay model, are given in this chapter to show how conceptual understanding may be developed within several of these topical areas.

Creative play in mathematics may occur in arts, crafts, music, and cooking activities. It may also take the form of inventive problem solving that goes beyond children's mathematical capabilities. Both of these kinds of activities are included in the creative play sections for mathematics.

## ACTIVITY 1. LIQUID VOLUME AND CAPACITY

**Concepts:** The space filled remains unchanged, despite the rearrangement of the parts or the shape (the principle of conservation). Volume refers to the amount of space in a hollow container.

**Learning Goals:** To promote understanding of the concept of conservation; to promote awareness that visual assessment of size and volume are not necessarily congruent

**Thinking Operations:** Observing, comparing, and interpreting data; designing investigations; suggesting hypotheses; examining assumptions; applying principles to new situations

**Materials:** Beakers of various sizes and shapes. (In order for the concept of conservation to be adequately explored, it is important to include several differently shaped containers that hold the same amount of liquid.) Also, plastic containers, measuring cups, a water table or a large dishpan of water, paper towels, newspaper.

139

## Activity Card

Use the materials in this center to conduct some investigations about how much water it takes to fill containers of different sizes and shapes.
- What do you observe about the amount of water it takes to fill the tall, skinny container?
- What do you observe about the amount of water it takes to fill the short, fat container?
- What do you observe about the amount of water it takes to fill the _____ container?

Talk together about your observations.

## Sample Debriefing Questions

*Asking Children to Reflect on Their Observations*
What observations did you make about the amount of water it takes to fill the tall, skinny container?
What observations did you make about the amount of water it takes to fill the short, fat container?
How do you explain it? How is it possible that these two differently shaped containers hold the same amount of water? What are your ideas?
If both of these containers (the short, fat and the tall, skinny) were filled with soda pop, which one would you want? How come?

*Challenging Children Beyond Their Observations*
How can you tell which container holds more water? What are your ideas on this?
How can you tell which container holds less water? What are your ideas on this?
How can you tell which containers hold the same amount of water? What ideas do you have?
How can you tell which container in the store holds more soda pop? Ice cream? Milk? Peanut butter? What are your ideas?

## Suggestions for Replay

Allowing for many more replay experiences with the initial investigative play task is a really good idea before adding new materials or activities.

In later replays, new containers of various sizes and shapes may be added, as well as new "pourable" substances for filling containers, for example, sand, colored water, and small solid objects (pebbles, marbles, buttons, paper clips, rubber bands, macaroni). These new materials may be used in conjunction with the following new activity cards:

> Use the materials in the center to conduct some more investigations about how much sand (colored water) it takes to fill containers of different sizes and shapes.

> Use the materials in the center to conduct some more investigations to find out how many pebbles (marbles, paper clips) it takes to fill containers of different sizes and shapes.

> Use the materials to conduct some investigations to find out which containers hold more (or less) water (sand, marbles, paper clips).
> * What observations have you made about the relationship between the shape of the container and its volume?

## Suggestions for Creative Play

Using paper and cardboard to make containers that hold the same amount of water (sand, rods, cubes, dominoes) as a container supplied

Figuring out a way to determine how much water it takes to fill up something with very large volume (a swimming pool, the classroom, a bathtub)

Designing containers to hold articles with irregular shapes (a 200-pound octopus, a baby giraffe, a slithery python, a giant helping of spaghetti)

## ACTIVITY 2.  DRY VOLUME AND CAPACITY

**Concepts:**   The space filled remains unchanged despite the rearrangement of the parts or the shape (the principle of conservation). Volume refers to the amount of space in a hollow container — the more volume, the greater the capacity.

**Learning Goals:**   To promote understanding of the concept of conservation; to promote awareness that visual assessment of size and volume are not necessarily congruent

**Thinking Operations:**   Observing and comparing data; suggesting hypotheses; examining assumptions; designing investigations; applying principles to new situations

**Materials:**   Boxes of various sizes and shapes (shoe boxes, candy boxes, cookie boxes, mailing cartons, stationery boxes); 1-inch plastic or wooden cubes. (For the principle of conservation to be adequately explored, it is important that some boxes of different shapes hold the same number of 1-inch cubes.)

### Activity Card

Use the materials in this center to conduct some investigations about how many blocks it takes to fill containers of different sizes and shapes.
- What do you observe about how many blocks it takes to fill the long, narrow box?
- What do you observe about how many blocks it takes to fill the short, fat box?
- What do you observe about the number of blocks it takes to fill the _____ container?

Talk together about your observations.

### Sample Debriefing Questions

*Asking Children to Reflect on Their Observations*
What observations did you make about how many blocks it takes to fill the long, narrow box?
What observations did you make about how many blocks it takes to fill the short, fat box?
How do you explain it? How come these two differently shaped containers hold the same amount of blocks? What are your ideas?
Suppose you tried to fill these boxes with chocolates. How many chocolates would fill the short, fat box? How many would fill the long, narrow one?
If both of these boxes (the short, fat and the long, narrow) were filled with cookies, which one would you want? How come?

*Challenging Children Beyond Their Observations*
When you look at these boxes, how can you tell which one will hold more blocks? What are your ideas on this?
How can you tell which one will hold fewer blocks? What are your ideas?
How could you tell which boxes hold the same amount of blocks? What ideas do you have?
How can you tell which box, in the store, holds more cookies? Candy? Marbles? Erasers? Pencils? What are your ideas?

## Suggestions for Replay

Replay with the same materials and the same activity card should be allowed to continue for several sessions, since children will find many new ways to investigate these concepts.

New and differently shaped containers, including those of odd shapes, may be added for later replay sessions, as well as new articles for filling containers: cuisenaire rods, dominoes, building blocks, Sterne cubes, and articles of different shapes (diamonds, hexagons, octagons, rounds; e.g., attribute blocks). These would be used in conjunction with the following new activity cards:

Use the materials in the center to conduct some more investigations about how many blocks (dominoes, rods) it takes to fill boxes of different sizes and shapes.

Use the materials in the center to conduct some more investigations to find out how many diamonds (hexagons, octagons) it takes to fill boxes of different sizes and shapes.

Use the materials in the center to conduct some investigations to find out which boxes hold more (or fewer) dominoes (cubes, blocks, hexagons).
- What observations have you made about the relationship between the shape of the box and its volume?

## Suggestions for Creative Play

Cooking (popcorn, cookies, muffins, jello)
Making butter (observing changes in form and volume)
Designing and making boxes using Origami or free-form shapes
Building with blocks, dominoes, 1-inch blocks, cuisenaire rods, or Lego

## ACTIVITY 3.  SHAPES AND SIZES

**Concepts:**  Some shapes, such as the square, triangle, and regular hexagon can be used to cover a surface without leaving a gap or overlapping. Two lines coming together at a point form an angle.

**Learning Goals:**  To promote awareness of the differences among the two-dimensional shapes of squares, triangles, and rectangles; to promote understanding of the concept of "fit without leaving a gap"; to develop awareness of the concept of angles

**Thinking Operations:**   Observing, comparing, and classifying data; designing investigations; applying principles to new situations; interpreting data

**Materials:**   Cut-out cardboard shapes of different sizes and colors (rectangles, squares, diamonds, triangles); if available, attribute blocks; large sheets of graph paper; rulers or meter sticks, scissors, and pencils

## Activity Card

Use the materials in this center and make some observations of these differently shaped pieces.
• What observations can you make about the squares? Rectangles? Triangles? Diamonds?
Talk to each other about your observations.
Use the pencils and paper to draw and cut out some shapes just like these.

## Sample Debriefing Questions

*Asking Children to Reflect on Their Observations*
What observations did you make about squares? Rectangles? Triangles? Diamonds?
How are squares like rectangles? How are they different?
How are triangles like diamonds? How are they different?
In what ways are all the squares (rectangles, triangles) alike? In what ways are they different?

*Challenging Children Beyond Their Observations*
How do you make a square (rectangle, triangle, diamond)? What kind of shape does it have? How do you know?
What observations did you make about the sides of these figures? About the corners?
In what ways are the corners (angles) of the squares and rectangles alike? How are they different?
What other things in the room that you can see have similar kinds of corners? How can you tell they are the same?

## Suggestions for Replay

Replay with the same materials and the original investigative play task should occur for several additional sessions, since the materials will yield many new investigations.

In later replays, new shapes (hexagons, octagons, pentagons, circles and half-circles) may be added to the center, in conjunction with new activity cards; for example:

Use the materials in the center to make a design with squares (rectangles, triangles, diamonds) on the graph paper.
- What observations did you make about how the squares fit together? The rectangles? The triangles? The diamonds?

Use the circles and half-circles to make a design on the graph paper.
- What observations did you make about how the circles fit together? The half-circles?

Use the octagons (pentagons, hexagons) to make a design on the graph paper.
- What observations did you make about how the octagons (pentagons, hexagons) fit together?

Use the materials in this center to design and cut out some squares and rectangles.
- Compare your squares and rectangles to the ones you see in the center.
- Compare the sides. Compare the shapes. Compare the angles.
- How are they alike? How are they different?

## Suggestions for Creative Play

Designing and comparing three doghouses, the first using only the shapes of squares; the second, only the shapes of triangles; the third, only the shapes of octagons

Working with partners and looking everywhere in the room to find objects containing triangular, rectangular, and square shapes; listing what has been found; and making some drawings of them

Creating designs using only diamond shapes

Designing and cutting out five different shapes that are neither square, rectangular, triangular, circular, or octagonal and inventing names for each of their shapes

## ACTIVITY 4.  AREA

**Concepts:**   The amount needed to cover a surface is its area. The area of a surface is different from its boundary, or perimeter. If you want to enclose a region, you calculate its perimeter. If you want to cover the surface, you calculate the area.

**Learning Goals:**   To promote understanding of the concept of area as meaning the amount required to cover a surface; to differentiate between the concepts of area and perimeter; to develop skill in solving problems requiring the calculation of area

**Thinking Operations:**   Observing, comparing, and interpreting data; suggesting hypotheses; examining assumptions; designing projects and investigations

**Materials:**   Large sheets of 1-inch graph paper cut into differently sized squares and rectangles; pieces cut into irregular shapes, but of the same area (see Figure 9.1); colored 1-inch square pieces of cardboard; additional sheets of graph paper; rulers and scissors

### Activity Card

> Use the materials in the center to conduct some investigations about the size of the surface of the squares, rectangles, and pieces of other shapes.
> • What observations can you make about how many colored squares it takes to cover the large squares?

**FIGURE 9.1**  Shapes and Area

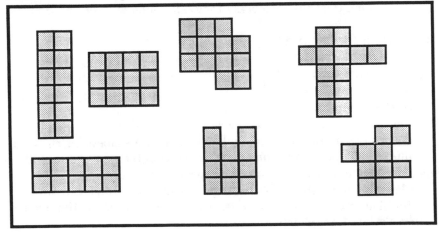

- What observations can you make about how many colored squares it takes to cover the rectangles?
- What observations can you make about how many colored squares it takes to cover the pieces of other shapes?
- Which surfaces need more colored squares to cover them? Which need fewer? Which are the same? What observations can you make?

## Sample Debriefing Questions

*Asking Children to Reflect on Their Observations*

What observations did you make about how many colored squares it took to cover the surface of the squares (rectangles, other shapes)?

What observations did you make about the surfaces that needed more colored squares? Fewer colored squares?

What observations did you make about the surfaces that needed the same number of colored squares to cover their surfaces?

How do you explain it? How come the irregularly shaped pieces had the same surface area as the rectangle, even though they looked so different? What are your ideas?

*Challenging Children Beyond Their Observations*

When you look at the surfaces of squares and rectangles, how can you tell which ones have the larger surface areas? What are your ideas about this?

When you look at the irregularly shaped surfaces, how can you tell which ones have the larger (smaller) surface area? What are your ideas about this?

If you wanted to cover this rectangle (square, irregularly shaped piece) with a piece of cloth, how would you know what size cloth to get? How might this surface area be measured? What are your ideas?

## Suggestions for Replay

Children should have many more opportunities to replay with the same rectangles, squares, colored squares, and irregularly shaped pieces, since many new investigations can be carried out with the same materials.

In later replays, new shapes (triangles, circles, half-circles, hexagons), cut from 1-inch graph paper (see Figure 9.2), may be added in conjunction with the following new activity cards:

**FIGURE 9.2**   Additional Shapes for Activity 4

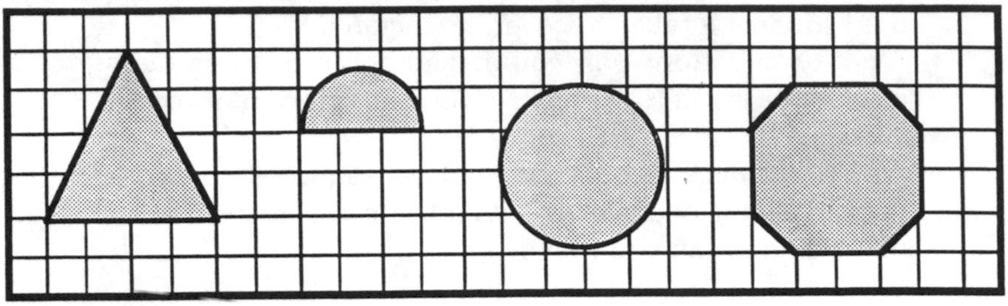

Use the materials in the center to conduct some investigations about the size of the surface areas of these shapes.
- What observations can you make about how many colored squares it takes to cover the triangle (circle, half-circle, hexagon)?
- How can you tell which have larger and smaller surface areas?

Use the materials in the center to make different shapes.
- Make as many as you can that have a surface area of 4 square inches.
- Cut your shapes out after you have designed them.
- Make as many as you can that have a surface area of 5 (then 6) square inches.
- Cut your shapes out after you have designed them.

Use the materials in the center to figure out the number of squares it takes to cover a book, a piece of paper, a box top, a desk top, a folder, and an envelope.

Place graph paper on the floor and draw around a shoe of everyone in the group.
- Whose shoe covers the largest surface area?
- Whose covers the smallest?
Figure out a way to calculate the area of each of the shoe surfaces.

Other replay opportunities may involve trying to determine the area of other surfaces in the classroom (blackboard, cupboard door, section of floor, pictures).

## Suggestions for Creative Play

Creating and inventing ways to figure out the surface area of leaves; hand
shapes; animal shapes; and the outside surfaces of boxes, coffee cans,
and soup cans
Creating and designing shapes with a given (fixed) surface area, for example, a shape that has an area of 9 square inches that would be a good
shape for a duck pond
Using shapes of certain area (e.g., 6 square feet) in artwork collages
Designing or creating space of certain specifications to plant a garden,
build a giant chessboard, design a maze, or design a kite

## ACTIVITY 5.  LINEAR MEASUREMENT

**Concepts:**   Linear dimensions of objects can be measured; standard
units of measure are agreed upon by common consent; they help us to
understand what we mean.
**Learning Goals:**   To promote awareness of the value of communicating to each other in quantifiable terms that others can understand; to
promote increased skill in using standard units of measure
**Thinking Operations:**   Observing, comparing, classifying, and interpreting data; designing projects and investigations; imagining and creating; suggesting hypotheses; examining assumptions
**Materials:**   Tape measures, inch and centimeter rulers, yardsticks and
metersticks, pieces of string and/or yarn, rubber bands, unit blocks, toothpicks, straws

### Activity Card

Use the materials in this center to make some observations
about how objects can be measured.
- What observations can you make about how to measure
  the top of your desk? The height of your desk? The
  height of the teacher's desk? The width of the classroom
  door? The height of the door? The width of the classroom window? [Teacher can substitute other objects for
  measuring.]
- What differences do you observe when you measure
  these objects with a ruler? A yardstick? A piece of
  string? Unit blocks? Toothpicks? Rubber bands?

## Sample Debriefing Questions

*Asking Children to Reflect on Their Observations*
What observations did you make about how to measure the top of a desk
(height of a desk, teacher's desk, door)?
What observations did you make when you measured these things with a
ruler? Yardstick? String? Unit blocks? Toothpicks? Rubber bands?
Which is easier to use when you measure? What are your ideas about it?
Why do you suppose we need to know the measurements of these objects?
What are your ideas?

*Challenging Children Beyond Their Observations*
When [child's name] measured the desktop, he found it was 18 inches
across. When [other child's name] measured the same desk top, she
found it was 23 rubber bands across. What are some of your ideas
about these two ways of measuring?
[Child's name] measured the length of the classroom with her feet. She
found that it was 74 of her feet long. Then [other child's name] measured it with his feet. He found that it was 86 of his feet long. How do
you explain this? What are some good ways to measure? What are
your ideas?

## Suggestions for Replay

The children will very likely want to replay with the same measuring
tools and objects for several additional sessions before they have exhausted
the possibility of investigations with these materials.
In later replays, paper and scissors may be added along with new activity cards to encourage new measuring investigations; for example:

Use the paper to make a tracing of one of your own feet.
Each member of the group should do this. Cut out your
tracings.
• Then each of you use your own foot tracing to measure
the blackboard, the bulletin board, and the length of the
room.
• How are your measurements alike?
• How are they different?
• How do you explain it?

Use the paper to make a tracing of one child's foot. Cut out
the tracing.

- Measure the length of the blackboard with that foot-shaped tracing.
- Then measure it with a yardstick or meterstick.
- What observations can you make about these two ways of measuring?

Use the paper to make a tracing of your own hand. Each member of the group should do this. Cut out your tracing.
- Then each of you use your hand tracing to measure the height of every other person in your group.
- How are these measurements alike?
- How are they different?

Use the measuring materials in the center to measure the height of every person in your class.
- Make a chart that shows the height of all the children.

### Suggestions for Creative Play

Creating and inventing ways to measure larger distances (the distance from school to a child's house, from a child's house to the shopping mall, from school to the library, from the classrom to the office)

Creating and inventing ways to measure how high different balls bounce

Creating and inventing ways to measure amount of snow fallen, amount of rain, the size of a puddle

Using linear measurement to build objects with blocks or wood (a boat that is 12 feet long; a house that is 10 feet high; a bird house that is big enough for three birds; a rabbit house that is big enough for two rabbits)

Using linear measurement in drawing and designing (a ship that is 8 inches long; an airplane that is 2 feet long and 14 inches wide; a person who is 3 feet tall)

## ACTIVITY 6. COUNTING

**Concepts:** Number is an attribute that represents a set of objects; numerals are names of numbers; counting is a way of determining *more, less, same, how many.*

**Learning Goals:** To provide opportunities for children to explore mathematical relationships in combining and removing sets and subsets; in determining *how many*; in examining the concepts of *more, less, same.*

**Thinking Operations:** Observing, comparing, and classifying; suggesting hypotheses; examining assumptions; interpreting data; designing projects and investigations; creating and inventing

**Materials:** Cuisenaire rods or other counting rods; cubical counting blocks; other counters such as buttons, stones, spools, dominoes, counting discs, toothpicks; about one dozen cut-out circles of colored cardboard or colored paper in different diameters. The counting objects can be varied, as can the colored circles, so investigative play with counting has extensive permutations with even these initial materials.

### Activity Card

Use the materials in this center to make some observations about numbers.
- How many rods can you fit onto the red circle?
- How many rods can you fit onto the orange circle?
- Which can hold more rods? Which holds less?
- How many toothpicks can you fit onto the green circle?
- How many toothpicks can you fit onto the yellow circle?
- Which circle can hold more toothpicks? Which holds less?
- What observations can you make about the number of counters that fit on the colored circles?

### Sample Debriefing Questions

*Asking Children to Reflect on Their Observations*
What observations did you make about how many buttons (pebbles, rods) fit on the yellow (orange, blue) circle?
What observations did you make about which circles hold more counters? Which hold less? How do you explain it?

*Challenging Children Beyond Their Observations*
How come the orange circle holds more stones but fewer buttons? How do you explain it?
How can you figure out how many buttons (discs, rods) can fit on the red and the orange circles? What are your ideas?
Do you think the blue circle will hold more stones or buttons? What is your estimation?
Which colored circles hold exactly 8 (or 9, 10, 7) buttons (spools, dominoes)? What's your estimation?
Which two colored circles together hold 9 (or 10, 8, 7) buttons (dominoes, unit blocks)? What's your estimation?

## Suggestions for Replay

Since there are so many permutations and combinations of colored circles and counters, replay with the original activity card might carry on over several days or even weeks. Children should be encouraged to carry on their extensive investigations with these materials.

When children are ready to move on, new colored circles of larger sizes and new objects for counters (toy cars, unshelled peanuts or hazelnuts, paper clips, crayons, pennies) may be added. These additional materials are used in conjunction with the following new activity cards:

- How many different combinations of paper clips (peanuts, crayons) can you make to show the number 8 (or 7, 6, 9)?

Write down the combinations you make.

Use the materials in the center to figure out an answer to these questions:
- How many peanuts would you need to give everyone in this class two peanuts?
- How could you record this information to show how many people and how many peanuts?

Use the materials in this center to figure out an answer to these questions:
- How many cookies would you need to give everyone in your group three cookies?
- How could you record this information to show how many people and how many cookies?

- Which circle in the center holds the most buttons, and which circle holds the least?

Try to figure out a way to write this down.

## Suggestions for Creative Play

Playing store, with real coins (100 pennies can go a long way), toy cash register, play money

Playing games in which counting and/or keeping score is used (ten pins, dominoes, dice, ball games)

Singing number songs ("This Old Man, He Played One," "Sing a Song of Sixpence," "Five Little Chickadees," "One, Two, Buckle My Shoe," "Roll Over"), creating skits around them where appropriate

Cooking or baking and "sharing out" cookies, muffins, popcorn
Drawing pictures to illustrate a "number sentence" $(3+4=7; 7-3=4)$
Planning, budgeting, and shopping for ingredients to make applesauce,
    pancakes, butter, strawberry shortcake

## ACTIVITY 7.  TIME

**Concepts:**   The passage of time can be measured; there are standard
units of measure for hours and minutes, days, months; our standard units
of time are measured by the rotation of the earth around the sun.
   **Learning Goals:**   To provide opportunities for experiences with standard units for measuring time; to increase appreciation for the usefulness
of standard units of measure in communicating our thoughts to others; to
promote awareness of what can be done in different time periods
   **Thinking Operations:**   Observing, comparing, interpreting data; designing projects and investigations; creating and inventing; suggesting hypotheses; examining assumptions
   **Materials:**   A variety of instruments that measure hours, minutes, and
days, for example, an hourglass, clocks (analog, digital, wind-up, alarm,
sweep second hand, wall), timers, and a stopwatch; cardboard clock with
movable minute and second hands

### Activity Card

Use the materials in this center to make some studies of
time.
   • How is time measured?
   • What kinds of instruments measure time?
   • How do clocks measure time?
   • How are clocks and timers alike?
   • How are they different?
Do some playing around with the materials and see what
observations you can make.

### Sample Debriefing Questions

*Asking Children to Reflect on Their Observations*
What observations did you make about how clocks measure time?
What observations did you make about how timers measure time?
What are some differences between digital clocks and analog clocks? What
    are some similarities?

What's a minute? A second? An hour? How are these measured? What are
your ideas?

*Challenging Children Beyond Their Observations*
How long do you suppose it takes to jump 100 times? What's your
estimate?
How long do you suppose it takes to drink a glass of water? What's your
estimate?
Does it take longer to read a book or to eat an apple? What do you think?
How do you know that is true?
Why do you suppose we need to measure time? What's good about being
able to do that?

## Suggestions for Replay

New activity cards may be added that involve different kinds of calcula-
tions with time; for example:

- How long do you estimate it will take [child's name] to
  jump 100 times?
  Use the materials in the center to figure out how long this
  does take.
- How long do you estimate it will take [child's name] to tie
  a shoelace?
  Use the materials in the center to find out how long this
  does take.

Use the materials in the center to find out how long it takes
to
- Bounce a ball 100 times
- Blow up a balloon
- Fill a gallon bucket with water
- Eat an apple
Think of some other things that you can measure in time,
and do these investigations, too.

New materials may be added to involve the children in measuring days,
weeks, months, years. Different kinds of calendars (day calendar, week,
month) may be used in conjunction with the following new activity cards:

Make some observations of the clock and the calendar.
- How are these time measures alike?
- How are they different?

Make some observations about how calendars measure
time.
- How are days, weeks, and months measured?

Use the calendars to figure out some ways of measuring
how long each person in your group will have to wait until
his or her birthday.
- Record your findings.

Other replay activities may involve gathering and classifying time schedules (TV schedules, airplane/train/bus schedules); keeping records of everybody's birthday; calculating how long it takes a child to walk to school
every day; designing investigations to determine the time at which the sun
sets every day in the month of January and in the month of May.

### Suggestions for Creative Play

Making a clock, a sundial, an hourglass, the calendar month of a child's
    birthday
Inventing ways to figure out how fast a bird flies, a balloon lets out air, a
    leaf falls to the ground
Engaging in dramatic play on time themes (I hate to wait for my mother to
    finish her shopping! I hate to go to bed at 7:00! I hate to have only 15
    minutes for recess! I hate to have to wait 10 months for my birthday!)

☆    ☆

These seven curriculum activities for serious play in mathematics represent only a fraction of what is possible. They will, of course, lead to many
rich and exciting investigations, in which children's concept development
will be enhanced. It is also hoped that they will serve as examples for other
serious plays in mathematics.

# CHAPTER 10

# Serious Play in the Language Arts

Generating examples of investigative play activities for language arts was more difficult than for any other curriculum area. It's not that there was a dearth of possibilities, but the opposite. Because I see language development holistically, and because all the investigative play activities already presented involve the use of language, it was instead an embarrassment of riches. Choosing from among such a variety of options was overwhelming.

Identifying those learning goals that would shape the investigative play was the starting point. One could, of course, chop up the language arts into discrete bytes of spelling, grammar, vocabulary, punctuation, phonics, comprehension, and penmanship, as it has been done for years. But I preferred a whole-language approach as more representative of how language is actually learned. I find excellent guidance in James Moffett's (1968) listing of basic language arts operations for Grades K–3: acting out, speaking up, becoming literate, reading, writing out, writing down, writing up, and playing games of language and logic. To learn to do all of these better is an unarguably viable and legitimate language arts goal for the primary grades. These operations, taken together, give rise to the curriculum activities that follow.

## ACTIVITY 1. WORDS AND SOUNDS

**Concepts:**  Words have auditory and visual relationships to each other; auditory and visual structures of words give us clues to decoding them.

**Learning Goals:**  To provide experiences with the analysis and manipulation of words; to promote awareness of auditory relationships; to promote use of auditory and visual analysis in decoding words

**Thinking Operations:**  Observing, comparing, classifying, and interpreting data; examining assumptions; evaluating and judging; making decisions; imagining and inventing

**Materials:**  Words of the following types, each printed on an individual card—may, say, pay, tray, pray, slay, sleigh, weigh, hay, play, today, hooray, stay; boat, coat, float, oat, goat, coal, load, oak, goal, loaf, roast, toast; rode, role, code, bone, hope, hole, home, hose, pole

## Activity Card

Work together and make some observations of the words on the cards. Then think of a good way to classify them.
- What kinds of groups can you make?
- How would each word fit into a group?
- In what other ways might you classify these words?

## Sample Debriefing Questions

*Asking Children to Reflect on Their Observations*
What observations did you make of these words?
How were some of these words alike? How were they different?
What kinds of groups did you make?
In what other ways could these words be grouped?

*Challenging Children Beyond Their Observations*
How are the words *road* and *rode* alike? How are they different?
What other words might you add to this group: *hay, say, pay*?
How are the words *boat* and *coal* alike? How are they different? What other words would you add to a group with the words *boat, coal*, and *load*?

## Suggestions for Replay

Children may, of course, replay with the same word cards and the original activity card, since many investigative opportunities are possible with these words. New words of the same type may be added to each original group, or new types of words with different phonic makeup (*ai* words, *ee* words, *ate* words, *at* words, *it* words, *in* words) may be introduced.

New activity cards may be added for use with any group of words, for example:

Make some observations of these words.
- Find some ways to classify them according to the way they sound.

Make some observations of these words.
- Find some ways to classify them according to what they mean.

Make some observations of these words.
* Find some ways to classify them according to how the vowels sound.

Make some observations of these words.
* Try to use them to make up some poems.
Write down some of your poems.

## Suggestions for Creative Play

Choosing a word and acting it out in a pantomime, to see if the other children can guess the word

Inventing words that rhyme with hard-to-rhyme words, like *octopus, hippopotamus, dinosaur, spaghetti*

Playing word games, for example, seeing how many words can be made using the letters shown in Figure 10.1

Writing as many words as the children can think of that begin or end with the letters *st*

Playing word games, such as doing anagrams, unscrambling words, or playing Scrabble

Writing words in patterns to form the shape of the objects they describe (dogs, cats, houses, violins, balloons), as in Figure 10.2

### ACTIVITY 2.  MEANINGS OF WORDS

**Concepts:**   Words convey meanings; we use words to communicate thoughts and feelings; some words and phrases create lovely mental images.

**Learning Goals:**   To provide experiences with the analysis of phrases in communicating meaning; to promote awareness of the mental pictures that some words and phrases generate

**FIGURE 10.1**   Letters to Use in Making Up Words for a Word Game

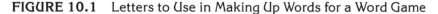
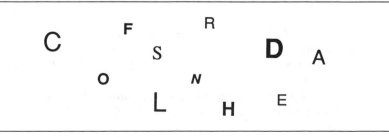

**FIGURE 10.2**   Words Repeated to Form the Shape Described

---

<pre>
                    tree
                 tree  tree
              tree  tree  tree
           tree  tree  tree  tree
        tree  tree  tree  tree  tree
     tree  tree  tree  tree  tree  tree
  tree  tree  tree  tree  tree  tree  tree
                 tree  tree
                 tree  tree
</pre>

---

**Thinking Operations:**   Observing, comparing, classifying, and interpreting data; applying principles to new situations; examining assumptions; evaluating and judging; creating and inventing

**Materials:**   Word cards with the following or similar types of phrases — running water, angry lion, singing bird, patting the duck, sunset sky, birthday cake, chasing the cat, melting snow, silly goose, scared stiff, chocolate cake, elevator door, after recess, cruel winter, messy room, puffing engine, raindrops, castle in the sky, fairy prince, wooden bridge, fire truck, ocean waves, mountain goat, speeding train, ghostly goblin, falling down, haunted house

### Activity Card

Work together and make some observations of the phrases on the cards. Then decide on a good way to classify them.
- What kinds of groups can you make?
- How would each phrase fit into a group?
- In what other ways could these phrases be classified?

### Sample Debriefing Questions

*Asking Children to Reflect on Their Observations*
What observations did you make about these phrases?
In what ways are the phrases *birthday cake* and *angry lion* alike? How are they different?
In what ways are the phrases *messy room* and *haunted house* alike? How are they different?

How could these phrases be classified? What other kinds of categories could be set up?

*Challenging Children Beyond Their Observations*
What kinds of pictures do you make in your mind when you hear the phrases *running water*? *Melting snow*? *Yowling cat*?
When someone tells you that he saw the sunset sky, what picture do you make in your mind? How would you describe the picture you see?
In what ways are the words *lion* and *angry lion* (*room* and *messy room*; *cake* and *chocolate cake*; *snow* and *melting snow*) alike? How are they different?
What phrases would you add to this group: *terrified cat, ugly monster, silly puppy, yucky food*? How do your phrases fit into that group?

## Suggestions for Replay

Children may play again with the initial investigative play task and the original phrases. New phrases may be added to the existing group, or the lot may be replaced with an entirely new set. Ideally these phrases should come from the children's own language usage, especially expressions used in their day-to-day communications with each other.

New activity cards may be added that reflect other dimensions of words and meanings; for example:

Some words make sounds: choo-choo, ding-ding, hissssss, ding-a-ling, boom-boom.
- Work together, and make up some words that sound like running water, thunder, birds singing, a car starting, an angry lion.
Write down the words you made.

Work together to make up some words and phrases that tell about
- Stars
- Birthdays
- Saturdays
Write your words and phrases down on a piece of paper.

Work together and think of as many words and phrases as you can to describe
- Your morning at school
- Your afternoon at school
Write down all the words and phrases you thought up.

Work together and think of as many ways as you can to complete each of these sentences:
- As happy as . . .
- As quiet as . . .
- As ugly as . . .
- As sad as . . .
- As beautiful as . . .
- As alarming as . . .
- As straight as . . .
- As perfect as . . .

Write down the sentences you made.

A photo with a strong visual impact may be added, along with the following new activity card:

Study the photo.
- Work together and think of as many words and phrases as you can to describe this photo.
- Write down all the words and phrases you thought up.

## Suggestions for Creative Play

Acting out: Each child or pair of children chooses a phrase and acts it out in pantomime, while the others try to imagine what the phrase could be.

Thinking about words: Children work in pairs and make a list of all the beautiful words they can think of, all the ugly words, all the scary words, all the mean and rotten words, all the gentle words.

Illustrating words: Many messages are now conveyed by illustrations, rather than with words. Children may work in pairs and think of ways to illustrate suggested messages (Danger — Thin ice! Don't feed the monkeys! It's bedtime; Clean up your room; Ride your bicycle carefully; Don't forget to feed the dog before you go to school).

Dramatizing on suggested themes (My aunt gave me a new dress for my birthday, and I hated it; Billy fell off his bicycle and broke his leg; The electricity went out right in the middle of my favorite TV program).

Writing e-mail messages (adapted from Moffett, 1968): The children may compose an e-mail message limited to 15 to 25 words about the following: You are trying to explain to your Aunt Sally the kind of game you'd like for your birthday, but you forgot the name of it. You must limit your message to no more than 25 words.

## ACTIVITY 3.  WORD POWER

**Concepts:**  Words are used to communicate thoughts and feelings; some words make us feel very good; some words make us feel quite bad.

**Learning Goals:**  To promote awareness of the power of language to hurt or help; to promote appreciation for the ways in which oral expression is structured to communicate ideas and feelings

**Thinking Operations:**  Observing, comparing, and interpreting data; suggesting hypotheses; imagining and inventing; evaluating and judging; making decisions

**Materials:**  Sets of cards with the following types of statements (It is important to avoid using names of children in your class):

> I don't want to play with you, William.
> Look at Harold. He looks stupid.
> Get off that swing, Bernice. It's not your turn.
> You can't come to my house.
> Fiona is dumb, dumb, dumb.
> I don't want Bertha for a partner.
> We don't want Marvin in our group.
> He can't play on our team.
> You are a very naughty girl.
> You'll never get to second grade.
> Your picture is gross. I hate it.
> Look at your work. It's a mess.

### Activity Card

Make some observations about the statements on all of the cards. Read them to each other, and talk together about how they make you feel.
- How would you feel if you were William? Harold? Bernice?
- How would you feel if you were some of the other children named in these statements?
- Why do you suppose people say these mean things?
- What ideas do you have to explain it? Talk together and discuss your ideas.
- Talk about a time when someone said something mean to you, that hurt your feelings.

Then put these cards into order, with the meanest one at the top and the least mean one at the bottom.

## Sample Debriefing Questions

*Asking Children to Reflect on Their Observations*
What observations did you make about these statements?
How come these kinds of words can be so hurtful? How do you explain it?
Will any of you tell about a time when someone said something mean to
    hurt your feelings? What happens when this occurs?
In your opinion, which was the meanest statement? Tell why you think
    that one was so mean.

*Challenging Children Beyond Their Observations*
Why do you suppose people say mean things to each other? What explana-
    tions do you have for it?
When do you say mean things? What happens afterward?
What's the difference between a mean statement and a nice one? What
    examples can you give of saying something nice?

## Suggestions for Replay

Sets of new cards with caring, helpful statements may be added; for
example:

> Oh, William, I want to play with you.
> I'm so happy to see you.
> Harold looks so great with his new haircut.
> We want Sarah on our team.
> Your poem is so beautiful. I loved it.
> I can help you with that. Don't worry.
> I'm so happy that you are my friend.
> Neil is a good friend to me.
> I appreciate Maureen. She is swell.
> Cole has great ideas. I'm glad he's in our group.
> Abbey is a great player. I'm glad she's on our team.
> I missed you very much when you were absent.

These statements may be used with the following new activity card:

> Make some observations about these statements. Read
> them out loud to each other, and talk about how they make
> you feel.
> • How would you feel if you were Abbey? Cole? Maureen?
>   Neil? The others?

Write down some of your ideas about how statements like these make you feel.

New activity cards may be introduced showing pairs of statements that the children are asked to compare, for example:

I can help you with that. Don't worry.
Look at your work. It's a mess.

You can't play with us.
I'm so happy to see you.

What a stupid shirt. It looks like your pajamas.
What a nice jacket. It looks great on you!

The following activity cards are examples of other studies of word power that can be introduced in subsequent replay activities:

Talk together and think of some very terrible, nasty things you might say to someone who hurt your feelings. Make a list of those statements.
• If you said any of those things, what do you think might happen next?
• What are your ideas?

Talk together and think of some very helpful and nice things you might say to make someone feel good. Make a list of those statements.
• If you said any of those things, what do you think might happen next?
• What are your ideas?

## Suggestions for Creative Play

Drawing pictures that are evoked by words with power to hurt or help (*stupid, dumb, gross, ugly, messy, beautiful, great, awesome, splendid*)

Engaging in dramatic play around the following suggested themes (Maureen is pushing on line; Sally won't give me my turn on the swing; Simon is having a birthday party, and I hope he invites me; James didn't help to clean up the painting corner; Margo took the best doll from our dress-up center)

Participating in Appreciation Day or No-Evil-Word Day, in which everyone remembers to say only genuinely nice and kind things to each
other, and every such remark is recorded on a chart
Writing stories and/or poems on themes related to words with power to
hurt or help (I feel bad when my teacher yells at me; I felt good when
my teacher said she liked my work)

## ACTIVITY 4.  PRETENDING

**Concepts:**    Feelings and ideas are expressed in words and actions; drama involves performance before an audience, for whose benefit effects are
calculated.

**Learning Goals:**    To promote expression in which words and actions
harmonize; to limber body, mind, and tongue; to forge drama into a
learning instrument for continued use; to develop appreciation for language as fun and meaningful; to promote intuitive understanding of style
as voice, role, and stance, and of rhetoric as having an effect on others; to
exercise and channel emotions (Moffett, 1968)

**Thinking Operations:**    Imagining and inventing, evaluating and judging, designing projects, making decisions, summarizing and interpreting

**Materials:**    Dress-up clothing of all types (see particularly the materials list for dress-up in Appendix A; be sure to include capes, scarves, hats,
and crowns); wooden blocks put together for a raised platform; activity
cards with suggestions for dramas, such as

We all went to live in a castle.
Our spaceship is going to the planet Jupiter.
The pirates want to take our ship.
A new baby came to our house.
Father (Mother) is going to work.
Frank has the chicken pox.
Stories from the class repertoire, such as *Cinderella, The Three Bears,
Little Red Riding Hood, Snow White and the Seven Dwarfs,
Dumbo, The Ugly Duckling, Pinocchio*

### Activity Card

Choose a topic from one of the cards, and use the materials
in this center to make up a play.
• Talk with each other and decide what the different characters will be.

- Decide together who will play each part.
- Then, act out your play.
When your play is over, talk together about what you liked about it.
- If you do this play again, what changes would you make?

## Sample Debriefing Questions

*Asking Children to Reflect on Their Observations*
Tell us about the play you made.
Tell us about who played the parts.
Tell us about the scary parts (funny parts, sad parts).
Tell us about the part you liked best.

*Challenging Children Beyond Their Observations*
If you do this play again, what else will you need?

## Suggestions for Replay

Since children reinvent the dramatic play each time they do it, repetition of even a single theme is encouraged. They also could replay with one of the other story ideas. As soon as children are ready to do so, they should be encouraged to suggest their own themes to play out.

More sophisticated dramatic play may include puppet theater and pantomime. In the latter case, children may mime such actions as closing a window, opening a jar of peanut butter, getting into the car, walking in the rain, pulling a wagon, eating lunch, getting bitten by a mosquito, and finding a five-dollar bill.

## Suggestions for Other Creative Play

Making props and scenery with paint, crayons, paper, and "notions" (bits of lace, feathers, buttons, bows, buckles, belts, jewelry, glitter, fur)
Performing group plays for the whole class

## ACTIVITY 5. SPEAKING UP

**Concepts:** We communicate with each other to express our ideas and feelings; telling each other what we think and how we feel is more "adult" behavior than acting out our thoughts and feelings; oral language is a medium that underlies reading, writing, and thinking.

**Learning Goals:**   To increase children's language power; to foster and promote speech as a medium of expression; to help children feel comfortable in expressing their ideas in a group

**Thinking Operations:**   Making decisions, evaluating and judging, summarizing, suggesting hypotheses, examining assumptions

**Materials:**   Pencil and paper for recording ideas; activity cards, each containing just one topic for group discussion, such as:

Should whales be captured and put in the zoo?
What are some good ways to train a dog?
Are dogs better pets than cats?
What are your favorite things?
My brother (sister) is a pain.
Should little kids have to do chores?
How do you suppose birds build their nests?
What are your favorite foods? Favorite dessert?
How do you figure out what to do if you are locked out of your house
    and your mom won't be home for another hour?
How do you take care of a pet snake?

Teachers should feel free to scrap these and substitute any topics of their own choosing that are relevant to pupil needs. The topic chosen, however, should provide for some emotional involvement on the part of the children, for it to be an effective discussion.

### Activity Card

Get together and talk about [topic].
• What are your ideas?
Write down your important ideas.

### Sample Debriefing Questions

*Asking Children to Reflect on Their Ideas*
Tell us about some of the ideas you had.
Tell us why you think that is true.
Tell us why you believe that is good.
Tell us more about where you got that idea from.

*Challenging Children Beyond Their Ideas*
Could you give us an example of what you mean?
Tell us why you think that would work.
What do you think might happen if you did that?

## Suggestions for Replay

Additions may be made to the list of topics for discussion. New topics can easily be lifted from current classroom concerns, and the children may be invited to come up with their own topics. A tape recorder may be used to record and play back the discussions, leading to group analysis and self-evaluation of the discussion.

The children may be asked to bring in objects to talk about, such as something they made, something they like a lot, or something that moves or works in funny ways.

## Suggestions for Creative Play

Writing stories or poems that are sparked from group discussions
Creating a class book of individual poems or stories
Illustrating stories

## ACTIVITY 6.  READING AND TELLING STORIES

**Concepts:**   Stories are ideas that are written down; people write stories to give information, to entertain and amuse, to make us think, and to give us pleasure.

**Learning Goals:**   To extend children's experiences with story; to begin a process of reading for meaning; to increase appreciation for and pleasure in story; to develop skill in asking thoughtful, intelligent questions

**Thinking Operations:**   Summarizing, interpreting, applying principles to new situations, creating and inventing, evaluating and judging, classifying, suggesting hypotheses

**Materials:**   The children are asked to bring their own library books. Replay requires a tape recorder and books with stories that are recorded on tape.

## Activity Card

Take turns and tell about the story you have brought to the group.
• Why do you think this is a good story?
• Why did you like it?
• Then read one page that tells about your favorite part.
When you have finished telling about your story, invite the others in the group to ask you questions about the story.

## Sample Debriefing Questions

*Asking Children to Reflect on Their Observations*
Tell about some of the stories you shared
Tell about the kinds of stories these were.
Tell about why you liked them.

*Challenging Children Beyond Their Observations*
What kind of character was _____? How do you know that?
Why do you suppose _____ did that? How do you explain it?
What do you see as the "main idea" of this story? What message is the
    author giving you?
What does this story mean to you?

## Suggestions for Replay

Replay occurs naturally in this activity, as the children always bring new
books to share.
The children may listen together to a commercially recorded story,
which is accompanied by the book for them to look at. They can discuss the
story using questions similar to those on the original activity card.
Variations of story sharing may include

    Making up and telling original stories
    Telling stories of things that happened in your life
    Tape recording original stories

## Suggestions for Creative Play

Writing original stories: Since this is one major goal of language learning,
    such activity should be encouraged as much as possible.
Illustrating original stories and binding them as books for the classroom
    library.

### ACTIVITY 7.  WRITING OUT

**Concepts:**  We "write out" to express our creative imagination, to
make visible what we are thinking, feeling, and imagining; writing is a
process of recording oral language.

**Learning Goals:**  To generate interest in and appreciation for the telling and writing of original stories; to stimulate creative imagination and
invention as an outlet for inner thoughts and feelings

**Thinking Operations:** Observing, creating, and inventing; evaluating and judging; making decisions; interpreting; summarizing

**Materials:** Four or five photographs with the potential for evoking deep and powerful affect; tape recorder; pencil and paper. It is best to use photographs that have some redeeming artistic quality. These are the ones that generate the most affect and the most powerful stories. To prepare your collection, see particularly books of photographs like *The Family of Man* (Steichen, 1955), *Family* (Mead, 1965), and *The Human Adventure* (Cousins, 1985). Check also local book shops and particularly book warehouses for other books containing collections of photographs.

### Activity Card

Study the photos in the center. Choose one photo that you like.
- Talk about the photo.
- Then make up a story that will go with the photo.

When you are all agreed on the story, tell it into the tape recorder and/or write it down.

### Sample Debriefing Questions

*Asking Children to Reflect on Their Observations*
What was it about that photo that made you choose it?
What did the photo say to you?
What details did you observe about it?
Tell about the story.

*Challenging Children Beyond Their Observations*
What kind of story did you create for the photo?
What do you see as the important message the story and the photo are telling?
What kinds of words might describe this photo?

### Suggestions for Replay

New and different types of photos may be added to the center, for use with the original activity card. Photos from family collections, with permission from parents, may be added. Children may also be asked to write captions for the photos as well as for cartoons that could be added.

Children may listen to the taped stories of other groups and raise questions about these stories.

**Suggestions for Creative Play**

Collecting original stories into books
Book illustrating
Book binding
Typing and word processing; desktop publishing (where computers and
    software are available)
Taking photographs in and around the school that lead to the generation of
    school stories

## ACTIVITY 8.  WRITING DOWN

**Concepts:**   We "write down" to record events, incidents, outcomes,
activities — something that happened. We also record sights and sounds.
We record directions to help people know what to do. We record so that
information will not be lost, so that we may have it to refer to when we
need it. Recording involves accuracy of observation.

**Learning Goals:**   To provide experiences with the activity of recording
information; to promote appreciation for recording information as a
means of ensuring future reference; to develop skill in recording information accurately; to raise awareness that events to be recorded are filtered
through our perceptual biases

**Thinking Operations:**   Observing and recording, interpreting, critically analyzing records, evaluating and judging, summarizing

**Materials:**   Pencils and paper

**Activity Card**

> Go with your group to the school office. On the way there,
> be careful to observe what route you take and everything
> you see along the way.
> - When you return to the classroom, write down the direc-
>   tions for getting from your room to the office.
> - Talk together first and decide what you need to write.
>   Then write.
> - Make sure you give the directions so that someone else
>   can read them and understand how to go.
> - When you have finished writing, take your directions
>   with you, follow what you wrote, and go to the office
>   again.

- Check your directions for accuracy. Make any corrections that are needed.
- Come back to the class and rewrite your directions as necessary.

## Sample Debriefing Questions

*Asking Children to Reflect on Their Observations*
What observations did you make about how to get to the office from this classroom?
What observations did you make about any "guideposts" along the way?
How were these included in your written directions?

*Challenging Children Beyond Their Observations*
When you followed your own directions on the second trip, what had you left out?
What did you find that was wrong?
How do you explain that?
Would someone new to the school be able to follow your directions? What are your ideas on that? How could you check that out?
What's hard about writing directions?

## Suggestions for Replay

Children may be asked to write down directions for other routes within the school (going from class to the bathroom, to the schoolyard, to the lunchroom, to the library or media center). Children may then practice writing down directions for routes outside of school (going from school to home, to a shopping mall, to the local library, to a recreational center).

Events can also be recorded such as those that occurred in and around school (in the schoolyard, lunchroom, library, classroom); particular events (a visitor to the class, a puppet show, the peculiar behavior of a class pet, a storm); an untoward event (lost lunch, broken movie projector, missing books). Children may be asked to write down events of a personal nature (My grandmother came to visit; We went to the park on Saturday to play frisbee; I lost my tooth, and a new one is growing in; I had a birthday party; My brother punched me in the nose for no reason). 

Each member of a group may be asked to record the same event. Then the group can compare different perspectives on this event by using the following new activity card:

Read each other's description of [event].
- How is [child's] description of that event like [other child's]?
- How is it different?
- What explains those differences?
- How do you know which is more accurate?

Replay of writing down can go on throughout the school year, as it should. All types of events can and should be recorded, as children gain skill in their ability to observe and record, and in their ability to record thoughtfully, creatively, and responsibly.

## Suggestions for Creative Play

Starting a class newspaper: The local paper is a good example of what a newspaper contains, as well as what events are recorded and how. Access to word processors may lead to more elegant products, but typewriters and even neatly hand-printed newspapers are fun, as well as highly productive thinking and learning experiences.

☆  ☆

The eight language arts activities included in this chapter may be put into direct classroom use. They may also serve as prototypes for what you might create to satisfy the instructional needs of your own program. Either way, shaping language arts activities in a play-debrief-replay structure contributes to both pleasure and skill development in the language learning of primary children.

# CHAPTER 11

# Creative Play Opportunities

In Chapter 4, I wrote about Breathing Out — the early morning creative play session that provides for a smoother and more satisfying transition from home to school. In this chapter some of these creative play possibilities are fleshed out. Because they do not have to be restricted only to Breathing-Out time, many creative play opportunities have already been included in the activities in Chapters 7 through 10. In fact, the dividing line between "creative play" and "play" may exist only in our own heads. What is important is that we give young children many opportunities that call on their creative and inventive talents, knowing that free, spontaneous, and unfettered play is at least as important, if not more so, than play that involves cognitive processing with a curriculum focus.

## DRAMATIC PLAY

Opportunities to dramatize — either purely inventive scenarios or those stories read and loved in class — should be a part of the daily life in a primary classroom. Dramatic play is greatly enhanced by props, dress-up clothes, hats, shoes, capes, gloves, crowns, swords, magic wands, kerchiefs and scarves, puppets, and uniforms (police, fire, medical), plus the spangles and bangles that lend novelty and glitter to the role-playing (see the materials list in Appendix A).

In spontaneous dramatic play, no focus is given. The children invent as they go along. Other, more structured dramas may be encouraged as well, but not one at the expense of another. For example, the playing out of a beloved story may begin with careful attention to the details of the story, but evolve into an entirely new script. Musical instruments may be added to introduce the idea of music and drama in partnership. Cassette tapes of good classical background music may also be added. A raised platform or even some wooden boxes pushed together to serve as a stage, a curtain, and a puppet theater with hand puppets all add incentive as well as inventiveness to the play.

## ARTS AND CRAFTS

Arts and crafts activities also represent an important dimension of what is critical in the creative life of a primary child. Opportunities abound, and many wonderful resources exist that add to the repertoire of what is included in the following list. These ideas may be conceptualized as "play centers" and integrated into curriculum activities to the degree that seems appropriate. At best, the following list of activities only scratches the surface of what can be done in early childhood programs with arts and crafts materials (see also Appendix A):

> Painting with water colors, pastels, fingerpaint, poster paint
> Drawing and coloring with crayons, felt-tip pens, soft pencils, charcoal, colored chalk
> Cutting and pasting in the making of colored-paper collages, paper sculptures, mobiles
> Printing with linoleum blocks; potatoes; hands, fingers, and feet; commercially available stamps
> Mask making
> Weaving with paper strips, yarn
> Sculpting with clay, soap, scraps of wood, paper
> Building with wood and tools, blocks, Lego
> Puppet making with paper and cloth, paper bags
> Gluing mosaics of seeds, stones, pasta
> Sewing and knitting

Especially good as a reference is the series *Art in Action,* by Guy Hubbard (1987), which contains dozens and dozens of inventive art projects for young children, and which makes a close connection between creative art and thinking.

## MUSICAL PLAY

One reason teachers stay away from including music in their classroom activities is their own perceived lack of musical background. Another is that, with music, there is sound, not an altogether welcome condition in some schools. If you have gotten this far in reading this book, you will have already demolished these arguments for yourself. Intrepid teachers who choose play-debrief-replay to encourage their pupils' thinking and creativity will not easily back off from new activities, in spite of more limited personal experience. They are more likely to go about finding out *how* to make them happen. If sound or noise is a problem for you, you are likely to reject not only musical activities but the entire concept of children learning through play.

It is, of course, wonderful if you can draw on some music in your background, and certainly what you would create for the children and how you would do it would be that much richer. Second best, however, need not be second rate. Even a musical virgin can inspire children to create, imagine, invent, and experience pleasure from music, in far-reaching ways. Having some good ideas is a start.

Musical centers, such as those described in the following, may be created that involve experiences with listening, singing, movement, and dancing. They may involve making and playing handmade instruments or playing commercially available ones. They may involve experimentation with sound and pitch, rhythm and beat, and melody line.

1. *Listening and singing along.* Materials such as tapes, cassette recorders, and listening earphones are included in this center. Tapes could include children's songs and sung stories, as well as selections from the classics. A good record shop will have an extensive collection of music that is appropriate for children. If you are a novice in the classical music arena, an informed source at the local record shop will point you in the right directions.

2. *Listening, singing, movement, and dancing.* Tapes and a cassette player are the primary tools in this center. Add long scarves, tap shoes, soft slippers, or socks for dancing. Tapes are chosen for rhythm and beat and include slow and fast dances, jiggedy and bouncy dances, and languorous dances.

3. *Playing along.* Simple rhythm instruments are added to the basics of tapes and cassette player, and children "thump" along with tambourines, sticks, drums, triangles, and cymbals. Cues to making rhythm may be included, and these don't have to be connected to the taped music. For example, children may be asked to make some rhythm that sounds like walking, running, hopping, skipping, or marching. They may be asked to make some beats that are like this DUM-da-da, DUM-da-da; or dum-DUM, dum-DUM; or dum-tiddy-dum-dum; or DUM-DUM-DUM-DUM.

4. *Creating original music.* Simple, basic instruments are included here, but without the tape recorder. An important addition is a keyboard instrument that allows for experimentation with melody. Paper, staff paper, and pencil may be included for writing down originally composed songs. Include, too, some of the rhythm and beat cues just mentioned.

5. *Making instruments that are pitched.* With 8 to 12 glasses or glass jars, a pitcher of water, and a metal spoon, children can experiment with sound and pitch, noting how pitch is elevated and lowered. Changing the jars (e.g., different thicknesses of glass) is likely to generate variations in sounds.

6. *Making instruments that are "stringed."* Rubber bands, string, scissors, fine wire, a few cans, several sturdy cardboard containers, wooden strips (about $1/4'' \times 1 1/4''$), and a stapler are primary ingredients for making stringed instruments. Experiments with homemade stringed instruments will yield insights into how pitch is changed as well as into other musical concepts such as vibration, plucking, and bowing.

7. *Playing around with instruments.* While teachers are not likely to place rare and treasured musical instruments into the hands of primary children for "free play," there are instruments that could and should be made available, with a few rules and guidelines set down in advance that provide for their care and well-being. In this center, children may "fiddle around" with guitars, ukeleles, violins with bows, bongo drums, flutes, recorders, and any other viable wind, percussion, or stringed musical instrument.

☆   ☆

Once again, opportunities for creative, inventive play abound. While what is offered in this chapter barely scratches the surface of what is possible, the activities at least point in the direction of how creative opportunities can enrich a serious play program, extending learning horizons for primary children in unlimited ways.

# CHAPTER 12

# Using Serious Play to Examine Moral/ Ethical Dilemmas

The teacher sits on the little chair in the circle, book in hand as the children gather on the rug around her, elbowing their way into more preferred positions. Lisa snuggles against Megan and puts her head affectionately on Megan's shoulder and Megan puts her arm around Lisa's waist. When the children have settled in, Ruby Freeman holds up the book so that all may see the title. Since most of these first graders have just begun their climb to literacy, Ruby believes that any experience of seeing words in print adds a stepping stone to that climb. The name of this story is "She Can't Be in Our Club," Ruby tells them. "I've chosen it because I believe it raises some important questions for this class to discuss. So are you all ready?" The children murmur assent and Ruby begins to read.

### SHE CAN'T BE IN OUR CLUB

"No, no, a thousand times no," squawked Petrus at the top of his chicken-voice. He wanted to make sure that everybody heard him. He wanted his friends to know that he was serious! He was not going to change his mind. "But why Petrus? Why can't Li Li be in our Tree House Club? asked Alice, the monkey.

"Why? I'll tell you why," Petrus sputtered and squawked. When chickens get excited, they have a hard time getting their words out. "She just can't! I don't want her. She'll spoil our club. This club is just for us—you, me, and Tooker," said Petrus, pointing his bony finger at Alice the monkey, and Tooker, the remarkable dog. "We don't want anybody new, especially frogs. Besides, all frogs do is croak. They can't even sing a tune." Petrus fluffed his tail feathers, puffed out his chest, and sat down with a final hrrrummmppph.

Alice was very distressed. She turned to look at Tooker, who was listening to his friends argue. Tooker could understand his friends' feelings. He could understand why Petrus, the chicken, did not want Li Li, the frog, in their club. He knew why Alice, the monkey, was upset. He also knew how Li Li would feel if the friends decided she could not be in their club. That's what made him so remarkable.

Tooker closed his eyes, and scratched his head. This was a big problem for the members of the Tree House Club. But this story is getting ahead of itself. We need to start from the beginning.

Tooker, the remarkable dog, Petrus, the chicken, and Alice, the monkey, had been friends for a long time. They all wore the same T-shirts with the Tree House Club logo. They all had fun singing in three-part harmony, on Saturday afternoons. They all liked to play hackey-sack. Every year, the three friends made lanterns and walked, single file, in the lantern festival at Trout Lake Park.

Tooker loved his friends Alice and Petrus, even though sometimes they could get into a lot of mischief.

For example, there was the day that the friends decided to make blueberry pancakes for lunch, and Petrus insisted that he mix the big bowl of batter all by himself. Tooker and Alice watched while Petrus splashed pancake batter all over the floor and the walls.

When Petrus saw what he had done, he sat down and tucked his head into his breast feathers. He didn't want to look at the mess he had made. Then he said sadly, "I can't believe I did that!"

The floor and walls were dripping with blueberry pancake batter. How were they ever going to get it cleaned up? Being friends with Petrus was not always fun.

Then there was the time that Alice chased a truckload of bananas down to the next town and it took her three days to find her way home.

When she finally got back, Petrus was furious. "Where have you been?" he yelled at her. "We've been so worried about you! It's just like you to lose your head over a bunch of bananas, Alice."

Tooker was patient with his friends. He had to be, because they depended upon him to help them keep safe and to remind them about what was the right thing to do. With Petrus and Alice, this was a full-time job. The real trouble started when Alice found an abandoned tree house that was almost completely hidden by the thick summer foliage of the old oak tree. When she brought her friends to see it, they were very excited. Alice told Petrus and Tooker, "This can be our special place. We can have our own club. We can call it the Tree House Club. And nobody will be able to find it. It will be just for us."

Petrus was excited too. "We can have secret meetings here," he told his friends. "We can decide on important things, like whether we want a bell or knocker on the front door, or what color we should paint the roof, or what our secret password should be."

Tooker thought that belonging to the Tree House Club would be fun for his friends. Even though normal dogs might have trouble getting up and down the old oak tree (dogs are not very good at climbing, you know), Tooker's magic cape made it possible for him to get up into the tree with no trouble. Besides, he enjoyed being up there in the high branches in that secret, wonderful hiding place.

One spring morning, the three friends were heading out to their secret meeting place when they met a frog on the street.

"Where are you going?" asked the frog. "My name is Li Li. I just moved to this neighborhood, and I haven't got any friends here yet. Do you think I could come along with you?"

"We're not going anywhere," said Petrus rudely. "And besides, even if we were, why should we tell you about it?"

"But even if you aren't going anyplace special," said Li Li, "could I come along anyway?" You could tell from the sound of her voice that Li Li was a little upset to hear how Petrus had spoken to her.

Alice looked at Li Li's sad face, and then she looked at Petrus. She wondered what she should say. Should she take Petrus' side? She was uncertain. So she looked at Li Li and said, "Maybe you could come another time, Li Li. Maybe tomorrow or next week." She could see that Li Li felt bad now. But she could also see that her answer didn't make Petrus any happier.

Tooker watched his friends walk down the path, leaving Li Li behind, all alone. His ears turned down as he said to himself, "I guess we're going to have to talk about this when we get to the Tree House Club meeting today."

Once they were safely perched in their secret hideaway, the argument began, with Petrus shouting, "I don't want any frogs in our club."

"But Petrus," answered Alice, "she's really nice. She could be fun to have as a friend."

"No frogs!" squawked Petrus at the top of his voice, his eyes bulging out of his head. "Besides, three of us is enough. Do you want this tree house to be so crowded that it will come crashing to the ground? Then, goodbye tree house and goodbye club."

Alice looked at Petrus and then she looked over at Tooker. She was very troubled. Maybe Petrus was right. But what about Li Li?

Then she looked at Tooker again. "What do you think, Tooker? What's the right thing to do?" (Excerpt from Wassermann & Wigmore, 1999)

The story about Tooker and his friends is one example of how children may be engaged in examining issues in an interpersonal dilemma with moral/ethical overtones. Questions such as: Who is right? Should Petrus' position about who is eligible to be in the Tree House Club be respected? What about Li Li? Should her feelings be considered? Is it all right to exclude someone from your club? Should everyone who wants to join your club be permitted to do so? Who will decide? Who should have the right to make the final decision? On what basis will the decision be made? What are some consequences of the choices being considered? What are the consequences of concern in decision making?—all are grist for the mill of classroom discussions around "critical moral/ethical issues."

Encouraging children to participate in thoughtful, informed discussion about "what's the right thing to do?" gives them opportunity to develop intelligent habits of thinking, use data in making decisions, and examine potential consequences of the actions they propose. It helps them to develop greater sensitivity to others' feelings, and others' points of view, and provides them with building blocks for developing moral and ethical behavior. For teachers who believe that character development and social responsibility are central to early childhood programs, the ideas in this chapter may prove helpful, for they demonstrate how the examination of moral/ethical issues may occur within a play-debrief-replay context.

## CHARACTER DEVELOPMENT AND SOCIAL RESPONSIBILITY

Life is about making choices. From the moment of waking, to the time we finish the day, we engage in actions that require choices to be made. Should I have oatmeal, or corn flakes? Should I wear my jeans or something more elegant? Should I hop on the bus, or take the car? Should I defrost the chicken or pick up some fish and chips on the way home from school? Fortunately, many of the decisions that stampede our consciousness each day of our lives are inconsequential, and we make them easily, without giving them the mind space that more weighty problems demand.

Decisions with moral and ethical implications are not so easily dismissed and it will come as no surprise that choosing what's "right" is both difficult and stressful. The *New York Times* has recently introduced a weekly column in their Sunday *Magazine*, "The Ethicist," which solicits moral dilemmas from readers and dispenses advice to go along with Sunday morning cafe latte. (Should we take this as a sign of our own lack of clarity about morality when we put our faith in an uncredentialed newspaper columnist to tell us about "the right thing to do"?)

It should be noted that how we make choices—that is, what we decide and how we choose to act—is an important indicator of who we are, and of what values we hold dear. The kinds of choices we make, and the implications of those choices define our "character" and our sense of "social responsibility." Some might call our choices, the way we choose to act, indicators of our "morality."

How do children learn to make choices? And how do they learn to make "good" choices? These are not simply rhetorical questions, for it is clear that making choices is a lifetime affair and that choices are "for better and for worse." Yet, despite the importance of learning how to choose wisely, classroom activities that encourage choosing and allow children to reflect intelligently on their choices are not found in abundance at any level of schooling (Gift, 1989).

As politicians at federal, state, and district levels press for more emphasis on academic achievement, formal testing, and standardization in early childhood programs, the need to nurture character development and social responsibility is in danger of losing ground. But should teachers neglect this vital component of children's growth and development, much would be lost. For at no time in the history of the world has the need for attention to the development of moral and ethical behavior been greater.

The promises of the new millennium loom large, but memories of children killing children in schools still resonate, the name Columbine written into the lexicon of twentieth century tragedies. In another era, children with automatic weapons would have been an aberration. In recent times, such events have occurred with horrifying frequency in schools throughout North America.

We live, as Dickens remarked, in "the best of times and the worst of times." Virtually every conceivable technological advantage now lies within our reach. We already take for granted heretofore unheard of medical and scientific procedures that make life easier, healthier, faster. Yet, as technology and science advances knowledge and skill at breakneck speed, ethics that guide decisions about "what's right" lag far behind. Scientists may be taking giant steps toward human cloning, but there are as yet no agreed-upon ethical principles that support, or fail to support, such procedures. For questions like, "Should we do this?" and "Why is this (not) good?" the jury is still in heated debate.

Events of the past years have thrust us deeply into a world of moral ambiguity, where questions of "right" and "wrong" are far from clear. A sitting president has been impeached, details of his sexual improprieties filling the media. The news is full of reports of the duplicity of government officials and leaders of big business, and it is hard to know who to trust and who to believe. As moral exemplars, our country's leaders have fallen short of our ideals—all of which has contributed to an overwhelming sense of dis-ease. Our world has grown more complex, and more morally ambiguous. Questions about "what is right" are less and less easy to answer.

Closer to children's lives than all of the above is the fact that thousands of children live below poverty levels, in conditions that are physically as well as emotionally unsafe (Kotlowitz, 1991). Drive-by shootings, crack cocaine, drug dealing, youthful offenders, AIDS, crime and violence are an integral part of children's culture in ghetto areas of some major cities (Simon & Burns, 1997). Add to that already insidious mixture issues of racism, sexism, child abuse, and dysfunctional families at all socio-economic levels, and the world of children begins to take on new meaning. Underscored by what Patricia Ramsey (1998) calls, "the world of contradictions in which children live," children, while taught that "all people are created equal" and that "each person has the liberty to pursue their happiness," and that "we as a nation are united to provide for the common good," observe, in their lives, the very opposite of what they are being taught: a world in which "exploitation of particular groups of people and of natural resources is accepted as the inevitable effect of unabashed competition" (p. 2). Ramsey argues that, "our children are growing up in a system that oppresses many and privileges some" and that these disparities are getting wider and deeper. Children "are learning about power and privilege in every interaction, in families, schools, and communities," and these issues permeate all our activities with young children, whether we like it or not (p. 5).

Distinguished child psychiatrist and writer Robert Coles tells us,

> Bringing up children is a long and sometimes trying haul for any of us. What really matters, of course, is decency, sound judgment, goodness of heart—a capacity for restraint with respect to some of one's impulses and an ability to help a daughter or son to know the need for, the satisfactions that go with, a constraint applied directly and for an understandable reason. (1999, p. 27)

Teaching children about exercising restraint over their impulses, making wise decisions, and helping them to navigate and address the challenges in their world will take not only the efforts of parents, but also the stability and professional orientation of the educational environment. For it is in the combined efforts of both groups that we have a fighting chance of bringing such goals to fruition.

Many teachers, despite other pressures, have already acknowledged the need to incorporate "character development and social responsibility" into their early childhood programs. Happily, educational goal statements handed down by local school boards and state departments of education support that choice. Charting a course marking how this might effectively be done, while respecting the principles of empowerment for all children, is the mission of this chapter.

## Some Caveats

When issues with moral/ethical overtones occur in classrooms, it is very tempting for teachers to take the high moral ground and advocate to children about "the right thing to do." Such preaching comes easy to the lips; but is less than effective. If preaching alone was enough to build moral character, no churchgoer would sin and no child would stray from the admonitions of concerned parents. What preaching can and does do is to identify what adults consider acceptable—which is valuable in it's own right. However, it is an inadequate strategy for building morality in others. The strategy is further undermined when adults are seen to behave in ways that are inconsistent with what has been preached. Learning about the "right thing to do" takes more than advice, admonition, and harangue.

Before launching into the classroom strategies that lead to building good judgment, informed decision making, and moral/ethical behavior, it is important for me to lay out my own caveats—to make my position about the goals of these suggestions clear. In no way am I advocating for children to learn only the rhetoric of moral behavior. It is easy to give voice to the words; but it is in one's actions that one's morality is finally determined. ("What you do speaks so loudly, I can't hear what you say.")

In no way am I advocating that moral behavior means "behaving nicely" in particular social situations—for this socially acceptable behavior is on par with rhetoric—children following a course of action without fully embracing the reasons behind their actions. Furthermore, such prosocial behavior may be motivated more by the rewards that are earned from such behavior—prizes, gold stars, praise—rather than coming from a child's own thoughtful reflection about why such behavior has been chosen.

Neither am I advocating that unquestioning obedience to the teacher's (or other adult's) authority is consonant with moral behavior—for such blind obedience has inherent problems of its own (Milgrim, 1983). DeVries and Zan's (1994) discussion of what they *don't* mean by "moral children" is instructive (pp. 29–31); I concur with them that moral behavior does not mean children who merely exhibit a set of moral traits, or behaviors; or those who are merely obedient, polite, or religious (p. 29). What I am advocating is children who are critical thinkers—who have learned *not* to accept the status quo, but to ask good, hard questions; children who are confident and persistent problem solvers ("can-do" children); children who have a growing sense of who they are and what they believe. To this I would add children who have learned to "think through" critical issues, who have the ability to examine different points of view, who understand potential consequences of their proposed actions, who understand the reasons behind their choices. Ramsey (1998) adds to my list the need to develop a strong sense of identity—of themselves as individuals, as members of their particular groups, and as living beings; a sense of solidarity with people and the natural world; an attainment of academic skills that give them access to the knowledge of our society and the power to make a difference (pp. 6–7). I would not argue with any of these additions.

The sum total of what is being proposed here comes under the rubric of "teaching for thinking"—in which teachers create opportunities for young children to develop those intelligent habits of thinking that inform their choices, and guide their actions and provide them with parameters about "right" and "wrong." For teachers who would embark on a program that develops such critical-mindedness in young children, I need to state outright that I am not promising a rose garden. There are "perils" connected with such development that should be made explicit.

Thinking involves critical examination of assumptions. It involves differentiating data from opinion and using data to inform positions of belief. It involves sifting through data to determine what is relevant, analyzing data to determine what "fits" with what. It involves being able to make evaluative judgments based upon data, and to know from what belief positions the evaluations are being made. It involves choosing actions that are consistent with data, and knowing about potential consequences of those actions. As children grow in these "habits of the mind," they are likely to become more critical of each other, of their teachers, books, school activities, political figures, and even their parents. They may uncover prejudices, values, and taboos. In short, children may become more questioning of certain actions and less "believers on faith." Is this what teachers want?

In the classic film, *Inherit the Wind*, the defense attorney pleads to the jury that his client be allowed the "right to think." When we think, we gain important ground in knowledge and in furthering the advances of humankind. But we also pay a price. We may learn to fly, but as we do, the birds lose their wonder.

Teachers may have thinking students, but they will certainly lose much of their ability to bend them to their authoritarian rules (Raths et al., 1986). Teachers have to decide for themselves "what's the right thing to do."

## PROMOTING INFORMED DECISION MAKING
## AND GOOD JUDGMENT

Chapters 7–11 in this book have included dozens and dozens of suggestions for investigative play activities that build children's conceptual understanding in various areas of the curriculum, extend their knowledge in those areas, and promote self-respect, personal power, and critical thinking through an instructional process labeled play-debrief-replay. In this chapter, strategies for playing with ideas are presented, as ways to inform children's decision making; to help them, through critical examination, to make judgments about "what's the right thing to do?" These mind-stretching activities begin with the obvious—children's literature.

Teachers will not be new to using written narrative to present children with multi-faceted dilemmas. There are literally hundreds of children's stories that could be used to fill this role, and the example of "She Can't Be in Our Club!" is just one of them. (A list of suggested stories is presented later in this chapter.) Playing with ideas takes a somewhat different form than the investigative plays presented in earlier chapters.

These plays begin with reading the selected story to the children. Because children are so easily immersed in stories, active engagement occurs naturally. Many children, in fact, "live" the story in their minds as it is read. Stretching minds, promoting the development of informed decision making and good judgment, comes during the debriefing stage of the process. As seen in the investigative plays in the preceding chapters, effective debriefing is strengthened by the preparation of questions that stimulate thinking about the issues.

### Debriefing

All the conditions of debriefing presented in Chapter 13 prevail. The skill of attending, for example—listening very closely to what the child is saying—is the bedrock of the debriefing process. It requires the ability to hear not only the words, but also the nuances of expression, discerning deeper and unstated meanings. It involves picking up the kinds of feelings underlying the statements—hearing and comprehending the "fullness" of what is being said. It also means freeing oneself from the desire to comment on or to judge the statements.

Such skills may come more easily in debriefing investigative play, where children are exploring with bubbles, or number sets, or consonant blend patterns—activities in which the content doesn't create tension between moral positions of right and wrong. There are few personal biases to be uncovered in the investigation of bubbles. But when the investigative questions lie in the moral/ethical arena, where personal preference, bias, values, and beliefs are being heatedly debated, it is more difficult for the discussion leader to assume that neutral stance, and allow children the freedom to state their own views without judgmental comment. How does a teacher learn to remain neutral?

Unfortunately, there is no short course, no single correct way to do this. But an effective approach lies in developing one's own ability to learn to listen to oneself critically during the debriefing process. Using videotape or audiotape playback adds a clinical perspective, and allows for more detailed study of one's debriefing skills in a context once removed from the actual event. Studying closely the way the discussion has been conducted, reflecting nondefensively on the extent to which neutrality has been maintained and in what situations it has been lost, the teacher gains insight about what steps to take in the next debriefing session. Like other developmental growth skills, this incremental process is slow and maybe a little painful, but in it lie the keys to teachers' professional growth as effective discussion leaders.

This is not to say that teachers *never* give an opinion, state a bias, tell what they think is "right." While not effective as a strategy that builds thoughtful reflection, teachers' opinions reveal the teachers' values. Teachers are the moral exemplars of their classes, and should, selectively and appropriately, tell the children what they think, what they believe, what values they hold dear. From such revelations, children do learn about the values of people they respect, and the importance of such learning should not be underestimated. But teachers' revelations about personal values do not occur during the debriefing, lest they torque the children's ideas into giving the teacher just what he or she wants to hear. This has the effect of making the debriefing the "teacher's game" and preventing children from thinking through the reasons for their own ideas.

Paraphrasing, asking questions that require analysis, and asking challenging questions are all part and parcel of debriefing inquiries into problems with moral/ethical dimensions. Questions, of course, are all of the "higher order" kind and allow for many points of view to be offered. They avoid calling for "right answers," since the discussion is centered more on what the children think than it is on "knowing the right answers."

In leading the discussion, teachers want to ensure that all points of view are heard and respected, that children feel safe about offering their opinions, and that they do not subtly "angle" for a particular point of view, or resolution. For a successful debriefing, it is imperative that children be allowed to express their own opinions, without being influenced by the teacher's thoughts on "what's the right thing to do."

There are, however, some important differences between debriefing a discussion involving a moral/ethical dilemma and debriefing an investigative play activity in the content areas. First, the nature of the discussion takes a different form. Instead of examining "how things work," making observations of data, and hypothesizing about theoretical constructs, children examine points of view, beliefs, opinions, concerns, positions, actions.

Second, contentious issues are more productively examined when debriefing questions follow a hierarchy that begins with the examination of data, and moves through analysis of data, to identification of value positions, and finally to determining action. In this intellectually healthy process children learn that proposals for action are informed by thoughtful consideration of data, rather than impulsive bursts of "off the cuff" suggestions.

Initially, young children will likely approach such discussions from quite naive perspectives. Perhaps moral admonitions will be advocated: e.g., "She should be good." Perhaps issues will be dealt with superficially: e.g. "They should all try to get along." Very likely, solutions will be offered before the data have been examined and analyzed. But after some time, and in the presence of questions that call for looking beyond the surface and digging for deeper meanings, children will grow in their critical skills and learn the "habits of intelligent thinking" in the same way they learn to read, through exposure and experience.

Teachers who would use stories to present children with moral/ethical dilemmas for discussion can make more of their chances to develop thoughtful examination with the preparation of debriefing questions. "She Can't Be in Our Club," taken as an example, might give rise to the following types of debriefing questions:

*Questions to Gather Data*
Who are the key characters in the story?
What do you know about Petrus? What do you know about Alice? What do you know about Li Li? What do you know about Tooker, the remarkable dog?

*Questions to Analyze Data*
What do you suppose are some reasons that explain why Petrus doesn't want Li Li in the Tree House Club?
What do you suppose are some reasons that explain why Alice can't make up her mind about what to do?
What do you suppose is "wrong" with frogs that would keep Li Li out of the club?

*Questions That Reveal Values*
If you had a club and someone wanted to join that you didn't like, what would you do?

Who would be invited into your club? Who would not be invited? How
    come?
Who has the right to choose who belongs to their club?

*Questions That Call for Identifying Actions and
Considering Their Consequences:*
What should the members of the Tree House Club do about Li Li?
Which members of the club would be happy with your suggestion? Who
    would not be happy? What makes you think that is true?
What should Tooker, the remarkable dog, say to his friends?

Before undertaking to lead a discussion involving moral/ethical dilemmas,
it's a good idea to read Chapter 13 for a grounding in debriefing skills.

## Replay

Replay activities follow debriefing in playing with ideas, as they do in investigative play, since follow-up activities, in which children have opportunities
to re-examine the situations, and the different points of view expressed in
debriefing, benefit from the perspective of time, coupled with ongoing reflection. Replay can take several forms, and are certainly not limited to the
following:

- Further discussion of issues, in small study groups
- Role playing the story, with characters' feelings highlighted
- Further discussion of issues, in whole-class follow-up
- Gathering data from class members about similar incidents in their
  lives, followed by whole-class discussion
- Discussion of similar incidents from classroom experiences
- Writing stories or drawing pictures presenting particular points of
  view
- Reading other stories with similar themes
- Creating other stories with similar themes

## Suggestions for Children's Literature that
## Examine Moral/Ethical Issues

From the classic fairy tales, like *Cinderella, Hansel & Gretel*, and *Rapunzel*,
to the more modern stories, a wealth of children's stories are available for
examining issues with moral/ethical dimensions. Teachers will have their
own favorites, but for those who are new to this venue, suggestions for some
that are particularly appropriate include the following:

Brown, Margaret Wise. (1986). *The Dead Bird.* New York: HarperCollins.
Carlson, Nancy. (1990). *Annie and the New Kid.* New York: Viking.
Carroll, Jessica, & Smith, Craig. (1995). *Billy the Punk.* Australia: Random House.
Heide, Florence Parry. (1971). *The Shrinking of Treehorn.* New York: Holiday House.
Kellogg, Steven. (1971). *Can I Keep Him?* New York: Dial.
Lasker, Joseph. (1974). *He's My Brother.* New York: Whitman.
Le Roy, Glen. (1981). *Lucky Stiff.* New York: McGraw-Hill.
Levy, Elizabeth. (1979). *Nice Little Girls.* New York: Delacorte.
Mathieson, Feroza. (1988). *Lost at the Fair.* London: Black.
Mendez, Phil. (1989). *The Black Snowman.* New York: Scholastic.
Staples, Sarah. (1990). *Cordelia Dance.* New York: Dial Books.
Teague, Mark. (1989). *The Trouble with the Johnsons.* New York: Scholastic.
Viorst, Judith. (1978). *Alexander, Who Used to Be Rich Last Sunday.* New York: Macmillan.
Wells, Rosemary. (1973). *Noisy Nora.* New York: Dial.
Wells, Rosemary. (1981). *Timothy Goes to School.* New York: Dial.
Wells, Rosemary. (1991). *Fritz and the Mess Fairy.* New York: Dial.
Winthrop, Elizabeth. (1985). *Tough Eddie.* New York: Dutton.
Wilhelm, Hans. (1986). *Let's Be Friends Again.* New York: Crown.

Reference books that contain lists of appropriate stories for children at all ages and in a variety of topical areas are particularly helpful in searching out what is available. Recommended reference books include:

Donavin, D. P. (Ed.). (1997). *Best of the Best for Children.* New York: Random House.
Sutherland, Z. (1997). *Children & Books* (9th ed.). New York: Longman.

In addition to children's books, films, television programs, videos, toys, and CD-ROMs are also useful tools for inquiring into critical questions of value; for example, What's the right thing to do? What's good about this? What's my opinion? Where do I stand on this issue? What's important to me? What are potential consequences of what I believe? What should be done about this? Once teachers have begun to look for appropriate material suitable for moral/ethical examinations, the chances are great that what is found will extend far beyond the time available for such inquiries.

## MORAL/ETHICAL ISSUES IN REAL-LIFE EXPERIENCES

Early childhood classrooms are rich with potential for examining moral/ethical questions and in-school, real-life experiences could easily fill the school-year agenda with vital and meaningful opportunities for children to address issues directly relevant to their lives. A wonderful resource for ideas is Rheta DeVries and Betty Zan's, *Moral Classrooms, Moral Children* (1994). Also recommended is Vivian Gussen Paley's *You Can't Say You Can't Play* (1992), an insightful and sensitive look at how young children make choices about playmates.

However, beyond these references are the critical incidents that occur daily in your own classroom. These are the products of normal interpersonal conflicts, and are golden opportunities for examining moral/ethical dilemmas. Their value lies in the fact that they come from the lived experiences of the children and require no projections into the realm of "what might be."

For the teacher who treads cautiously into this territory of real-life experience, the following suggestions of where conflicts/tensions arise around moral/ethical dilemmas might be helpful:

- Getting along together—including interpersonal conflicts, who may join the group, fights
- Friends—including what's a friend, changing friends, characteristics of good friends
- Accepting others' points of view—including the need to believe that "I" am right, what happens when other people's ideas differ from mine
- Possessions/possessiveness—including determining "what's mine," setting parameters for sharing
- Rejection of a child—including situations in which children express sentiments such as: we don't want to sit near him; we don't want her to play in our game; he's not invited to my party
- Insistence on being right—including determining who is right, how do we know, feeling safe about being wrong
- A friend in trouble—including what is a child's personal responsibility when a friend is in trouble
- The new child who doesn't speak English—including how is a non-English-speaking child treated by others; how is she accepted; what are some barriers to acceptance
- Getting even—including getting revenge on someone who has hurt or done a child/children "wrong"; how does that even the score; what are the motivations for getting even; what does it accomplish
- Calling names—including names that are used; how are they hurtful; what is behind name calling; what is the goal of name-calling
- Tattling—including when is it right to tell; when is it not right; is tattling ever right
- Discrimination—including rejecting a child or children because of race,

ethnicity, religion, appearance, dress, socio-economic class, physical handicaps
- Borrowing and not giving back—including guidelines for borrowing
things from others; when borrowed things are lost; length of time appropriate for borrowing
- Consequences of broken rules—including appropriate consequences; jus-
tifications for "punishment"; appropriate "punishment"
- Breaking rules/breaking the law—including the differences between
rules and laws; establishment of classroom rules; where rules come from;
where laws come from
- What's fair? —including determinations of rules and fairness for games
and other social interactions
- Dangerous play—including making determinations of what is dangerous;
how is danger determined; how to avoid dangerous situations; what dangerous situations tempt us
- Getting into fights/settling arguments—including how fights start; what's
behind fights; what are the goals of fights; in what other ways can arguments be settled
- Punishments—including types of punishments; what are punishments
for; if they work; how they make a person feel
- Stealing—including determinations of stealing when something is missing; why people steal; what are some consequences of stealing
- Cheating—including the differences between stealing and cheating; what
is cheating; why people cheat; what behaviors are included in the act of
cheating
- To tell or not to tell—including when is it appropriate to tell; when is it
inappropriate; what are some potential consequences of telling
- Littering—including what does littering mean; in what areas do children
see littering occur; why do people litter; what's bad about littering; how
might we prevent littering
- Consumerism (I want that!)—including advertising that is particularly attractive to children; creating the desire in children to buy and own certain
toys, products; expenses involved in buying a product; product durability;
trusting that what is being advertised is what you get
- Taking the blame—including owning up to one's responsibilities in something that has gone wrong; shifting the responsibility to others; need to
shift the responsibility; fear of owning up to one's role
- Lies, honesty, "white lies," truth—including what's the difference between lies and white lies; between lies and truth; why people lie; what
are some consequences of lying; the meaning of being trustworthy; taking
responsibility to tell the truth

- Keeping a promise—including being faithful about doing what you said you would do; reasons for broken promises; the feelings of those who are on the down side of broken promises
- Need to win; need to be first—including aggressive acts that ensure a person will be first; unprincipled acts that ensure that a person will win; what's behind the need to win/be first
- Responsibility for the environment—including assuming responsibility for protecting not only the environment in one's home and in one's classroom, but in the larger world; what does this involve; what will this mean in a child's life
- Playing tricks; being tricked—including being deceitful; playing tricks for "fun"; how does the person who is on the down side of "tricks" feel
- Keeping secrets; telling secrets—including what are secrets; when is it not okay to keep a secret; when is it not okay to tell a secret
- Bending to the pressure of the group; taking an individual stand—including taking the responsibility of making up one's own mind; why some children bend to the pressure of the group; what's behind that behavior; what are some consequences
- Handling anger—including expressions of anger; violent expressions of anger; what are some frustrations that cause people to become angry; how people handle anger; what are some better, some worse ways to express anger

☆       ☆

The early childhood classroom is a gold mine of opportunity for children to learn to examine moral/ethical issues, and to grow in their awareness, their understanding that reasons for their actions betray who they are, and who they hope to become. These are the building blocks of character development and social responsibility. It is for primary teachers to mine that gold, to make the most of these opportunities that enable children to take important steps on the pathway to their growing morality.

## Part IV

# AFTER PLAY

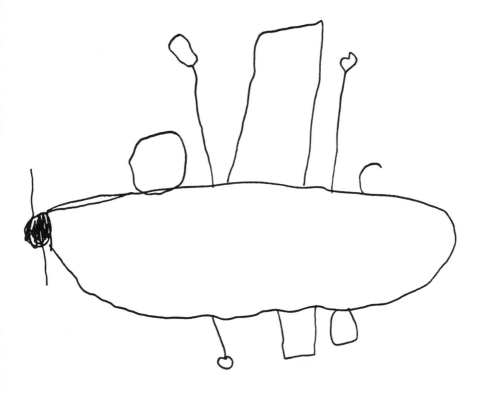

# CHAPTER 13

# Debriefing: Using Interactions That Promote Reflection

He stands with his nose pressed against the glass of the fish tank. The lion fish, with their porcupinelike dorsal fins and warrior faces, swim indifferently past him, ignoring the small cloud of his breath on the window. He is so fascinated by these sea creatures and their spectacular colors that he has forgotten his classmates and his teacher, who are heading for another part of the aquarium. His teacher looks back, sees him there, and calls, "William. Come along now, please." Reluctantly he separates himself from the glass and moves slowly over to where the rest of his first-grade class is waiting.

"I saw the lion fish, Miss Tanner."

"I know, William, I saw you watching them."

"They got all those prickly things on their backs."

Which one of at least a hundred different ways of responding will the teacher choose in replying to William? How will that response affect William's thinking, his sense of personal power, his appreciation for lion fish? And how will the teacher's response help William to understand more about lion fish, about life in the sea, about the miracles of biology?

These questions are at the heart of effective debriefing interactions, for different responses have different effects—upon thinking, upon children's sense of can-do, upon their attitudes about the subject, and upon how children learn to make meaning from their experiences. A teacher's response can be for better or for worse; helpful or hurtful. As a teacher, your key to effective interpersonal functioning is learning to formulate helpful responses, to hear what you are saying as you are saying it, to make your interactions count in building children's self-esteem and developing their thinking capabilities. If designing rich and provocative curriculum experiences for investigative play is the top side of the teacher's job, the use of appropriate interactive skills for debriefing is the underbelly. It takes the two to tango.

## DIFFERENT RESPONSES HAVE DIFFERENT EFFECTS

Classroom teachers interact with their students hundreds of times each day, choosing from an extensive repertoire of possible responses to individuals and groups that attend to specific children's concerns, to particular events, to organizational and management matters, and to students' ideas. These responses are formulated quickly and often in rapid succession within the give and take of great numbers of verbal interchanges. This interactive process, intense and demanding, asks a lot of the teacher: to respond thoughtfully, appropriately, and sensitively, in ways that are helpful (not hurtful), when the environment is charged with activity and other institutional demands. It is no wonder that teachers feel exhausted at the end of each teaching day. The interactive process of teaching alone demands great energy, as well as the highest level of professional functioning.

*Child:*   She took my pencil.
*Teacher:*   How can I help you with that, Todd?

*Child:*   I just ripped my pants on the playground, teacher.
*Teacher:*   I have an extra pair in the closet. See if they fit you, Max.

*Child:*   I don't understand this math.
*Teacher:*   Show me where you are having trouble, Debbie.

*Child:*   I'm finished. What am I supposed to do now?
*Teacher:*   What ideas can you suggest?

In teachers' repertoires there are responses that give information:

*Child:*   What page is the math homework on, Miss Pilpul?
*Teacher:*   You'll find it begins on page 72.

*Child:*   What's the name of the bird we saw yesterday, Mr. Frank?
*Teacher:*   Do you mean the woodpecker, Darlene?

There are responses that direct and demonstrate:

*Child:*   How do you fold this origami pattern?
*Teacher:*   First you fold the top down, like this. Then you fold the sides over, like this. And then, pull the entire piece inside out and — voilà!

There are responses that are confrontational and that "manage" behavior:

*Teacher:*   If you do that one more time, Jeff, I'll have to ask you to take some time out!

There are responses that are evaluative:

*Child:*   Is my work good, teacher?
*Teacher:*   [Possible responses]
- That's good, Phyllis.
- No, Roger. That's not quite right.
- I think it's the best picture you've ever done. William.
- You spelled three words wrong.
- I liked your work very much, Jessica.

Sometimes, teachers are called upon to respond with empathy:

*Child:*   I feel mean. I hate the whole world.
*Teacher:*   [Possible responses]
- You're very upset about your family's moving. Just when you began to make new friends in this class.
- You are very angry because the other boys wouldn't let you play in their game. They were very mean to you.

Other responses require children to think about issues, ideas, and concepts, calling for reflection-on-action or reflection-on-observation. They may also ask children to generate new ideas:

*Teacher:*   [Possible responses]
- Tell me a little more about what you observed.
- When you put that heavy piece of wood into the water, you expected that it would sink. You were surprised that it floated! I wonder how you could explain that?
- When Billy measured it, he found that it was 13 cm wide. When Alice measured it, she found it was 14 cm wide. How could that be, do you suppose?
- You say that lemons are exactly like eggs. I wonder if there are any differences between them?
- Which would be the better way to go? What are your ideas?
- Which one would you choose? Why would you choose that one?

Whichever response teachers choose from their full repertoire, that response has power for the children. Because it comes from a person in authority, a respected teacher, the response has power to hurt or to help. It has power to be additive or subtractive; to empower or to disempower; to enhance or diminish thinking. Teachers' responses can be inviting, appreciative, and respectful, and they can be rejecting, cruel, and punishing. They can foster autonomy, and they can cultivate dependency. Perhaps you think this is overstating the case, assigning too much weight to the statements people make to each other in human interactions. Of course, none of us is likely to die from a single hurtful response ("That's a stupid question, Jill!"). Yet, any of us who has been at the butt end of sustained hurtful statements dished out by thoughtless and insensitive adults (or children) will know, from personal experience, the power of such statements to diminish us. After long exposure to such interactions, we begin to believe less of ourselves: that we *do* ask stupid questions, that we are "bad," that we "will never learn," that we are unworthy, that we are unable to do things for ourselves. These negative self-feelings do not come from the ethers. They occur as a consequence of significant adults' disrespectful, hurtful, and diminishing responses to who we are and what we do. That there are corroborating data to support these ideas is hardly necessary for those of us who have had such punishing interactive experiences. (For further reading, see Aspy & Roebuck, 1977; Carkhuff, 1969; Carkhuff & Berenson, 1976; Combs, Avila, & Purkey, 1971; Gazda, Asbury, Balzer, Childers, & Walters, 1977; Purkey, 1978; Truax & Carkhuff, 1967.)

Knowing as we do what tremendous power lies in the things teachers say, and given that teachers have hundreds of potential responses tucked away in their "response repertoires," which one may be chosen to respond to William, the 6-year-old who tarried with the lion fish while the rest of his class went on to another part of the aquarium? As in most other decisions teachers make, it depends! It depends first upon whether the teacher wishes to address William's *behavior* or his *thinking*. In either case, certain guidelines apply when a response is contemplated. The response should be *respectful*, particularly of William's feelings about self. The response should *empower*, that is, it should promote the child's autonomy, rather than foster dependence. The response should *attend* to what the child has said.

If Miss Tanner, William's teacher, chooses to address William's behavior, she has several options that incorporate guidelines of *attending, empowering*, and *respecting*; for example:

- "I know you were very interested in those lion fish, William. But I was very worried that you might get separated from the group and we would lose you."
- "Those lion fish were fascinating. I can understand that you wanted to

watch them for a long time. I know it's hard for you to come away when you prefer to stay here."

Both responses are respectful of William's self and his interests. They both attend to his feelings. Both tell him that his option to remain with the fish has been foreclosed. Yet they do so with consideration. In that way, they are both additive and empowering. Alternatives that are disrespectful, inattentive, and disempowering include

- "We don't have time for that now, William."
- "They *have*, William — not *got, have.* Can you say 'they have'?"
- "Save your questions until we get back to class."
- "We've all been waiting for you, William. It wasn't very nice of you to keep us waiting."

If Miss Tanner chooses to engage William's thinking about the lion fish, she also has options available in which the criteria of *respect, attending,* and *empowerment* are evident in the response. Each of the following responses engages William's thinking by asking him to *reflect* on his observation; however, each directs the study of lion fish along potentially different pathways.

- "Those prickly things stick right up on the top of the fish." This response *paraphrases* William's statement. It communicates implicitly that his teacher has heard and is attending to his idea. William's idea is thus respected. Paraphrasing allows William to hear his idea "played back" in a different form. He may then reflect further on that observation, or extend his ideas. Either way, his thinking is engaged. When all of these conditions are met, the experience is empowering for William.
- "They seem to be very prickly — sharp to the touch." This response also *paraphrases*, yet adds the detail of "sharp to touch." This response attends to William's idea and is respectful of him and his idea, and is therefore empowering. It gives William a chance to build out his idea, using "sharp to the touch" as a means of extending his observations.
- "Tell me some more about what you saw those prickly things do." This response attends to William's statement and is respectful of his observation. It asks him to think more about what he has seen and to articulate his ideas. All of these conditions are enabling and empowering.

How do teachers learn such facilitative interactive skills? How do teachers learn to choose appropriate responses, while at the same time monitoring what they say and watching for the effect? How do teachers learn to make their interactions count?

## LEARNING THE INTERACTION SKILLS FOR DEBRIEFING

A beginner practicing her golf swing is told, "It's all in the wrist!" A newcomer to debriefing is told, "It's all in attending!" While both are overstatements, both point up important clues to mastery.

All successful interactions begin with learning the skill of attending, a simple but vastly neglected tool in human interactions. Attending means listening very closely to what the other person is saying. It means "clearing your ears and head" of extraneous "noise" (your own intruding thoughts) so that you may hear exactly what is being said. Attending involves more than just listening; it involves the ability to hear not only the words but the nuances of expression, to discern deeper and unstated meanings. It involves picking up on the affect, so that the statement is heard in context. It means hearing and comprehending the "fullness" of what is being said and freeing oneself from the desire to comment or to judge it (Carkhuff, 1983). These are the first steps in learning to attend:

1. Make and hold eye contact with the student speaking.
2. Listen to what is being said. Be naturally interested. Show in your body language that you care about what the student is saying.
3. Discern the tone, the nuances of expression.
4. Look for evidence of any affect (verbal or nonverbal) that the student is revealing.
5. Be aware of indicators of stress shown by the student.
6. Avoid commenting on the student's idea.
7. Avoid giving your own idea in response to what the student is saying.
8. Take in the full meaning of what is being said. *Apprehend* the student's idea.
9. Make it safe for the student to present the idea.

As you engage in all of these actions, you will come to a fuller apprehension of the student's statement. You will be able to take in the larger meanings of what is being said. While you are in the process of doing all of this, begin to think about formulating a response that

1. Does not evaluate the student's idea, in either tone or word
2. Thoughtfully and accurately paraphrases the student's idea

3. Is respectful; shows natural interest; is nonjudgmental; and helps student feel safe, nondefensive, and nonthreatened

As you respond, observe the effect of what you said on the student. Especially watch the eyes, to discern how your response has been "received" — whether it helps the child "work" the idea, or if it has caused stress and a defensive reaction.

It's funny that attending behaviors should require so much concentrated effort. We all perceive ourselves to be very good listeners, when, in fact, many of us are so busy trying to get our own ideas out that we rarely pay heed to what the other person is saying. This is especially true when we work with young children, since very few of us make the time to listen fully and appreciate their ideas, so busy are we with trying to give them the benefit of our own wisdom.

### Responses That Paraphrase

One does not wait to master attending skills before developing one's skills in formulating thoughtful and "on-the-mark" facilitative responses. These are done in concert. However, it is suggested that if you are new to debriefing interactions, you begin by formulating responses that paraphrase students' ideas. There are several reasons why this makes sense. First, the paraphrase response is the most natural to master. It is not a response that has to be struggled with. It is formulated from the framework of the student's idea. Second, it allows you to concentrate on your attending skills at the same time, without having to worry about formulating more complicated responses. Third, it sets the debriefing interactions in motion. You can practice attending, pacing, paraphrasing and reflecting on the impact of your response, all the while engaging in productive debriefing. Fourth, while the paraphrase responses seem less challenging to pupil thinking, they are nevertheless responses that require reflection. Used effectively, they are enormously productive in encouraging and extending pupil thinking.

A paraphrase can be a quite straightforward "saying back" in different words what the child has said:

*Child:*    Sometimes you find sharks in the deep parts of the water.
*Teacher:*    Sharks live in the deeper parts of the ocean.

A paraphrase can interpret what the child has said, by "reading into" the statement:

*Child:*    Sometimes you find sharks in the deep parts of the water.
*Teacher:*   So sharks are not likely to be found in the shallow parts. Is that
       what you mean?

A paraphrase can interpret, as well as "read in" affect:

*Child:*    Sometimes you find sharks in the deep parts of the water.
*Teacher:*   So it might be safer to swim in the shallow parts of the ocean
       and more dangerous to swim in the deep parts.

The closer one stays to the child's statement in formulating a paraphrase response, the more accurately will that response capture the child's idea. The more one reads in and interprets, the greater the risk of misinterpreting the child's idea. Paraphrased responses that read in also have the tendency to shift the discourse into new territory, as seen in the previous examples. From "sharks in the deep ocean," the last paraphrase shifts gears to the idea of swimming, which may radically change the course of the inquiry. Yet, the richer the interpretation of the child's statement, in a well-formulated paraphrased response, the more potential for digging into substantive concepts.

A debriefing session in which teachers attend to students' ideas and use paraphrasing responses in reply can work effectively to illuminate the "big ideas" in the area of inquiry (refer to Chapter 6 for discussion of "big ideas"). Here's an example of how this works:

A first-grade teacher is using the operation of comparing (see Chapter 6 for discussion of the higher-order thinking operations) to help children discern different artistic approaches to mask making. The "big ideas" that the teacher is working toward include how different media (in this case wood and papier maché) are used to create works of art and that masks are used in different cultures to different effects.

*Teacher:*   [Opening statement] You have had a chance to work together in
       your groups, to compare and discuss these two masks. What observa-
       tions did you make about how they are alike and how they are differ-
       ent? What can you tell me about this?
*Tanya:*    They both have big noses.
*Teacher:*   So the noses are something you noticed first. [Paraphrases]
*Kirsten:*   They both have their mouths open.
*Teacher:*   Open mouths. That's another feature that you noticed. [Para-
       phrases]
*Byron:*    They're both Indian masks.

*Teacher:*   There's *something about them* that tells you they have been made by Indians. [Interprets]

*Byron:*   Yeh. I think that Indians use masks.

*Teacher:*   So it's the masks themselves — because Indians use masks. I guess they couldn't be Japanese. Is that what you mean? [Reads into student's statement]

*Byron:*   No. They look like Indian masks to me. [He begins to be a little unsure; looks at masks again and maybe is examining his assumption.]

*Sam:*   I could see that they are made of different material. They both look like they're made of wood, but they're not. This one is wood (knocks on it), but this one is something else.

*Teacher:*   This one is wood. You seem pretty certain. And this one is some other material. You're not sure. [Reads in]

*Sam:*   I don't know. It's too light for wood. (Continues to finger as he observes the papier maché mask)

*Arlyn:*   It could be a light wood. I saw some light wood. It hardly weighs anything.

*Teacher:*   Maybe it's a very lightweight wood. [Paraphrases]

*Sam:*   I don't think so. Look at this. It's like a little piece of paper is pulling off this edge. (He peers at a place where the paper is beginning to pull away.)

*Teacher:*   You think the mask is made of paper. [Interprets]

*Sam:*   But it can't be paper, unless it's very thick paper. Otherwise the paper would tear. It's too hard for just plain paper.

*Teacher:*   If it's paper, it's got to be very thick paper. Otherwise, it couldn't last very long. [Paraphrases]

*Sam:*   Yeh. [He is reflecting on it.]

*Teacher:*   You want to think about it some more? [Reads into Sam's non-verbal behavior]

*Sam:*   Yeh.

The dialogue continues in this fashion until the teacher sees a natural waning of interest.

Using only paraphrasing in her responses, the teacher skillfully opens out the children's observations and comparisons, in an examination of the use of mask-making media. She does this without inserting any of her own ideas, or directing the children, or judging the quality of their ideas. She does this without raising "why" questions (e.g., Why do you think so?) or any other question that challenges children's thinking prematurely, before they have had a chance to examine and compare data. Paraphrasing, used skillfully, can lead to rich and provocative debriefing sessions, in which big ideas are illuminated. It can also lead nowhere of importance; for example:

*Teacher:* Tell me about the similarities and differences in these two masks.

*Martin:* They both have big noses.

*Teacher:* You see big noses in both.

*Carol:* They both have their mouths open.

*Teacher:* Both have open mouths.

*Joe:* They're both Indian.

*Teacher:* You think that they are both Indian artwork.

*Tamara:* It looks like the eyebrows are more further away from the eye on this one and this one is closer to the eye.

*Teacher:* When you look at this one, you can see the eyebrows far away from the eye, and when you look at this one, you see them close to the eye.

*Christa:* The eyes look sort of open.

*Teacher:* You see that the eyes are open. (Lifts the masks up)

*Judy:* Yeh, but if you are looking at a different angle, they're closed.

*Teacher:* And if you look at them at a different angle, they look closed.

In this second transcript, the teacher paraphrases in each response, but the inquiry does not get at "big ideas" or important meanings. Instead the dialogue barely moves beyond surface observations, addressing trivial bits of information about the masks. Sometimes this occurs when teachers have not identified, in advance, the "big ideas" — what is important for the children to examine. The answer to that question guides the teacher's use of paraphrashing, and the art lies in bringing these big ideas under examination without telling, directing, or judging. The skills for doing this grow over time, as we teachers open ourselves to repeated and long-term self-scrutiny of our debriefing interactions, in other words, learning to hear ourselves as we speak.

More sophisticated responses, both from the teacher's perspective of formulating them and from the children's perspective of having to dig more deeply to reply, include those that require the making of analyses and the generation of new ideas. Both of these categories of responses are used much more sparingly than paraphrasing (the *basic* response), and they are interspersed in and among paraphrase responses, as appropriate.

While there is no hard evidence to support this claim (since researchers cannot easily look into a child's brain to determine the amount and extent of mental processing occurring), educational theorists such as Bloom (1964) have pointed to a hierarchy of cognitive skills, identifying some as less taxing (e.g., comparing) and others as more challenging (e.g., applying principles, interpreting data, evaluating). While these claims are arguable, observable experience with children does, in fact, point to the relative ease with which most respond to the *basic* paraphrase responses. Children appear to be more uneasy when asked for analysis, and they are considerably more stressed in the presence of responses that call for generation of ideas. While this is certainly not true of all children in every situation, field experiences in teaching-for-thinking programs with primary children have allowed for such generalizations and have led to these hierarchies (Raths et al., 1986). It appears to help and does not appear counterproductive in debriefing to adhere to them. What is clear, however, is that debriefing sessions that make extensive use of analysis and/or challenging responses often stump children and lead to disjointed or unfocused inquiries.

## Responses That Require Analysis

Responses that require children to make analyses ask them to dig more deeply and beyond their firsthand observations. These responses include asking that examples be given, asking if assumptions are being made, asking where a child got that idea from, asking if the child has thought about alternatives, asking that comparisons be made, and asking the child to give some data to support the idea.

This does not exhaust the list of possible responses that call for analysis. You will likely think of others that are particularly appropriate in responding to a student's idea. There is also no hierarchy within this category with respect to which of these is more difficult than others. Difficulty (and challenge) is likely to vary from situation to situation, from child to child. The happy news is that, as children get more experience with being responded to in these ways, they learn habits of thinking. That is, when at first a child may blanch upon being asked for an example, in later sessions, after extended experience with thinking, examples are likely to come more easily. That, of course, is the great reward of teaching-for-thinking interactions: Children learn habits of thinking. They learn to take responsibility for what they say, to base arguments on data, to examine alternatives before choosing, and to think about ideas, rather than merely collecting bytes of information. These habits of thinking do not appear after one, two, or three play-and-debrief sessions, but the data are clear that they do appear, over time, in the presence of such teaching-for-thinking classroom practices (Wassermann & Ivany, 1988).

The following transcript shows how responses calling for analysis are interspersed with basic paraphrasing responses. This is a Grade 2 class, and the teacher is conducting a debriefing session following group play centered on ideas that were introduced in a science film seen in class. The focus of the debriefing session is on the "big idea" of the importance of water in our lives. Eventually this will lead to other big ideas such as where water comes from and what we need it for.

*Teacher:* Tell me about some of your discussions. Tell me about the ocean.

*Margo:* It's salty.

*Teacher:* The ocean has salt water. [Paraphrases] How did you discover that? [Calls for analysis: Where did that idea come from?]

*Margo:* When I went swimming, I got some in my mouth and it tasted very salty. Ugh.

*Teacher:* So tasting the water would be one way of telling that it was salty. [Paraphrases]

*Margo:* Yeh.

*Teacher:* I see. [Accepts student's idea nonjudgmentally] Thanks, Margo. [Appreciates student's idea] Are there other things that you can tell me about the water in the ocean? [Returns to the initial question; therefore, is not a response]

*Jason:* Well, sometimes the water is very rough. If it's stormy, boats can sink.

*Teacher:* Ocean water can be rough. [Paraphrases] You're also telling us that the ocean can be used for boat travel. [Paraphrases, by reading into what the student has said]

*Jason:* Yeh. For boats, and seaplanes can land on it, too.

*Teacher:* For boats and seaplanes. Different vehicles can travel on it. [Paraphrases] I see. [Accepts student's idea] Any other ideas about ocean water? [Returns to the original question]

*Nicole:* There are parts that are very deep. Very deep. Sometimes you find sharks in the deep part.

*Teacher:* You are saying, Nicole, that sharks may live in the deep part of the ocean. [Paraphrases]

*Nicole:* Yup.

*Teacher:* How would you know that, Nicole? [Asks that an analysis be made: What data support that idea?]

*Nicole:* I saw it on television.

*Teacher:* The television program helped you to know about the sharks that live in the ocean. [Paraphrases]

*Billy:* Other fish live in the ocean, too, you know.

*Teacher:* The ocean's a place where other fish live as well. [Paraphrases]

*Billy:* Yeh. Salmon and whales, too. My father caught a salmon when he went fishing.

*Teacher:*   [Does not work with the idea that Billy's dad caught fish, although she does not reject it; focuses instead on the bigger idea of marine life] You are telling me that many different kinds of fish live in the ocean. [Paraphrases] Children nod.

*Teacher:*   So let's see if I've got your ideas now. The ocean is used for travel. We swim in it. Fish — lots of different fish — live in the ocean. I wonder, what else is it good for? Any ideas? [Asks that analyses be made: Why is this good?]

Compare this transcript with the following one, in which the teacher calls for specific pieces of information, in which the discussion seems to ramble around but does not address any "big idea," and in which none of the students' ideas is "worked."

*Teacher:*   What kind of water is in the ocean?

*Ken:*   Salt.

*Teacher:*   Salt water. [Agrees with the student] Right. [Rewards the student's response] Now, how do we get fresh water? [This new question moves the inquiry immediately away from the study of oceans, to another, tangentially related issue; deeper relationships are not uncovered in the debriefing.]

*Alison:*   We could get it from the rain.

*Teacher:*   But how would you get the rainwater? [Looks for an answer]

*Marty:*   Clouds.

*Teacher:*   But it would just fall to the ground. How would you get some? [She is looking for a particular answer; Marty's response of "clouds" could be productively "worked," but she chooses instead to pursue her own line of inquiry.]

*Farah:*   In a cup.

*Teacher:*   Okay. We could have a bowl. Do you think there is any other way of getting fresh water? [Corrects Farah's idea, by translating *cup* into *bowl*, but still doesn't like it and is still searching for the "right" answer]

*Jason:*   Take some salt water and put it on a stove to boil it.

*Teacher:*   When we boil it, it's going to be plain water? [Subtly tells Jason that's a wrong idea]

*Jason:*   Yeah.

*Teacher:*   Nancy disagrees with you. [Puts the burden of correcting Jason's idea onto Nancy]

*Nancy:*   I tried that once. But it tasted salty. That's all.

*Teacher:*   It wouldn't be fresh water. It would still be salty. [Tells the group that Jason's idea was wrong] Got any other ideas? [Is still looking for the "right" idea]

*Peggy:*   But we don't know if we could have a stove, though. [Examining Jason's idea from another perspective — Is the assumption correct that a stove is available?]

*Teacher:*   Never mind. We're pretending that we did have stoves. [Rejects Peggy's idea to examine that assumption]

*Sam:*   Put it on the stove and then in the fridge.

*Teacher:*   Okay. First hot, then cold. Then it's going to be pure water. Okay. [Finally has the answers she was waiting for, although the validity of the process is highly dubious; rewards Sam by telling him his idea is okay]

*Jason:*   But the glass would break. [Thinking about the variables in such an experiment]

*Teacher:*   But we could use metal. We wouldn't have to use glass. [Subtly tells Jason to forget his idea; gives him the answer]

*Jennie:*   Get a pump and pump the salt water out.

*Teacher:*   Good idea, Jennie. [Rewards Jennie's idea, even though the theory is factually incorrect]

*Jessica:*   Maybe somebody could invent a salt magnet and stick it in the water. (Children laugh)

*Teacher:*   Jessica has an idea. A salt magnet and take the salt out. Now we are getting somewhere. [Rewards the idea, which, although inventive, is factually incorrect] (Produces two containers) I wonder which container has the salt water and which has the fresh. How could we tell? [Asks children to gather data from a very simple and straightforward test]

*Children:*   (In chorus) We could taste it.

*Teacher:*   (Chooses several children to come up and taste the water from both containers and tell which is salt) Okay. How could we prevent that water from evaporating? What could we do? [Focus precipitously shifts from how salt is extracted from salt water to the concept of evaporation.]

*Kevin:*   Put a lid on.

*Teacher:*   Put a lid on. [Repeats Kevin's idea to show agreement, but does not "work" with it] What do you think, Lianne?

*Lianne:*   Put it in the fridge.

*Teacher:*   Does it not evaporate in the fridge? [Looks for the answer]

*Lianne:*   It might, but . . .

*Teacher:*   (Cuts Lianne off) Well, we can do it. (Puts a lid on and labels both containers; also makes a red line to indicate where the water level is. The children sit and watch her.) [The teacher shows that she is in full control of the experiment and the action.]

*April:*   When you put it there, it's going to have stuff on it like on the window. Like on the turkeys in the supermarket. [April is generating a new theory about how frost is formed.]

*Teacher:*   Shall we wait and find out what it's going to have on there? [Dismisses April's idea, by the use of a rhetorical question] Let's take a vote. How many say the salt water is going to evaporate? (Some children raise their hands.) How many say the fresh water will evaporate? (Other children raise their hands.) Well, we'll see, won't we?

## Responses That Challenge

Responses that challenge children's thinking in the most sophisticated ways are those that call for the generation of new ideas. These ask children to extend their thinking far beyond their firsthand observations, into new and "uncharted" territory. They put students at the highest cognitive risk and are used very sparingly during debriefing, interspersed appropriately within the basic paraphrase response patterns. These challenging responses include asking children to

> Generate hypotheses
> Interpret data
> Identify criteria used in making judgments
> Apply principles to new situations
> Make predictions about what is theoretically possible
> Explain how a theory may be tested
> Create new and imaginative schemes

Once again, this list far from exhausts the range of more challenging questions that may be asked; however, it gives an idea of what kinds of questions constitute such a challenge to children's thinking and demonstrates the complexity of what is being asked.

There are important caveats to the use of challenging questions. Not the least of these is that they be used very selectively, perhaps never more than one or two in a short debriefing session. Challenging questions invariably shift the focus of the discourse onto new and different planes. So, when one is asked, the inquiry shifts from what has been under discussion into new territory. Too many challenging questions then give the discourse a jerky and erratic flow, jumping from one idea to another. It is the paraphrase that grounds the inquiry, allowing for a slower, more studied examination. Since challenging questions are cognitively complex and require more sophisticated data processing, if they are used too soon in debriefing, they tend to stump the children, especially those who are new to thinking about complex issues, and may frustrate them more than enable them. While some teachers may wish to believe that the greater challenge, the better, in-school experiences with empowering children as thinkers suggest otherwise.

The first-grade teacher in the following transcript is conducting a debriefing session following children's play with the concepts of volume and capacity (See math Activity 1 in Chapter 9).

*Teacher:* Tell me about some of the other observations you made as you played with the water and these different containers.

*Peter:* The tall one held the biggest water.

*Teacher:* You observed that the tall container held the most water. [Paraphrases; uses her own adult vocabulary to inform Peter, without directly "correcting" his English]

*Children:* (Several nod in response to teacher's statement.)

*Teacher:* So the tall container held more than any other container. [Paraphrases by interpreting the intent of the statement]

*Children:* (Nod in response.)

*Teacher:* Tell me, how did you figure that out? [Asks for analysis: What data support that idea?]

*Chi Chi:* I could see how much there was.

*Teacher:* You could use your own eyes, and you could see how much there was. Your eyes told you that the big, tall container held more water. [Paraphrases and interprets]

*Chi Chi:* Yup. (Open her eyes wide and oogles them.)

*Teacher:* (Laughs) That's one way of figuring it out! [Accepts Chi Chi's strategy for making the determination] I wonder if there are other ways. [Not looking for the one "right" answer, but for an examination of several ways in which these determinations may be made]

*Aidan:* Here's what I could do. I could fill up the tall container. Then I could pour it into this other big one, here. Then I could see if there was any left over, or if it was the same.

*Teacher:* So you would check it out. You'd see if this short, fat container could hold as much water as the big, tall one, by pouring the water in and seeing if it held the same or not. [Paraphrases]

*Aidan:* Yup! That's what I did, too.

*Teacher:* And what did you observe? [Tell me more.]

*Aidan:* The same. It was the same for both.

*Teacher:* They both held the same amount, even though the big, tall one looked like it held more. [Paraphrases and interprets]

*Aidan:*    (Nods in assent)

*Teacher:*    Aidan disagrees with Peter and Chi Chi. Well, what do we do now? How can we know who to believe? [Asks that analyses be made by asking that corroborating data to support these two different ideas be presented]

*Deidre:*    We can do what Aidan says. Pour it in and see. Then we can know it.

*Teacher:*    So do the same as Aidan did? Then we will know? [Paraphrases] But wait a second. Chi Chi says, "Our eyes tell us that the big, tall container holds more." Do your eyes tell you something that's wrong? [Challenges: Asks students to apply principles to new situations] (Students get quiet. Teacher waits.)

*Arlyn:*    (Tentatively) Sometimes we can't believe our eyes.

*Teacher:*    Tell me more about that, Arlyn. [Asks for more]

*Arlyn:*    When we think we see something and it's not really there.

*Teacher:*    Our eyes can play tricks on us? [Paraphrases] (Several children want to get in on this discussion.)

*Ricky:*    You think you see it. You think it's small. But it's not.

*Teacher:*    How does that work, Ricky? [Asks that analyses be made; asks for an example]

*Ricky:*    Like in a car. When you first see it, it looks so small, puny like. Then you come close, and wow! It's this big, giant thing.

*Teacher:*    So if you are far away, something that is really large can look quite small. [Paraphrases]

*Ricky:*    Yup. (The other children nod.)

*Teacher:*    I wonder how this applies to this container? [Challenge: Asks that principles be applied to a new situation]

*Chi Chi:*    It could look bigger with your eyes, but maybe it's not as big as it looks.

In this transcript the teacher works with the children to examine the mathematical principle of conservation — the big idea that the space remains unchanged despite the rearrangement of the parts or the shape. Note particularly how the paraphrase response is used to help the children examine the observable data and how paraphrasing allows students to examine and to reflect upon their statements. Note how softly the calls for analysis and challenges are worded (not, "What other ways are there?" but, "I wonder if there are other ways?"), the points at which they are introduced, and how the examination of the observable data leads naturally to the next steps of analysis and challenge. Note, too, how artfully the teacher uses paraphrasing, analysis, and challenging responses to help students in the examination of the big idea.

## The Art of Responding Naturally

Having learned the skills of attending and paraphrasing, having recognized the nature of questions that call for analysis and the generation of new ideas, and having understood how all these pieces fit together is the equivalent of learning all the vocabulary words and phrases of a foreign language. With the words and phrases in mind, the art of speaking in that foreign tongue in a way that can be understood calls for putting the words and phrases into sentences that communicate your thoughts. This comes with greater fluency, after experience in using the language.

This is also true of learning the skills of debriefing. Fluency comes after many, many sessions of using these questioning strategies and learning to listen to yourself talk to children. Practicing this is very much helped if you tape record your debriefing interactions and listen, during after-school hours, to how the session worked. This allows you to study your interactive style, to be cognizant of your strengths and identify areas of needed growth. Unfortunately, there are no shortcuts to mastering the art of debriefing interactions, as there are no shortcuts to learning French. (How do you get to Carnegie Hall? Practice, practice, practice!) Some self-study tools are included in Appendix B, designed to facilitate this professional growth. The Coding Sheet allows you to see the kinds of responses you are using and the extent to which you use them. The Analysis Sheet helps you to analyze your interactive style critically and to decide on plans for improvement.

In observing and monitoring your professional growth in the use of debriefing interactions, try to remember these very important pieces of advice:

1. Allow yourself adequate "growth time" in developing these skills. It's impossible to learn to speak French in a day or even a week. Have realistic expectations about your skill development.
2. Practice, practice, practice; and continue your examination of how your skills are being used. Debriefing interactions do not grow via spontaneous generation, but through hard work.
3. "Give yourself a break" while you are learning. Don't get down on yourself because you haven't mastered the skills as quickly as you had hoped. Be as nice to yourself during your practice time as you would to a friend who was struggling to learn French. Remember to notice how much growth you have already made, instead of always focusing on how much growth is still needed.
4. Pace yourself by attempting only as much as you feel you can handle. Don't try to do everything at once. Never undertake so much that you

are going to feel overstressed in working on these skills. If you do, you are likely to give up the whole idea before too long.

Paul Winchell's (1954) advice to aspiring ventriloquists is equally applicable here: Don't rush; don't get impatient; don't get discouraged; don't ever give up.

## USING DEBRIEFING SKILLS TO EXAMINE THE BIG IDEAS

In a play-debrief-replay program where much control is given over to the students during play, debriefing allows the teacher to assume control. In these sessions, the teacher is fully "in charge," engaging the children's thinking by using questions and responses that call for their study of those ideas that the teacher considers important. In debriefing, the teacher's questions and responses set the pathways for this examination. The more prepared the teacher is, the more debriefing will yield to the study of important issues.

Before debriefing the children's play, it is essential that you already know what important concepts are to be examined. It is helpful, too, to make a "crib sheet," with two or three questions that focus the debriefing on the big ideas. In that way, you will be armed with some tools, should you need them to refocus your own thinking, especially if the debriefing has gotten sidetracked.

How you respond — whether you paraphrase or ask for analysis, whether you question or make statements, whether you choose to put a specific idea under scrutiny and which idea you choose for that scrutiny — contributes to the effective examination of the big ideas. In the following transcript, it is possible to see how the teacher's choice of response directs the debriefing down a particular pathway. In each passage, two or three options for response by the teacher are presented, and the response actually chosen is marked with an asterisk.

The Grade 3 students are studying a photo of a weather station in the Arctic. The teacher has focused the study on the big idea of understanding more about the conditions of life in the Arctic zone.

*Teacher:*    What observations did you make about the photo?
*Della:*    Cold.
*Teacher:*    [Options for responding]
  • It's cold there. [Paraphrases]
  • What do you mean? [Asks for more information by challenging in a critical way]

- Tell us a little more.* [Asks for more information in a gentle and inviting way]

Whichever option the teacher chooses in response to Della has implications for the direction of the inquiry. Choosing thoughtfully, therefore, allows the teacher to direct the inquiry toward the big ideas.

*Della:* Icebergs.
*Teacher:* [Options for responding]
- There are icebergs in the photo. [Paraphrases]
- What are icebergs? [Asks student to come up with an answer that gives information about icebergs]
- Icebergs tell you how cold it is.* [Paraphrases by reading into student's statement]

Once again, the way the teacher chooses to respond has implications for how the inquiry is to proceed. Paraphrasing allows for additional examination; the information question redirects the inquiry toward a discussion of icebergs and away from the more general discussion of the Arctic zone; paraphrasing by reading in allows Della to examine how icebergs are one indicator of cold weather. The teacher chooses.

*Della:* It's got to be very very freezing cold for there's to be icebergs.
*Teacher:* [Options for responding]
- Where the climate is very cold, you will find icebergs. [Paraphrases]
- Thank you, Della. Anyone else want to comment?* [Shifts away from Della and invites others to participate in discussion]
- What makes you say that it would be cold? [Challenges by asking for supporting data]

If the teacher chooses to paraphrase, she will keep the inquiry focused on Della and on her idea of freezing cold. If the teacher wishes to invite others to respond, she can opt for the second response. If the teacher wants to risk calling for analysis, she may ask Della to give data to support the idea. The choice the teacher makes will, of course, direct the pathway of the inquiry.

*Jim:* I see lots of snow. It's got snow and maybe sometimes you got blizzards, lots of wind in the Arctic.
*Teacher:* [Options for responding]

- Blizzards, snow, and wind. If you lived in the Arctic, you could expect a lot of that kind of weather. [Paraphrases and interprets Jim's idea, by bringing it back to the teacher's big idea]
- It sounds as if there's going to be very cold weather, with lots of snow, ice, blizzards, and wind. Hmmm. I wonder how it would feel to live there — like where this picture is taken?* [Paraphrases Jim's idea and moves subtly into asking for an examination of how these arctic conditions affect life]

*Karen:*   Hard to find food.
*Teacher:*   [Options for responding]
- Say a little more about that.* [Asks for more information]
- It would be a tough job to find food. [Paraphrases]
- Why do you say that? [Challenges by asking for supporting data]

How you choose to respond to each child's idea is influenced by your goal of examining the big ideas. Your responses are also guided by the need to allow children adequate time for reflection of the surface or observable data, before challenging their thinking at higher levels. In every response above, respect for children and for their ideas is clearly manifest. Time for thinking, for reflection on ideas, and a climate of safety for children to express their thoughts without fear of being wrong are all incorporated into the interactions. These skills combine to form the masterful art of debriefing interactions.

Studying your interactive style, learning to make the most of debriefing sessions, so big ideas are examined and reflected upon, is very much helped by the tedious but highly productive task of making verbatim transcripts of your debriefing interactions. This is about as much fun as copying lines, but the benefits are enormous. After taping a debriefing session, select a 10-minute segment that shows your *very best* interactions. Transcribe the entire sequence, using the verbatim transcript form shown in Figure 13.1. You will not have to do this tedious task more than two or three times before it begins to pay off for you. Writing out every word you say is virtually a guarantee that you will examine and study your responses in the most detailed way, noticing how they are formulated and how effectively they lead to children's examinations of the big ideas. Writing out possible alternate responses helps you to apprehend and to formulate more appropriate responses. Analyzing your responses helps you to become more critically aware of the kinds of responses you are actually making.

The following passage provides an example of how to transcribe and analyze a debriefing session. This sequence records debriefing interactions with Grade 2 students. During their investigative play task they had been

**FIGURE 13.1**   Form for Verbatim Transcript of a Debriefing Session

| Student Statements | Teacher Responses | Analysis of Response and Resulting Student Response | Alternate Response |
|---|---|---|---|
|  |  |  |  |

working with sound-making materials and examining ways in which sounds can be made and altered. The two big ideas underlying the activity were, there are a variety of ways sounds can be made and changed; different sounds can be made using the same objects. The following thinking operations were incorporated in the play task: observing, comparing, hypothesizing, classifying, examining assumptions, and gathering data.

| Student Statements and Teacher Responses | Analysis of Response and Alternate Response |
|---|---|
| T: It looks like you were having lots of fun playing with different sounds. You made lots of sounds, and I was wondering if you would tell me about some of the observations you made. | Opening statement, not a response; a little wordy. *Alternate:* Tell me about some of the observations and discoveries you made about sound. |
| S: I found this. (Rubs sandpaper and wood together enthusiastically) | |

T: (1) Ah. So you found out that by rubbing sandpaper and wood together you make an interesting sound. (2) Do you like that sound, Jeffrey?

(1) Calls for reflection by paraphrasing both Jeff's idea and his action. (2) Low-level response calling for a single answer, quite irrelevant to the inquiry at this stage. Jeffrey responds with a single answer that effectively terminates his thinking. *Alternate* (delete the second part and stay with the paraphrase): You found that by rubbing sandpaper and wood together you make a particular kind of sound.

S: No, not really. (Laughs)

T: Tony, you had your hand up.

Group management; invites another child to respond.

S: I discovered that you can take two tinny things and go like this. (Bangs tinfoil pie plates together)

T: By banging the two tinny things together you get a noise sort of like this. (Bangs pie plates together)

Paraphrases student's observation about sound and uses a demonstration of how it was done. Tony appears interested in this response, but he seems reluctant to continue the examination.
*Alternate:* You discovered that by hitting the two pie plates together you get a distinct noise.

S: (Laughs)

T: I wonder how these sounds are different. How is Jeffrey's sound different from the one you made?

Calls for analysis by asking Tony to compare the sounds made by the pie plates and the wood and sandpaper. Too early for this kind of challenge, and it dead-ends Tony's participation.
*Alternate:* The kind of sound that makes you laugh. You like the sound of it.

S: Hmmm.

T: That's a little tough, isn't it?    Reflects Tony's inability to respond and tries to recoup the "loss" of the challenge. Tony seems to feel understood, and he is taken off the spot. *Alternate:* (None; this one is okay.)

S: Yeah.

T: That's okay.    Reassures Tony. *Alternate:* (None; this one is also okay.)

T: Let's see . . .

S: I got an idea. Maybe this sounds louder than that. (Hits pie plates and points to wooden blocks)

T: So the pie plates sound louder than the block and sandpaper rubbed together.    Calls for reflection by paraphrasing the student's idea. Tony has recouped and come up with a response to the challenge. Maybe responding to his feelings helped to reassure him? Could have asked him to demonstrate, though. *Alternate:* Show me how that works.

T: Chuck?

S: I know why that happens. Those are hollow, and these things aren't.

T: The pie plates are hollow, and these (wood blocks and sandpaper) are solid.    Paraphrases Chuck's idea and calls for further reflection on it. Chuck responds with new information. *Alternate:* (None; this one seems to work, too.)

S: Solid sounds are different.

T: Hollow sounds and solid sounds make different sounds.    What I should have said is hollow *objects* and solid *objects*! But the paraphrase is there. It accurately reflects Chuck's idea.

*Alternate:* Hollow objects and solid objects make different sounds.

S: Yeah.

T: I wonder if there is anything else you want to say about the differences you found in these sounds?

Opening up the inquiry to examine differences. I'm on the right track. *Alternate:* (None)[1]

Although transcribing your debriefing session is not an altogether enchanting experience, the written transcript provides such a valuable tool for examining each response you make, and allows for such powerful insight into how each response works in the interactive process, that you will find it definitely worth your time and effort.

## THE INTERACTIVE FLOW

The interactive flow in effective debriefing reveals a different pattern of teacher-student interactions from that of a "correct-answer" lesson. In the latter, the pattern of interactions looks like this:

*Teacher:* Why did the car stop? [Asks a question]

*Karen:* It ran out of gas. [Gives an answer]

*Teacher:* Right! [Evaluates student's answer] And how did that happen, Susie?

*Susie:* He forgot to get gas. [Gives an answer]

*Teacher:* Right! [Evaluates student's answer; asks another question, directed to other students] But why did he forget?

*Mark:* He was absentminded. [Gives an answer]

*Teacher:* Who knows what *absentminded* means? [Asks another question]

*Emory:* You forget things. [Gives an answer]

*Teacher:* Right! [Evaluates student's answer]

In this pattern, the teacher raises a question and elicits an answer from a student. When the answer is forthcoming, the teacher generally evaluates it. Then, either another question is asked of another student, or the same question is asked of another student, if the first answer was incorrect. Or, the teacher may tell the students what she thinks, perhaps giving a "mini-

---

1. Transcript adapted with permission of Bernie Kollischke.

lecture" about the meaning of *absentminded*. The objective of the lesson is to elicit the answers that reflect correct information in the story. The objective of the interactive dialogue is to get as many students to give answers as possible. The pace is rapid, and the students are expected to respond quickly, or lose their turn to respond. Waiting for an answer to be forthcoming is an anathema to this form of lesson. The teacher does not probe into meaning in any depth with any one student but jumps from one student to the next, to the next, and so forth.

In debriefing, where the objective is to help students examine their ideas, the interactive flow follows another pattern.

*Teacher:*   What observations did you make about the car? [Raises an opening question]

*Sharon:*   It ran out of gas on the highway. [Gives her idea]

*Teacher:*   It stopped right on the highway. [Paraphrases, thus calling for student to reflect on this idea]

*Sharon:*   Yeah. [Reexamines her idea]

*Teacher:*   Say some more about how that happened. [Asks student to think more about it]

*Sharon:*   They forgot to put the gas in. [Offers more ideas]

*Teacher:*   Hmmm. I guess they were surprised. [Responds in a way that reads into the student's idea and thus calls for her to examine it further]

*Sharon:*   Yeah. He was so absentminded. [Works with her idea a little more]

*Teacher:*   Anyone want to say some more about that? [Invites others to give ideas]

This teacher opens the dialogue by raising a similar question, but works with the ideas of a single student for several interactions before inviting other students to participate. The interactions with individual students are more prolonged and more intense. There is considerably more "wait time," as teachers allow students the time they need to think about what they are going to say and to get their ideas out. The pace is much slower, so fewer students participate orally in a given amount of time.

The objective in debriefing is to require students to think more about their ideas and about what they are saying. In this situation, the idea is not to elicit "correct answers," but to have students come to a fuller understanding of what is happening and why.

Both the objectives and the interactive pattern of this kind of lesson have implications for the size of the group in a debriefing session, and it is immediately seen that, the fewer children in the group, the more possible it is to work with every child's ideas. The teacher who would organize groups for debriefing will doubtless want to work with smaller groups. That means finding ways of keeping the other children purposefully engaged. This is a matter of class organization and orchestration.

In a "correct-answer" lesson, the pattern and the rapid pace allow for involvement of more children in a given period of time, although the pressure of having to come up with the "right" answer frequently deters many children from participating. Usually it is only the few more certain and more active children who actually do become involved.

Teachers may point to the slower pace and the need to work closely with one child at a time in debriefing as "problems" that militate against this interactive style. Yet, once again, teachers have to make choices based upon what they consider important. What are the goals of teacher-student interactions? If numbers of children participating and giving correct answers rapidly is the goal, then the choice is clear. If thinking and examining ideas is the goal, then the choice is also clear. Wouldn't it be swell to have both thinking *and* rapid-fire responses? But thinking requires time. What's more, good thinking takes lots of time. This may be the single most compelling reason for smaller class size.

## DEBRIEFING THE DEBRIEFING

In an in-service workshop on the use of a play-debrief-replay program, a group of 25 teachers was given the task of playing with balloons and straws and designing investigations to study air pressure. After the play, a demonstration debriefing session was conducted in which 8 teachers worked with the instructor, while the rest of the group observed the process of debriefing. After the debriefing demonstration of the teacher's balloon-and-straw play, the entire group of 25 engaged in a debriefing of the interactive style of teaching seen in debriefing. The teachers, who experienced debriefing from the "inside" of the process, expressed their comfort with what occurred. None of their ideas was judged "right" or "wrong," and this absence of evaluative comment made them feel safe in expressing their ideas. The teachers also felt their ideas were accepted and appreciated. This made them feel respected and good about participating. They felt their thinking had been challenged, and they saw this as exciting. The absence of closure provided impetus for their wanting to continue with the experimentation, to replay, to test new ideas that sprang from debriefing, and to gather more data. All of the benefits attributed in this text to debriefing were noted by the teachers who participated in the workshop, and these observations came only from their own experiences inside of the process.

One teacher, however, who had been an observer to the debriefing dem-onstration, was exceedingly discomfitted. He felt that the workshop leader had neglected her chief obligation to the teachers who were playing stu-dents' roles. As he saw it, she had neglected to manipulate their thinking, to bring them around to the "right answers" about air pressure. She had neglected to finish the session with a minilecture about air pressure. In that way, the workshop leader had been derelict in her duty as a leader, and he, as a teacher, could never subscribe to such a process. It was not the teach-er's job to leave the students thinking! It was too open and too untidy! It was the teacher's job to see that the students got (from him) the important information!

While most teachers have already discovered the sad truth that students do not develop conceptual understanding from having concepts "ex-plained" to them, some teachers will nevertheless insist that, since we have "always done things this way," we must continue to "give" students the concepts by telling them what they are. This may come more from the teacher's need to inform and bring closure (to "tidy up") than from sound educational theory. Debriefing does, of course, not seek "right answers" or end with giving students the "right concepts." Debriefing ends on a note of unfinished business. That kind of ending begs for replay, so the children can find out for themselves. That is empowering. When we bring closure, there is no need for replay. The teacher has the answers and the teacher has the power. For some teachers, debriefing without bringing closure to the issues under examination will clearly be a new and different way of work-ing with children. But is it good? Can classrooms operate where correct answers are not the be-all and end-all of the instructional process? Further-more, are there no times in a play-debrief-replay program when right answers are appropriate?

Teachers will certainly want children to know some facts: that $3+4=7$, that elephant is spelled e-l-e-p-h-a-n-t, that the Earth is round and not flat, that Trenton is the capital city of New Jersey. When facts are stressed, it is important for children to know what is what; which answers are "right" and which are "wrong."

There are other times when teachers will want children to examine issues, ideas, and concepts and where "right" answers are far from clear; for example:

> What should we do about pollution in the environment?
> Who deserves to get my vote?
> Are apples safe to eat?
> Is it better to live in the city or the country?
> Should people be allowed to burn the flag?
> What should we do about the problem of drugs?

On issues that matter most to us, there are rarely any clear-cut, "right" answers. In fact, there are usually many possible answers to each question, depending upon circumstances. Life's most interesting and important questions rarely have single, correct answers, only better and less-good choices. It's for the trivial questions — Does three plus four equal seven? — that we can say with any certainty, yes, that's right. But it's the big questions around which our lives turn.

Learning how to make better choices is one important goal of thinking, and the path to that goal is to promote greater tolerance in children for a variety of responses and a critical attitude in examining those responses, with an eye toward what seems more appropriate. Knowing the right answers rarely helps us to deal with the big questions; in fact, it may do the very opposite. Thinking calls for raising our tolerance for ambiguity, at a different end of the cognitive spectrum from certainty, for certainty in matters where thinking is demanded speaks of dogmatism, rigidity, and anti-intellectualism.

If all teaching efforts aim at children's knowing only the "right" answers, students will never have reason to work their minds to examine what is unknown, to reach those new and inventive breakthroughs that take us to new planes of knowledge. In the final analysis, teachers will have, once again, to choose: What's worth knowing, and what's worth learning, and what is education really for?

# CHAPTER 14

# Evaluation of Serious Players

The determination of judgments of value continues to confound educators. It may not be the most profound question on the Planet Earth to ask if something is good, but it is certainly one of the most perplexing. It lies at the heart of evaluation practices. Its partner is, How does one know? Given that these are the two questions evaluators struggle with in all professions—from those who judge art, music, film, literature, drama, and design, to those who judge livestock at county fairs—teachers are in very good company. Evaluation poses terrible burdens on the judge: to hold up standards of excellence while at the same time being fair, just, and reasonable. Evaluation practice is helped by being clear about the criteria used in making judgments. It is helped by being aware of biases held and by attempts to keep them from excessively infiltrating and corrupting judgments. Evaluation is also helped by examining performance over time, since every performer has good and bad days.

In educational practice, evaluation provides learners with some means for advancing their understanding and skill. Teachers, therefore, acknowledge and accept the professional responsibility of using evaluation as feedback to enable a learner's subsequent growth. The piano teacher who points out (evaluatively) that the trill is better played with the third and fourth fingers, rather than the second and third, enables a student to incorporate this evaluative feedback into successive performances. Teachers, too, assume the burden of insuring that evaluative feedback is offered in humane and psychologically nonhurtful ways, so that students are never crushed or humiliated by the assessment. While a film, theater, or literary critic may feel justified in evaluating a work with scathing sarcasm, teachers are not in the business to kill or maim. They *are* in the business of providing feedback that helps children grow and learn. Evaluation practices that promote subsequent growth and that are facilitative, rather than punitive, are empowering.

## WHAT'S EVALUATION FOR?

Evelyn, a Grade 2 student, is working in a group with four other students. They have, on their table, about a dozen pieces of fabric which they are examining for color, texture, design, weight, and elasticity. When the children have finished their investigations, they set to work recording their observations. These papers are collected by the teacher, who responds evaluatively on each. Evelyn has written,

I saw some is pretty.
I saw some is red and some flowers.
I saw some is tick [sic].

Her teacher reflects on the kind of evaluative response she is going to put on Evelyn's paper. In giving her feedback, the following questions are uppermost in the teacher's mind:

1. What aspects of the child's work do I want to address; that is, on what do I want to focus the feedback?
2. How can I phrase my evaluative response so that the child continues to think productively about the fabric?
3. How can I phrase my response so that it does not diminish the dignity of the child?
4. How can I, through my feedback, show the child that I value her and her efforts?

The teacher writes the following on Evelyn's paper:

Dear Evelyn: You looked at the colors of the fabrics. You saw that some were thick. Maybe some were soft? Do you think so? Maybe some were stretchy? Do you think so? How could you put these fabrics into groups? What kinds of groups could you make? Try it, and tell me about it.

In her response to Evelyn, the teacher does not point out the spelling or grammatical errors. Although this might be an option, this teacher instead chooses to spell the word *thick* correctly in her note to Evelyn. The teacher's response is respectful of the child's work and her efforts. She does not praise falsely, nor does she condemn. She does not mark or grade the paper. She gives the child questions to think about, a task that she hopes will push Evelyn's thinking further along in her examination of the fabric. What's important to this teacher, on this paper, is *not* the correction of Evelyn's spelling or grammar. What the teacher concentrates on is the promotion of

Evelyn's habits of thinking. She believes that Evelyn's language skills will improve more readily through her demonstration of correct language use in her feedback, rather than through correcting Evelyn's errors.

When Evelyn receives this feedback, she returns to examine the fabric. She tests for stretchiness, and she touches some to her face to determine softness. She asks her friend Charlotte to help her, and together they create some groups. They discuss whether they should group according to color, or by whether a fabric is a pattern or a solid color. Evelyn suggests that they could categorize according to "soft" and "hard." They choose the latter and spend considerable time determining which pieces belong to each group. Evelyn comes to tell the teacher how this has been done. The teacher's feedback has given rise to this subsequent learning. In this small scenario, the first purpose of evaluation is seen: to provide feedback for the learner to grow on. What is also seen is that evaluation occurs in the absence of measurement. Evelyn's teacher does not attempt to mark or grade what Evelyn has done, judging it against a single, arbitrary standard (e.g., "You have made 73 points out of 100 on your comparison."). Teachers may evaluate without measuring, and some would argue that it is the art of evaluation that informs learning, while the act of measurement impedes it (Eisner, 1994). When children feel able to take the next steps in learning, they are empowered. When evaluation practices penalize children for making errors, they are diminished.

What I am suggesting here as the "art of evaluation" has very little if anything to do with measurement, with behavioral objectives, with mastery learning, with the standardized testing of children, with marking and grading. While there is considerable political pressure to adopt such measurement techniques to evaluate young children, these methods deserve our severe critical scrutiny as being antithetical to our most cherished educational goals. Goodman, Goodman, and Hood (1989) go so far as to claim that such practices are "synthetic, contrived, confining, controlling and out of touch with modern theory and research" (p. xi). As teachers, if we are serious in our desire to empower children, the evaluation practices we choose must provide feedback for learners to grow on, rather than marks and grades that quantify children's performance, like eggs, into "jumbos, mediums, and cracks."

## LEARNING THE ART OF EVALUATION

In the classic film *Diner* (Levinson, 1982), an affectionate portrait of a group of immature young men wrestling with problems of growing up, the character played by Steve Guttenberg designs a 100-item, short-answer test of football arcana for his bride-to-be to determine if she is an acceptable life partner. She needs a score of 65 to pass. If she fails the test, the wedding is off. In one of the film's memorable scenes, Guttenberg's buddies gather in his home, listening to the test being administered orally by Guttenberg to his anxious fiancee. One friend is obviously doubtful about this means test of acceptability, but others accept this procedure as perfectly normal. When one question stumps the hopeful bride, Guttenberg's father says proudly, "That's *my* question."

The audience response is palpable, the painful edge of the comedy heard in the uneasy laughter. We know there is something wrong with this picture.

Choosing a life-time partner does require critical judgments, but a football quiz or any other paper and pencil test is not usually the preferred means of making assessments. So how do we know? How do we make a choice in such a critical matter as mate selection? Generally, we rely on observations of behavior over time, forming our judgments by comparing how the behavior we see meets our explicit or implicit criteria—those standards upon which prospective mates either triumph or fall short.

The determination of whether a child's performance is "good" in the play-debrief-replay program relies on similar intelligence procedures: the identification of criteria against which judgments are made and the gathering of behavioral data over an extended period of time and in many different contexts. These are, of course, *subjective* judgments, but all evaluation is more-or-less subjective. Subjectivity is not necessarily bad or a poor means of evaluation. When the intelligence procedures are thoughtful, sensitive, and informed, and when personal bias is identified and managed, subjective judgments add enormously to our understanding of how children learn. Subjective judgments are suspect when the procedures used to obtain data are unintelligent, when assumptions are made that go unexamined, when generalizations are accepted as facts, when labels are used instead of explanations, when the intelligence is gathered by an unskilled observer, and when personal bias is disowned and corrupts the findings.

In all of this, the assumption is being made that we teachers are competent professionals, capable of carrying out intelligence-gathering procedures and using these to make thoughtful, informed judgments. As in most other professional teaching tasks, these are not skills we are born with. We do, however, grow in such skills, with reflection on practice, over time. And while we are learning to improve our intelligence-gathering skills and strengthening our confidence in our ability to make informed, intelligent judgments, we must be careful not to succumb to the razzle-dazzle of the test-making hucksters, who, with their promises of "easier and more scientifically accurate" evaluation methods, seduce us into joining the pretense that testing and grading are objective measures (which they are not) and that tests will give us the important data we need to help promote children's learning (which, in most cases, they do not). Measuring children does not empower them. In evaluating children we must, as in all other classroom practices, choose procedures that will deliver the goals of empowerment we claim to value.

## Being Clear About Criteria

In choosing a prospective spouse, it is helpful for a person to be very clear about the criteria for what a spouse should be. When the criteria are clear, intelligence can be gathered that affirms or denies whether the candidate's behavior "measures up" to those criteria. As a teacher in a primary program, it is helpful for you to be very clear about the criteria you have for children's growing and learning. When you are clear about what you hope children will become as a result of your teaching, you are in a position to gather intelligence to affirm the extent to which each child has shown behavior that reflects your standards.

In almost all primary programs, growth criteria are linked to program goals, and a good starting point for determining these is to refer to the goal statements that have been issued by your local school board or state department of education. Not only will these provide help with articulating standards, they also serve as a good way for you to demonstrate that the intent of your teaching program is the fulfillment of district-sanctioned goals. Most goal statements for primary grades are categorized into specific emphasis groups, such as social development, personal and emotional development, physical development, cognitive and intellectual development, and attitudinal development. Categories may have different emphases from district to district, and they may be called by different names. In many districts, criteria are identified within different curriculum areas. Yet, in spite of the many different ways in which primary-level goal statements appear across the continent, it is safe to assume that most school districts want, at the very least, primary teaching that emphasizes the social, emotional, physical, cognitive/academic, and attitudinal development of young children. In British Columbia, Canada, where early childhood programs have been the hallmark of the educational system, Ministry of Education goal statements that include the intellectual as well as human and social development of students serve as guides to classroom practice and evaluation methods. The goals begin with an articulation of a profile of educated citizens:

- thoughtful, able to learn and think critically, and to communicate information from a broad knowledge base, in order to be able to solve problems efficiently and effectively;

- creative, flexible, self-motivated, and possessing a positive self-image, in order to be able to make choices confidently and to take advantage of opportunities as they arise;
- capable of making independent decisions in order to participate fully in society's democratic institutions;
- skilled and able to contribute to society generally, including the world of work;
- productive, able to gain satisfaction through achievement, and to strive for physical well-being;
- cooperative, principled, and respectful of others regardless of differences; and
- aware of the rights and prepared to exercise the responsibilities of an individual within the family, community, Canada and the world. (British Columbia Ministry of Education, 1990, pp. 3–4)

Examining selected lists of goal statements for various school districts reveals that most statements are written in ways that call for the gathering of behavioral data. These include, of course, performance data—the behavior seen in children's performance on cognitive/academic tasks. For example, in the category of "social development," the criteria (can work cooperatively with others, shows respect for the ideas and opinions of others, shows increased self-reliance, shows increased ability to function independently) indicate those standards against which a child's social behavior is examined and assessed. In the category of "cognitive/academic development," the primary mathematics learning goals (knowledge of number relationships and number facts, place value, basic computation skills, understanding of standard units of measure) allow for the evaluation of a child's performance behavior in relationship to these standards. In making their evaluative judgments, teachers use their most valuable professional tools—their eyes, their ears, and their intelligence—which yield the best possible evaluative data. Teachers who observe children's interactive and performance behavior day after day, and in many different contexts, are in the very best position to know what they have seen and to make intelligent judgments. In fact, performance assessment—the process of gathering data by systematic observation for making decisions about an individual—has been described as "an authentic way to acquire accurate information about students' performance and comprehension" (Pierson & Beck, 1993, p. 29; see also Cizek, 1991). The criteria, however, help us to know what we are looking for, what is important.

## Gathering Behavioral Data over Time and in Different Contexts

One of the more important and vastly undervalued resources teachers have is their observational skills. A teacher who works in the reflective practitioner mode is a student of classroom behavior, observing, studying, intuiting, and making intelligent meanings from what is seen. A teacher *knows* when a child is "having a bad day," because the teacher sees behavior that is different from the child's pattern. A teacher *knows* when to intervene, to offer assistance, and when to hold back and let the child figure it out without help. A teacher *knows* when a child's performance on a learning task reveals difficulties with that task. A teacher *knows* that the class is "high" and needs to expend some energy in gross motor activity. A teacher *knows* that a child needs quiet time, to settle down. Teachers know all of these important things because they are sensitively tuned in to their children, their classes. They know these things through the subtle art of observing, studying, intuiting, and interpreting interactive and performance behavior — "reading into" what is seen and making meaning from it. These processes are the means by which most professionals function in their jobs. Evaluative judgments based upon them inform subsequent actions.

Our eyes and ears — indeed, all our senses — are the tools of evaluation. Teachers need to learn to use their senses more wisely and more effectively. They also need to learn to trust their judgments. Professional observations not only provide a wealth of data about children and how they learn and how successfully they are "measuring up" to standards, they also guide teachers in making decisions about what next steps to take with individual children.

Observation skills are sharpened when they are focused on specific learning goals. Instead of trying to look everywhere and at everything at once, two or three children at a time are singled out for study in relationship to certain behavioral standards. The teacher decides in advance what is being looked at, and a checklist is developed that is generated from the learning goals for the class. Observations may focus on performance behavior in certain curriculum areas and/or on interactive behaviors. The teacher identifies the important learning goals and uses these as standards in assessing children's interactive and performance behaviors.

For example, a teacher observes, through the gathering of behavioral data, that Alice frequently "gets stuck" in the formation of groups and that she is dependent upon others for help in classifying. This diagnostic information helps the teacher understand that Alice must work with classifying objects at a lower level of abstraction. That would mean many more "hands-on" experiences in classifying objects before moving on to the more abstract "minds-on" classification of items presented on a piece of paper. When the teacher observes that Philip has great difficulty in making choices from among many alternatives, and that this causes both him and his group great consternation in "getting things moving," the teacher understands that Philip is likely to profit from having his options initially limited to two or three. The teacher also observes how these interventions work to solve the problems they are aimed at.

Observational data, gathered with intelligence and wisdom over the course of many months and in many different contexts, provide information on the extent to which individual children are growing and learning, according to our specified criteria. With these data, the teacher can diagnose where and how children are having difficulty and decide on subsequent teaching strategies. In these ways, evaluation practices become additional tools in the empowerment of young children. The evidence is clear, moreover, that systematic and rigorous performance assessment produces significant and substantial learning gains, in studies that range across age groups from 5-year-olds to university graduates, across several school subjects, and in several countries (Black & Wiliam, 1998).

## Providing Thoughtful Feedback

Every young child wants to know if the teacher likes his work — and that is even true of some adults as well! Valuing children and valuing their work enables and empowers them. It feels good to know that the teacher likes you! As Albert Cullum (1971) puts it, "When you don't like me teacher, I feel the whole world sees me in wrinkled pants" (p. 36). Yet, in valuing a child's work, excessive praise may be as detrimental as excessive condemnation, since the child may become "hooked" on the praise and work for the sake of it alone, instead of for the sake of learning (Elkins, 1981; Kohn, 1999).

Feedback, to be empowering, begins with rejecting altogether the idea of marking and grading children's classroom work. This is not a frivolous suggestion, nor is it intended to lose teachers their jobs. It is urged for many reasons, not the least of which is that marks and grades are, at best, arbitrary. They in no way give information back to the child that enables that child to take the next steps in learning. What, after all, does a B+ tell a child about what he or she needs to do next? Grades diminish pupil thinking, rather than encourage further study. They punish error, rather than allowing children to learn from error. Grades encourage children to be competitive rather than cooperative. They develop the worst attitudes in children — that the purpose of learning is to get good grades, not for the sake of thinking and knowing (Wassermann, 1989a). As if that were not enough, grades explicitly set up status hierarchies in classrooms, in which whole groups of children are doomed never to succeed.

If grading and marking are so bad, so wrong, so patently counterproductive to educational ideals, how is it that the practice has persisted for so many years? This is not easy to answer, but it brings to mind the epoch in medical history when it took over 50 years after germs were found by Semmelweiss to be the cause of disease, for surgeons to embrace the practice of antisepsis. It took over 50 years before leading surgeons of the medical profession would give up their wearing of street clothes, covered with the detritus of earlier operations as a badge of their status, in favor of sterilized garments. After all, Semmelweiss, considered a heretic for preaching antisepsis, was only advocating that surgeons wash their hands before operating—a very minor change indeed, compared to the change being advocated here in marking and grading students' papers.

In the place of marking and grading, feedback is being suggested that (1) focuses on those aspects of the child's performance that the teacher considers important, (2) raises questions that the child ought to think more about, and (3) appreciates the child's work (Perrone, 1991). For example, suppose a child has compared butterflies and bees by writing,

| *Bees* | *Butterflies* |
|--------|---------------|
| sting  | no sting      |
| honey  | no honey      |

The teacher may provide the following feedback:

> Dear Adrian: You note that bees have a sting and that they make honey, while butterflies neither have a sting nor make honey [reflects what the child has done]. If bees use their sting to protect themselves, what do butterflies do, I wonder? If bees make honey, I wonder what butterflies make? Do you have any ideas? [focuses the child's thinking on the more specific ways in which butterflies are different from bees and raises questions that ask the child to think more about these]. Thank you for showing me your work [appreciates the child's work].

What occurs in this type of evaluative response is an ongoing dialogue between teacher and student that is private, personal, and tuned in to the child's performance. Note especially that judgments of value, such as *good, good work,* and *excellent,* are absent from the feedback. Nor are comments such as *wrong, poor work,* or other remarks that highlight error used. If a teacher wishes to place value on a child's paper, it is more in keeping with the principles of empowerment to write, "I loved your ideas," than to write "Good!" This reflects the difference between personal prizing and judging to an arbitrary standard, and it is significant in promoting autonomous learners, as opposed to those who remain dependent on teachers' affirmations of what is good before they can carry on.

Several other examples of teachers' responses on student work are given here to show how the principles of highlighting, provoking thought, respecting, and appreciating are applied in different curriculum areas.

> Dear Arlo: I liked your picture very much [prizes, appreciates]. I liked your use of color in making your flowers [highlights use of color]. I'd like to hang it

up in the classroom [prizes, values]. I wonder if you could make a frame for it [invites the child to consider this aesthetic addition to his work].

Dear Carmen: I saw that you placed the pictures of foods in two groups: food you liked and foods you did not like [highlights the kind of classification set up; respects the child's system]. Suppose you were the owner of a supermarket. How might you group the foods then? What are your ideas? [gives the child something new to think about in classifying foods].

Dear Cheryl: I loved the story you wrote [appreciates and values]. I especially liked the part where the boy found his cat. The way you wrote it made me very happy [highlights]. I hope you will want to put your story in the class book. If you do, you will want to do some editing of your spelling [highlights area of need]. Let me know if you need some help with this.

Dear Pamela: I see that you have fit 9 rods into the red circle and 8 rods into the orange circle. When you added up the rods in both circles, you counted a total of 15 [respects what the child has done; highlights attention to number facts]. I wonder how you could figure out if that is correct [asks child to think about ways of determining accuracy of the computation]. I will be very happy to hear how you figured it out [shows interest and appreciation].

Dear Marsha: You wrote that one good way to train a dog to carry a newspaper is with a bone. I wonder if you could explain to me how this works [asks child to think more deeply about the issue and to articulate ideas more clearly]. I will be so interested in hearing your ideas [appreciates].

Dear David: I saw in your paper that you said you were going on a holiday with your family to Nassau and you were going there by car [respects what the child has written]. Do you have some ideas about how you get the car to go across the water? Can you help me to understand how this works? [highlights a discrepancy in the child's thinking about geography]. I hope you tell me soon! [shows interest].

Negative evaluative comments — "careless spelling," "10 wrong," "you are not trying," "sloppy work" — have no place in a can-do classroom where empowering children is the teacher's main concern. No matter how well intended, these punitive, demeaning, and hurtful responses wound children for all time and teach them not that they *can*, but the very opposite, that they can*not*.

But what about report cards? What if, by district fiat, teachers have no choice but to write grades on report cards? Where there are no options, and report card grades must be submitted, teachers will find, to their great surprise, that the ongoing gathering of intelligence about children's behavior on learning tasks will provide the very richest resource for making wise judgments (also see Chapter 3 on this issue). If report cards are a fact of life in your school, you don't have to love them. You can, however, make the very best and wisest judgments about children's growth, based on your intelligence-gathering procedures. Whenever possible, moreover, children should be included in the determination of report card grades. (More is written about the self-evaluation process later in the chapter.)

### Reporting to Parents

One of the three important purposes of conducting evaluation is to provide feedback to parents about their child's progress and growth. Every concerned parent wants to know, Is my child learning? Many parents also want answers to the more global question, How's my child doing? This encompasses considerably more than academic performance.

For teachers who report to parents in face-to-face conferences, learning outcomes serve as guidelines for evaluating a child's interactive and performance behaviors. Instead of resorting to educational jargon (e.g., "He's working up to his potential."), a teacher can be much more specifically focused; for example:

> As you can see, Mr. and Mrs. Conti, one of the skills we work to develop in Grade 1 is classifying. This is an important thinking skill, and Paulo is given many classifying tasks so that he may learn this skill. I have observed his work, and I can see that he can classify with great sophistication. He knows how to create groups, and he knows which objects belong in those groups. He has many good ideas for classification systems.
>
> We also work on developing the skill of comparing. This, too, is an important thinking skill. I have watched Paulo work in making comparisons, and he is still a bit impulsive in his judgments. I am working with him on this skill, and I am confident that he will make good progress. If you wish, you may help by asking him to make some comparisons at home. This can be done informally, as part of your everyday habits. For example, if he is asked to choose whether he'd like a peanut butter or cheese sandwich for lunch, he can be asked how these are alike and how they are different.

Parents who receive evaluative feedback (either in written or oral form) that speaks clearly about their child's strengths and areas of needed development, and does so respectfully and with full caring about the child in evidence, will be satisfied to have a greater understanding and appreciation of how their child is functioning in the classroom.

### Being Aware of Biases Affecting Professional Judgment

"I'm not prejudiced," says Mr. Camrose, "but . . . " At once you know, as you listen to him in the staff room, that not only are his biases deep and far-reaching, but that he is unable to face the fact that he has them. We teachers, who are among the world's most caring professionals, are not neutral. We hold values and personal beliefs, and these form a perceptual screen through which we view the world. No suggestion is being made that teachers *should* be neutral or value-free. If we were, we'd be a bloodless, uninteresting lot. What is being suggested is that we find ways of recognizing our biases, especially those that get in the way of sound professional judgment, and learn to manage them. By "manage" I mean control them to the extent that they no longer influence how we view particular children. While this is difficult to do, learning to do it well opens up doors to self-awareness that are important for professional growth.

Perhaps such growth for you could begin with learning about your biases in favor of some children and against others. One way to do this is to write a short profile of each child in the class, as spontaneously as you can, without editing out any of your thoughts. In the profile, write about how you perceive this child's behavior as a group member. Two days after you have written the profiles, read them, but with an eye to the kind of thinking that you did in each one; for example:

1. What value judgments were made? Were they negative or positive? Mark all the value judgments you made with the letter *V*, using a plus (+) or minus (−) next to the *V* to indicate a negative or positive slant.

    *V+*

    Mark is a *wonderful* boy.

2. What labels did you use? Were they negative or positive? Mark all labels with an *L*, also adding positive and negative indicators.

    *L−*

    She's *immature*.

3. What generalizations did you make? Find them and mark these with the letter *G*.

    *G*

    She's a *low achiever*.

4. What extreme words did you use? Mark these with an *X*.

    *X*

    He *never* finishes his work.

5. What qualifying words did you use? Mark these with a *Q*.

    *Q*

    It *seems* he doesn't even care.

As you read and "code" these profiles to reveal your patterns of thinking about each student, you will have a clearer awareness of the biases you already hold against and/or in favor of that child. This is the first step in managing your feelings.

The next step is to select out the profiles of those children for whom you hold positive biases. Keep these profiles at your elbow, particularly when you are making written evaluative comments on these children's papers. Ask yourself,

1. Am I being fair here?
2. Am I overlooking aspects of performance that need attention?
3. Am I being overly generous in my feedback?
4. What self-talk do I hear myself making as I read this child's paper?

Also select out the profiles of those children for whom you hold negative biases. Keep these at hand as well when you are making written evaluative comments on their papers. Ask yourself,

1. Am I being fair here?
2. Am I emphasizing negative facets of performance that should be overlooked?
3. In my heart, do I expect this child to do poorly?
4. Am I being overly negative in my feedback?
5. What self-talk do I hear myself making as I read this child's paper?
6. Have I shown appreciation for this child and her work in a way that is truly genuine?

These simple procedures will not guarantee an evaporation of all biases. They will, however, help in promoting your own awareness of their existence and give you some beginning tools in their management.

## CHILDREN EVALUATING THEMSELVES: A KEY TO EMPOWERMENT

One important indicator of can-do adults is their ability to be critically and nondefensively aware of their own performance. They do not turn to others to ask, "Is my work good?" They may like to hear that others think so, but it is not their desperate need to hear it. For most very creative adults — painters, composers, writers, research scientists — this locus of evaluation must be within them, if they are ever to go on with their creative and original endeavors. It does little good for them to depend on external authorities for judgments of value, since even the best critics have notoriously condemned the most brilliant and innovative creative work (see, for example, Slonimsky, 1981). To know, within oneself, that "my work is good" and that "my work needs to be improved in these ways" is the hallmark of adults who hold personal power.

In too many classrooms the locus of evaluation is not allowed to grow within the learner. It is generally the teacher who holds evaluative control, exercising judgments and informing children about whose work is good and whose is less than good; where the weaknesses and where the strengths are. In these classrooms, teachers act as both judge and jury. Children learn very quickly to bow to these judgments, and eventually internalize them. Little by little, their own confidence to make judgments about self and work is eroded away. Without experience at it, the ability to know the extent to which one's work is good is never successfully developed. By Grade 12, students have learned that they do not have the ability, the resources, or even the right to make these self-assessments. In the process of educating them, we have taught them to look to others to evaluate their work. We cannot expect this behavior to change radically on graduation day. Where such personal power has been eroded, students emerge with limited capacity to function as creative, inventive, original thinkers. Creative people know for themselves that what they do is good, and why.

The primary years is not too early to begin work on shifting the locus of evaluation to students. Not only is this important to their present and future health and welfare, this is also part of enabling and empowering them as can-do people. To hold power for deciding for oneself about the quality of one's work, including what its strengths and weaknesses are, is more than just a way to advance one's critical thinking. It is the greatest level of personal power.

The play-debrief-replay classroom, where students are offered a wide variety of options and where they are encouraged to choose for themselves, sets the stage for the development of self-evaluative capabilities. When children choose, they are evaluating what is good for them. In accepting ownership of their choices, they learn that choices have consequences. In this process, self-evaluation is an implicit, ongoing act. It can and should be made explicit, and the procedures discussed in this section identify some ways of doing this.

## Conferences with the Teacher

There will be many opportunities for teachers to talk with individual children in a personal conference that has an evaluative focus. In conferring with the child, the teacher asks, in a respectful and nonjudgmental tone, that the child make an assessment of his or her work. The questions the teacher chooses to ask highlight those aspects of interactive or performance behavior that the teacher believes are important. As the child engages in self-assessment, the teacher never betrays the child by disagreeing or agreeing. (This is not an adversarial relationship, nor is it a game to guess what the teacher thinks about it.) The teacher paraphrases or interprets, requiring the child to reflect on his or her assessment, and then responds respectfully to what the child has said. If the teacher wants to offer data that are discrepant with what the child is saying, this, too, is offered nonjudgmentally, rather than as a means of telling the child, "Aha! Gotcha!" The more children are asked to reflect on their own performance, the more they feel safe about owning their judgments about self, and the more they grow capable of making informed, intelligent judgments about their work; the more, too, is knowledge increased and understanding improved (Black & Wiliam, 1998). Self-evaluation may be carried out with even the very youngest primary children. While they will not be very skilled to start, they will learn to do this better as they get experience with it over time.

Some questions and invitations to respond used in conferences that help children grow in their self-evaluative capabilities include

> Tell me about how you worked in your group today.
> Tell me some of the things you liked about your work.
> Tell me about some of the things that did not work well for you.
> What are some things you could do for yourself?
> What were some things you needed help with?
> When you had some trouble, tell me about how you solved the problem.
> Tell me about some of the new ideas you had.
> What did you think you did the best of all? How did you feel about that?
> Were there things you didn't try? Tell me about them.
> Which work made you feel very proud? Tell me about it.
> Tell me about how you helped with the clean-up.
> Tell me about how you classified those plants.
> Tell me what you did when you saw David crying.

An evaluative conference in which a child was being asked to reflect on her work might proceed in this fashion:

*Teacher:*  Tell me about the way you worked with the plants in your group.
*Marcy:*    We needed to decide who was going to use the magnifying glass first.

*Teacher:*   And how did you do that?

*Marcy:*   I told them that everybody had a turn for 2 minutes. I could check them with my watch.

*Teacher:*   So you were in charge of the play.

*Marcy:*   Yeh. I was the boss.

*Teacher:*   Tell me if you think this worked well for your group.

*Marcy:*   They like for me to be the boss. To tell them what to do.

*Teacher:*   Hm. I was wondering about that. Could you tell me, if they like it, how come they were fighting with you? I don't seem to understand that.

*Marcy:*   They weren't fighting. [Denies] They're just being silly.

*Teacher:*   So it's okay for you to boss them around. They really like it.

*Marcy:*   Well, they may not like it too much.

*Teacher:*   Oh? Maybe they don't like it.

*Marcy:*   They don't like it, but I have to tell them because I'm older.

*Teacher:*   The oldest person gets to tell?

*Marcy:*   Yeh. That's the right way.

*Teacher:*   So I have to watch out for the oldies, I guess, to tell me what to do.

*Marcy:*   (Grins)


This is obviously a recurrent theme with Marcy, and the teacher is giving her a lot of "space" to examine and reflect on her behavior in the group. Needless to say, this will be discussed again in later conferences.

These self-evaluative conferences help children to grow more comfortable with their skill needs, as they and the teacher perceive them. They learn to understand about curriculum goals and standards of performance, as they are called upon to reflect on the relationship between those goals and their performance. They don't have to be defensive about poor performance. They learn to see weaknesses not as errors deserving of reproach, but rather as indicators that more work is needed. They learn to value error as a natural concomitant of taking cognitive risks and making inroads onto new learning pathways. In such practices the very healthiest growth toward personal self-awareness and self-acceptance is fostered.

### Self-Evaluation Reports

Self-evaluation may also be carried out in written form, although such reports do not preclude the use of individual conferences and both usually work well in tandem. Written self-evaluations may begin as soon as children can express their thinking in writing, and the teacher is the best judge of when this may begin.

Self-evaluation report forms should be simple and uncomplicated. They should require children to examine their work in relationship to some articulated standard. They should not be so general as to be unfocused and hard to interpret. Lest they become a terrible and despised chore, they should not be required too frequently. About once a month may be a reasonable expectation. Self-evaluation reports may highlight larger learning goals, such as those in the following general report form:

*Students' Self-Evaluation Report*
  1. Tell about how you see yourself learning to
     a. Make good observations.
     b. Carry out good investigations.
     c. Suggest good hypotheses.
     d. Work well with others in the group.
     e. Come up with good ideas.
     f. Take responsibility.
     g. Make good decisions.
  2. Tell about what you think you can do best.
  3. Tell about where you think you need more help.
  4. Tell about your plans for next month.

Other self-evaluation reports may address specific learning goals within a subject area, as in the following two examples:

*Self-Evaluation Report for Language Arts*
  1. Tell about
     a. How you see yourself as a reader.
     b. How you see yourself as a story writer.
     c. How you see yourself being able to make your ideas understood.
  2. Tell about your printing.
  3. Tell about how you are able to record your observations.
  4. Tell about what you think you can do best.
  5. Tell about where you think you need help.
  6. Tell about your plans for next month in language arts.

*Self-Evaluation Report for Science*
  1. Tell about how you see yourself as an observer in the science world.
  2. Tell about your skill in
     a. Asking good questions.
     b. Gathering data.
     c. Classifying data.

      d. Designing science investigations.
      e. Inventing new ways to do things.
  3. Tell about what you think you can do best in science.
  4. Tell about where you think you need help.
  5. Tell about your plans for next month in science.

In one Grade 2 class, Candice completed her self-evaluation report, commenting on how she saw her performance in specific language arts activities:

> *Reading*: I think I am good at reading but I could improve by [sic] expression more. I can read smoothly.
> *Listening*: Most of the time I am a good listener. When I listen I know what to do.
> *Printing*: The last 2 weeks my printing is much better then [sic] before. I get it done too!
> *Story writing*: I can do good ending stories sometimes if I try.
> *Reports*: When I do reports they are pretty good. I know how to do notes. (MacDonald, 1982, p. 143)

There are many possible forms for self-evaluation reports, and what you choose to include on them should reflect those dimensions of learning that you consider important. For, as sure as the sun sets in the west, the evaluative items you include will teach explicitly and implicitly what's worth knowing, and all curriculum will inevitably tilt in that direction. Consider, too, that there is no one perfect form, and that you are likely to want to try different forms, evaluate how children respond to them, and modify them as appropriate. (For an extensive list of self-evaluation materials, see Adam et al., 1991, especially Chapter 3.)

## Parent-Teacher-Child Conferences

If children are to be given responsibility for evaluating their own performance in school, why not allow them a voice in parent-teacher conferences? Could this work at the primary grade level? Would children demonstrate thoughtful self-awareness in public disclosure of academic and behavioral strengths and weaknesses? What would be some problems in setting up such conferences?

When Cheryl MacDonald (1982) attempted such an innovative practice for the first time, she found that problems of logistics — of scheduling time, for example, were easily solved. She found, too, enthusiastic support for this procedure from parents, who were impressed with their children's abilities to participate in such self-evaluation.

In MacDonald's program, the children personally invite their own parents to come to school at an individually scheduled time, and each child actually brings his or her parents to the classroom. Once there, the child and parents view a videotape of the class in action, observing how the child interacts and works in the classroom setting. The parents also look at many still photographs that show the children of this class engaged in various activities throughout the school year. The child then shows his or her parents around the classroom, pointing out the work he or she has done at school. The child may also teach the parents some of the things he or she has learned. Portfolios, collections of self-selected children's work, may also be shown, to demonstrate the developmental progress of a child in different subject areas since the last performance period (Herbert, 1998). After these introductory activities, the child shares with the parents a report he or she has written describing perceived strengths and/or weaknesses in each subject area and personal goals for the rest of the year. The student's self-report follows an open-ended format for each curriculum area, similar to the examples given earlier. In each area, important learning activities are listed for the child to comment on.

The teacher then shares the report she has written about the child's observed strengths and weaknesses. The teacher has already shown this report to the child, so there are no surprises.

☆　　☆

How well do children respond to these challenges to examine and evaluate their work in school? Some of the following comments (unedited for spelling errors) indicate that not only do even very young children know about themselves, but they can write with astonishing frankness and perception. Allowing for this self-awareness to grow, uncorrupted by the need to impress others for good marks, is a key to empowerment.

> I think I am a good reader, but I just need to practice a little to get faster. (*Enida*)
> My goal on reading is to be a very good reader by the end of spring break. Right now I am an eaven reader. (*Michael*)
> I am a good reader because I read smoothly. I am a bookworm. (*Nicole*)
> I listen good, then I know what to do. (*Christopher*)
> I think I am a good listener because I get lots of things right. (*Jimmy*)
> I am improving buy consontrating. (*Glen*)
> I'm not good for printing but I do my beast. (*Christopher*)
> Most of the children are better printers than I am, but I have improved since September. (*Heather*)
> I print beautifully. But sometimes when I'm mad I don't print very good. (*Lance*)

I have no trouble with my speaking, but sometimes I forget what I am going to say. (*Lance*)

I am good at doing arithmetic. I can borrow and carry now. I know how to tell time and factoring. (*Jamie*)

I am slow on substraction and speed drills and carrying. I am fast on 1,2,3,5 and 10x. I am fast on fractions. (*Alykhan*)

I work by myself and don't look at other people's books. I am nice to friends. I never hurt other people's feelings and whenever anyone wants help I tell them how to figure it out. (*Jimmy*)

I think if I'm a little bit kinder I will have more friends. (*Ethan*) (MacDonald, 1982, p. 143)

In reviewing the journal articles about evaluation that appeared in the last ten years (1989–1999), I found, not surprisingly, that issues about the "what" and "how" of evaluation practices are still argued, reflecting the "same old, same old" conflicts. Politicians, bureaucrats, and even some school boards at regular intervals still push for the use of standardized tests to measure the extent to which a child has met grade-level expectations, as if such practice was the magic bullet that would quickly solve all the problems of poor classroom performance and school accountability. No early childhood teacher who has spent any time in the classroom is persuaded of such a preposterous premise. In spite of accumulated data that point clearly to the inadequacy of standardized tests as accurate measures and their counterproductivity in fostering what we all claim to want: the improvement of students' learning (Black & Wiliam, 1998; Neill, 1997; Wiggins, 1993), the arguments continue. Nor do the data seem to persuade advocates of standardized testing otherwise. "Don't confuse me with the data! My mind is made up!"

Elliott Eisner (1999) has written eloquently about evaluation, from both educational theory and practice perspectives and his words inform our thinking and give focus to where we need to go on these contentious issues. I cite them here to bring this chapter to a close:

Under these circumstances, what is required to give pride of place to an assessment system that both facilitates teaching and learning and reveals the distinctive intellectual achievements of individual students? From my perspective, what we need is a change in the public's conception of the mission of the schools. Of course, bringing about such a change is no small task. Yet a shift needs to be made from a conception of schooling as a horse race or a kind of educational Olympics to a conception of schools as places that foster students' distinctive talents. The good school, as I have suggested, does not diminish individual differences. It increases them. It raises the mean and increases the variance. . . .

Our priorities for schools in America have not grown out of a deep public debate about the mission of education; they have grown out of a desire to improve test scores. Test scores are widely regarded as proxies for the quality of education. But they are utterly inadequate. (p. 660)

Never underestimate young children, for, if you do, you are bound to be surprised. In a classroom where principles of empowerment underlie all children's learning experiences, the potential for children's growth is vast, and the surprises in store for teachers who would choose to follow this course of action are heady. Perhaps that is what makes teaching young children so worthwhile.

# APPENDIXES
# REFERENCES
# INDEX
# ABOUT THE AUTHOR

# Materials List
# for a Can–Do Classroom

The materials listed below are grouped by the type of activities for which they would be used. This list was drawn from Brown and Precious (1968), Howes (1974), and Wassermann and Ivany (1996). These texts are especially recommended for a more complete listing.

*Arts and Crafts*

aluminum foil
balloons
balsa wood
boxes, all sizes
cardboard tubes
cartons
carving tools
cellophane paper
chalk, different colors
charcoal
clay
clay tools
clothespins
coat hangers
collage materials
corks
corrugated cardboard
cotton
crayons
doweling
drinking straws
dyes
easels
egg cartons
fabric scraps, all sorts
feathers
felt pens
finger paints
food coloring

fur
gauze
glass beads
lace
leather scraps
materials for mosaics
mobile-making materials
modeling tools
newspaper
paint
paintbrushes
paper, all kinds
paper clips
paper fasteners
paper punch
papier maché materials
paste
pastels
pencils, all kinds (colored, grease, soft, charcoal)
pins
pipe cleaners
plaster of Paris
plasticine
poster paint
poster paper
powder paint
printing ink
printing and stenciling

materials (potato, felt, and linoleum blocks; cutting tools; pencils; cork; spools; stamp pads; ink)
ribbon
scissors
sculpting and modeling materials (soap, plaster of Paris, small cardboard boxes for molds, clay, clay tools)
sequins
sewing thread and needles
shells
sponges
spools
stapler
straws
tape
tins
tissue paper, all colors
tubes from paper towels and toilet paper
wallpaper sample books
wire
wood

### Dress-Up and Housekeeping

aprons
baby carriage
blankets
capes
chairs
clothing (hats, ties, dresses, shoes)
crowns
cushions
dolls and dolls' clothes
fans
glasses
gloves
handbags
housekeeping equipment for sweeping, dusting,
washing, ironing, and cooking (kettle, knives and forks, tea set, pots and pans, tea towels)
jewelry
kitchen equipment, large (cupboards; sink units; chairs and stools; "play" refrigerator and stove, possibly of cardboard; ironing board)
kitchen equipment, small (toasters, coffee pots, irons, mixers, old or broken appliances)
mirrors
old costumes
scarves
shaving kits
shawls
stethoscope
stuffed animals
suitcases
telephone
toy cars
umbrellas
uniforms (doctor, nurse, firefighter, sailor, police)
wallets

### Cooking and Baking

basins
cake tins
colander
cookie sheets
egg whisk
kitchen scales
measuring cups and
spoons
mixing bowls
mixing spoons
muffin tins
oven gloves
pie tins
pots and pans, all kinds
recipes
tea towels
timer
washing-up materials
wooden spoons

### Music Making

bells
castanets
charts and pictures of the history of musical instruments
chimes
cymbals
drums
glockenspiel
guitar
homemade instruments
ideas for making
instruments
ideas on how to write music, blank music paper
instruments from olden days and instruments from other countries
music books and sheets of easy-to-play music
music boxes
orchestral instruments
piano
recorders
record player
records (classical, popular, and children's songs and dances)
tambourine
tapes and tape recorder/player
triangles
tuning forks
ukelele
xylophone

### Construction

basic tools (hammers, saws, screwdrivers, drill, files, plane, sandpaper, vise, pliers, twist drills, metal saw, coping saw, square, straight edge)
brads
cardboard, different sizes and thicknesses
construction booklets, pictures of things to make
glue
hinges
nails
pieces of garden hose
pieces of wood, all sizes and shapes (bamboo,
balsa, dowels, pegboard)
rope
screws
wheels of various sizes, cans, spools, wheels from broken toys
wire
workbench

## Dramatic Play

boxes (sturdy) for a stage
dress-up clothes and other
    props from the house-
    keeping materials
jewelry

makeup
marionettes
musical instruments
poster paints
puppet stage

puppets, either store-
    bought or handmade
tapes and tape player

## Reading and Writing

camera
catalogues
children's homemade
    books
children's library books,
    covering a wide range
    of abilities and interests
"how-to-do-it" books
magazines, children's and
    others
materials for making

books (paper, card-
    board, staplers, art sup-
    plies)
microphone
newspapers
paperback books
picture collections
reference books (encyclo-
    pedias, dictionaries,
    atlases, maps, tele-
    phone directories)
scribblers and blank

books
skillbuilders (games to
    practice language
    skills, enlarge vocabu-
    lary)
tape recorder and blank
    tapes
tapes with children's sto-
    ries
typewriter
word processor and ap-
    propriate software

## Measuring and Numbering

assorted paper (graph,
    plain, large sheets and
    small)
assorted writing tools
    (pencils, pens, chalk)
balance scales
blocks (dienes blocks, at-
    tribute blocks)
calipers
candles
click wheel
clocks
compass
containers of all sizes

cuisenaire rods
dominoes
games and puzzles
kitchen scales with
    weights
machines (adding ma-
    chine, calculators, cash
    registers)
math reference books
measuring cups, spoons
measuring tools for linear
    measurements (rulers,
    yardsticks, meter sticks,
    string, rope, rods, tape

measure, wire)
micrometer
miscellaneous objects for
    counting (beans, seeds
    of all kinds, cones, pa-
    per clips, marbles, bot-
    tle caps, nuts, shells,
    corks, pebbles, nuts
    and bolts, washers,
    clothespins)
play money
protractor
thermometers, different
    kinds

## Sciencing

absorbent cotton
air pump
alcohol
aluminum foil
ammonia
animals, small (mice, liz-
    ards, hamsters, guinea
    pigs, chicks, gerbils,
    fish, turtles)
apple juice
atomizers
baking soda
balance scales
ball bearings

balloons
balls
barometer
basins
bathroom scale
batteries
beans
bells
binoculars
block and tackle
blocks
blotting paper
bobs
bones

bottles
bowls
boxes
brace and bits
bricks
bubble pipes
buttons
buzzer
calipers
camera
candles
can opener
carbon paper
cardboard tubes

cement
chalk
cheesecloth
chopsticks
clocks
clothespins
colander
comb
compass, magnetic
compasses, measuring
concrete blocks
corks
cornstarch
detergent
doweling
drums
dry cells
dry ice
earthworms
egg cartons
egg whisk
eggs
electric fans
electric motors, toy
electric push buttons with
    lamps and sockets
electrical appliances, for
    taking apart (toasters,
    coffee pots, mixers, ra-
    dios)
extension cords
eyedroppers
eyeshades
fabrics, all kinds
feathers
fertilizers
filmstrip projector
fired clay tiles
fish weights
flashlights
flour
flowerpots
flowers
fly wheel
foam rubber
food coloring
foods
forceps
fruits
funnels
fur

fuses, burned out
geometric shapes
glass
glass beads
glass cutters
glass tubing
glue and paste
glycerine
gravel
gyroscopes
harmonica
height measure
holograms
honey
hourglass
ice cream sticks
ice cubes
instant coffee powder
insulated copper wire
iodine
iron filings
jacks, automobile
jars
jugs
kaleidoscope
kazoos
knives (carving, paring,
    dissecting)
lamp
leather scraps
leaves
legumes, dry
lenses, all kinds
light bulbs, working and
    burned out, various
    sizes
limewater
logs
lumber
machines, for taking
    apart (adding ma-
    chines, typewriters,
    calculators, pencil
    sharpeners, clocks, tele-
    phones)
magnetic wire
magnets of all shapes and
    sizes
magnifying glasses
mallets
maps

marbles
marking pens
measuring cups
measuring implements
    (yardsticks, meter
    sticks, tape measures)
medicine dropper
metal items (scraps, sheet-
    ing, wire)
metals, all kinds and
    weights
microscopes
milk powder
"minibeasties" (spiders,
    ants, caterpillars, worms)
mirrors
model windmill
modeling clay
molds
motors
mousetraps
muffin tins
nails of all sizes
needles
newspaper
newsprint
nuts and bolts
overhead projector
pails
paper, all kinds
paper clips
paper cups
paper punch
paper towels
paraffin
peanuts
peas
pebbles
pencil sharpener
pendulum frame
pendulums
picture collections
pillows
ping-pong balls
pins
pinwheel
pipe cleaners
pitchers
plants
plaster of Paris
plastic (sheeting, tubing)

plastic containers (buckets, basins, tubs)
plasticware (cups, dishes)
playing cards
poster board
poster paints
potatoes
potting soil
printing ink
prisms
protractor
pulleys, double and single
rheostats
ribbons
rice
rock salt
rocks
rope
rubber bands
rubber suction cups
rulers
salt
sand
sandpaper
saws
scissors
screen
screws, all sizes
sealing wax
seeds
seesaw balance on a fulcrum
shells
skeletons
skins, animal
Slinky
snail shells
soap flakes
soldering iron
spinning tops
sponges
spools

spoons, graded sizes
sprayers
spring scales
springs
squid
staple remover
stapler
star charts
steel wool
stethoscope
sticks
stones
stopwatch
straws
string
styrofoam chips
sugar
sunlamp
switches
syringes
tape
tape measures
tape recorder
tapes, musical
teapot
tea strainers
telegraph key
telegraph set
telescope
test tubes
thermometers (clinical, room, cooking)
thread, string, twine
thumbtacks
timers (egg, 10-second)
tin cans
tissue paper, all colors
toilet plunger
tongue depressors
tools (see "Materials for Construction")
toothpicks

toys (cars, airplanes, furniture, utensils)
transistor radios
transparent flexible tubing of various diameters
trays
tree parts (bark, leaves, twigs, branches, driftwood)
triangles
trundle wheel
tubes from paper towels and toilet paper
tuning forks
turntable
umbrellas
unglazed clay tiles
vacuum cleaner
vegetables
vinegar
vise
washers
watch
water containers
watering can
waxed paper
wedge
weights
wheels of all sizes
whistles
wire
wire cutters
wooden balls
wooden beads
wood, scraps of different types
"wormarium"
xylophone
yeast cakes
yeast, dried
yo-yos

*Other Activities*
blocks

sand and water tables

toy cars and trucks

# Self-Study Tools for the Teacher

## CODING SHEET

Use the Coding Sheet to examine the kinds of responses you have made during the debriefing sessions.

When you have tape recorded a debriefing session, listen to the tape and check the kind of responses you hear yourself making. When you have completed your analysis, the Coding Sheet should give you a profile of your overall response pattern and the extent to which each response type has been used.

A. Responses That Inhibit Thinking by Bringing Closure

    Agrees/disagrees _____

    Doesn't give student a chance to think _____

    Tells student what he/she (teacher) thinks _____

    Talks too much/explains it her/his way _____

    Cuts student off _____

    Other closure responses _____

    Heckles/is sarcastic/puts down idea _____

B. Responses That Limit Student Thinking

    Looks for single, correct method/answer _____

    Leads student to "right" answer _____

    Tells student what to do _____

    Gives data _____

    Other limiting responses _____

C. Responses That Encourage Thinking

    1. Basic teaching-for-thinking responses

    Repeats statement so student may consider it _____

    Paraphrases to reflect main idea _____

    Interprets student's idea _____

    Asks for more information _____

    2. Responses that call for analysis

    Give me an example. _____

    What assumptions are being made? _____

Why do you suppose that is good? _____

What alternatives have you considered? _____

How does (that) compare with (this)? _____

How might that be classified? _____

What data support your idea? _____

3. Responses that challenge

What hypotheses can you suggest? _____

How do you interpret that? _____

What criteria are you using? _____

How would those principles be applied in this situation? _____

What predictions can be made? _____

How would you test that? _____

What new scheme or plan can you envision for that situation? _____

4. Responses that accept student's idea nonjudgmentally

I see. _____

Thank you. _____

D. Unrelated Responses

Classroom/behavior management _____

Speech mannerisms _____

Other _____

## ANALYSIS SHEET

Use the questions in this Analysis Sheet in conjunction with the Coding Sheet to examine the effectiveness of your debriefing skills. This clinical analysis of how you debrief the play will promote thoughtful reflection on your interactive style, as well as help identify strengths and areas of needed skill development.

1. Describe your response pattern during the debriefing. What responses were most used? Least used?
2. What "big ideas" did you want the students to examine? How did your responses help to promote this examination?
3. To what extent did your responses attend to students' ideas?
4. To what extent did your responses stay in the "basic teaching-for-thinking" response category?
5. To what extent did your responses move into the "analysis" and "challenge" categories?
6. How did this response pattern serve the goals of debriefing?
7. To what extent were you able to use nonthreatening responses while at the

same time working with students' ideas, helping them examine the issues of consequence?

8. Based upon your observations of students' responses during the debriefing, what do you see as some good features of your interactions?

9. What aspects of your interactions need more practice?

10. What new insights did you acquire about debriefing from your work in this session?

# References

Adam, M., Chambers, R., Fukui, S., Gluska, J., & Wassermann, S. (1991). *Evaluation Materials for the Graduation Program*. Vancouver, BC: Faculty of Education, Simon Fraser University.

Arnoud, S., & Curry, N. (1971). *Play: The Child Strives Toward Self-Realization*. Washington, DC: National Association for the Education of Young Children.

Ashton-Warner, S. (1963). *Teacher*. New York: Simon & Schuster.

Aspy, D., & Roebuck, F. (1977). *Kids Don't Learn from People They Don't Like*. Amherst, MA: Human Resources Development Press.

Barnes, L. B., Christensen, C. R., & Hansen, A. J. (1994). *Teaching and the Case Method* (3rd ed.). Boston: Harvard Business School Press.

Berlak, A., & Berlak, H. (1981). *Dilemmas of Schooling*. London: Methuen.

Bettelheim, B. (1987, March). The Importance of Play. *Atlantic*, pp. 35–46.

Black, P., & Wiliam, D. (1998). Inside the Black Box: Raising Standards Through Classroom Assessment. *Phi Delta Kappan, 80*, 139–148.

Bloom, B. (1964). *A Taxonomy of Educational Objectives*. New York: McKay.

Bracey, G. (1998). Minds of Our Own. *Phi Delta Kappan, 80*, 328–329.

Bredecamp. S., & Copple, C. (1997). *Developmentally Appropriate Practice in Early Childhood Programs* (rev. ed.). Washington, DC: National Association for the Education of Young Children.

British Columbia Ministry of Education. (1990). *Year 2000: A Framework for Learning*. Victoria, BC: Author.

Brown, M., & Precious, N. (1968). *The Integrated Day in the Primary School*. London: Ward Lock.

Bruner, J. (1985). *On Knowing*. Cambridge, MA: Belknap Press.

Bruner, J. (1966). On Teaching Thinking: An Afterthought. In S. F. Chipman, J. W. Segal, & R. Glasser (Eds.), *Thinking and Learning Skills* (Vol. 2; pp. 597–608). Hillsdale, NJ: Erlbaum.

Cadwell, L. B. (1997). *Bringing Reggio Emilia Home: An Innovative Approach to Early Childhood Education*. New York: Teachers College Press.

Carkhuff, R. (1969). *Helping and Human Relations* (Vol. 1). New York: Holt, Rinehart.

Carkhuff, R. (2000). *The Art of Helping* (8th ed.). Amherst, MA: Human Resources Development Press.

Carkhuff, R., & Berenson, B. (1976). *Teaching as Treatment*. Amherst, MA: Human Resources Development Press.

Cizek, G. J. (1991). Innovation or Enervation? Performance Assessment in Perspective. *Phi Delta Kappan, 72*, 695–699.

Coles, R. (1999, October 17). Make Room for Daddies [Review of the *Velveteen Rabbit*.] New York Times Book Review, p. 27.

Combs, A., Avila, D., & Purkey, W. (1971). *Helping Relationships*. Boston: Allyn & Bacon.

Cousins, N. (1982). *The Human Adventure*. New York: W. W. Norton.

Cuban, L. (1982). Persistent Instruction: The High School Classroom, 1900–1980. *Phi Delta Kappan, 64*, 113–118.

Cuban, L. (1986). *Teachers and Machines*. New York: Teachers College Press.

Cullum, A. (1971). *The Geranium on the Windowsill Just Died But Teacher You Went Right On*. Holland: Harlan Quist.

DeVries, R., & Zan, B. (1994). *Moral Classrooms, Moral Children: Creating a Constructivist Atmosphere in Early Education*. New York: Teachers College Press.

Dewey, J. (1916). *Democracy and Education*. New York: Macmillan.

Eisner, E. (1994). *The Educational Imagination: On the Design and Evaluation of School Programs* (3rd ed.). Paramus, NJ: Prentice Hall.

Eisner, E. (1999). The Uses and Limits of Performance Assessment. *Phi Delta Kappan, 80*, 658–660.

Elkind, D. (1978). *A Sympathetic Understanding of the Child* (2nd ed.). Boston: Allyn & Bacon.

Elkins, R. (1981). Too Much Praise Is Abuse. *Educational Leadership, 38*, p. 482.

Erikson, E. (1968). *Identity: Youth and Crisis*. New York: W. W. Norton.

Fadiman, D. (1992). *Why Do These Children Love School?* Santa Monica, CA: Pyramid Film & Video.

Feynman, R. (1985). *Surely You're Joking Mr. Feynman*. New York: W. W. Norton.

Freire, P. (1983). *Pedagogy of the Oppressed*. New York: Continuum.

French, M. (1985). *Beyond Power*. New York: Summit.

Gardner, H. (1991). *The Unschooled Mind*. New York: Basic Books.

Gazda, G., Asbury, F., Balzer, F., Childers, W., & Walters, R. (1977). *Human Relations Development* (2nd ed.). Boston: Allyn & Bacon.

Gift, J. (1989). *Opportunities for Students to Make Decisions Affecting Their Learning in Four Elementary School Classrooms*. Unpublished master's thesis, Simon Fraser University Faculty of Education, Vancouver, BC.

Gilbert, J. C. (1990). *Performance-Based Assessment and Research Guide*. Denver, CO: Department of Education. (ERIC Document Reproduction Service No. ED 327304)

Gizek, G. J. (1991). Innovation or Enervation? Performance Assessment in Perspective. *Phi Delta Kappan, 72*, 695–699.

Glasser, W. (1985). *Control Theory in the Classroom*. New York: HarperCollins.

Goodman, K., Goodman, Y., & Hood, W. (1989). *The Whole Language Evaluation Book*. Portsmouth, NH: Heinemann.

Gorman, M., Plucker, J., & Callahan, C. (1998). Turning Students into Inventors. *Phi Delta Kappan, 79*, 530–535.

Grace, C. (1992). *The Portfolio and Its Use: Developmentally Appropriate Assessment of Young Children*. Urbana, IL: ERIC Clearinghouse in Elementary and Early Childhood Education, EDO-PS-92–11.

Gruen, Arno. (1986). *The Betrayal of the Self*. New York: Grove Press.

Hargreaves, A. (1988–1989, Winter). The Maturation of Educational Measurement. *E + M Newsletter*. Toronto, ON: Ontario Institute for Studies in Education.

Herbert, E. (1998). Lessons Learned About Student Portfolios. *Phi Delta Kappan*, 79, 583–589.

Howes, V. (1974). *Informal Teaching in the Open Classroom*. New York: Macmillan.

Hubbard, G. (1987). *Art in Action*. San Diego: Coronado.

Isenberg, J., & Quisenberry, N. L. (1988). Play: A Necessity for All Children. *Childhood Education*, 24, 138–145.

Jennings, W., & Nathan, J. (1977). Startling/Disturbing Research on School Program Effectiveness. *Phi Delta Kappan*, 59, 568–571.

Jersild, A. (1955). *When Teachers Face Themselves*. New York: Teachers College Press.

Jervis, K. & Montag, C. (1991). (Eds.). *Progressive Education for the 1990s: Transforming Practice*. New York: Teachers College Press.

Jones, E., & Reynolds, G. (1992). *The Play's the Thing: Teachers' Roles in Children's Play*. New York: Teachers College Press.

Kohn, A. (1998). Choices for Children: Why and How to Let Students Decide. *Phi Delta Kappan*, 80, 9–20.

Kohn, A. (1999). *Punished by Rewards: The Trouble with Gold Stars, Incentive Plans, A's, Praise and Other Bribes*. Boston: Houghton Mifflin.

Kotlowitz, A. (1991). *There Are No Children Here*. New York: Doubleday.

Langley, L., & Wassermann, S. (1988). Alternatives to the Gumdrop: More Effective Inservice Programs for Teachers. *Teacher Education*, 32, 31–42.

Levinson, B. (Dir.). (1982). *Diner*. New York: MGM-United Artists.

Lewin, T. (1999, January 24). A Push to Reorder Science Puts Physics First. *New York Times*, p. 1.

Lortie, D. (1975). *Schoolteacher*. Chicago: University of Chicago Press.

Lortie, D. (1986). Teacher Status in Dade County: A Case of Structural Strain. *Phi Delta Kappan*, 68, 568–575.

MacDonald, C. (1982). A Better Way of Reporting. *B.C. Teacher*, 61, 142–144.

Manley-Casimir, M., & Wassermann, S. (1989). The Teacher as Decision-Maker: Connecting Self with the Practice of Teaching. *Childhood Education*, 65, 288–293.

Mead, M. (1965). *Family*. New York: Macmillan.

Milgram, S. (1983). *Obedience to Authority*. New York: HarperCollins.

Moffatt, D. (1968). *A Student-Centered Language Arts Curriculum, Grades K–6*. Boston: Houghton Mifflin.

Neill, D. M. (1997). Transforming Student Assessment. *Phi Delta Kappan*, 79, 34–58.

Nolan, J., & Huber, T. (1989). Nurturing the Reflective Practitioner Through Instructional Supervision: A Review of the Literature. *Journal of Curriculum and Supervision*, 4, 126–145.

Paley, V. G. (1992). *You Can't Say You Can't Play*. Cambridge, MA: Harvard University Press.

Perrone, V. (1991). *A Letter to Teachers*. San Francisco: Jossey Bass.

Piaget, J., & Inhelder, B. (1969). *The Psychology of the Child*. New York: Basic Books.

Pierson, C., & Beck, S. (1993). Performance Assessment: The Realities That Will Influence the Rewards. *Childhood Education, 70*, 29–32.

Purkey, W. (1970). *Self Concept and School Achievement*. Englewood Cliffs, NJ: Prentice Hall.

Purkey, W. (1978). *Inviting School Success*. Belmont, CA: Wadsworth.

Quinn, S. (1982, January). The Competence of Babies. *Atlantic*, pp. 54–62.

Ramsey, P. (1998). *Teaching and Learning in a Diverse World: Multicultural Education for Young Children* (2nd ed.). New York: Teachers College Press.

Raths. L. E. (1969). *Teaching for Learning*. Columbus, OH: Charles Merrill.

Raths, L. E. (1998). *Meeting the Needs of Children*. New York: Educator's International Press. (Original work published in 1973)

Raths, L. E., Wassermann, S., Jonas, A., & Rothstein, A. (1986). *Teaching for Thinking: Theory, Strategies and Activities for the Classroom* (2nd ed.). New York: Teachers College Press.

Rogers, C. (1961). *On Becoming a Person*. Boston: Houghton Mifflin.

Saltz, B., & Saltz, E. (1986). Pretend Play Training and Its Outcomes. In G. Fein & M. Rivkin (Eds.), *The Young Child at Play* (pp. 155–174). Washington, DC: National Association for the Education of Young Children.

Schön, D. (1983). *The Reflective Practitioner*. New York: Basic Books.

Schön, D. (1987). *Educating the Reflective Practitioner*. San Francisco: Jossey-Bass.

Seligman, M. (1991). *Learned Optimism*. New York: Knopf.

Sharon, Y., & Sharon, S. (1992). *Expanding Cooperative Learning Through Group Investigation*. New York: Teachers College Press.

Slonimsky, N. (1981). *Lexicon of Musical Invective: Critical Assaults on Composers Since Beethoven's Time*. Seattle, WA: University of Washington Press.

Simon, D., & Burns, E. (1997). *The Corner: A Year in the Life of an Inner-City Neighborhood*. New York: Broadway Books.

Spitz, R. (1949). The Role of Ecological Factors in Emotional Development in Infancy. *Child Development, 20*, 145–156.

Steichen, E. (1955). *The Family of Man*. New York: Museum of Modern Art.

Stevens, L. J., & Price, M. (1992). Meeting the Challenge of Children at Risk. *Phi Delta Kappan, 74*, 18–23.

Stigler, J. N., Gonzales, P. A., Kowalsky, T., Knoll, S., & Serrano, A. (1999). *The TIMSS Videotape Classroom Study: Methods and Findings for an Exploratory Research Project on Eighth Grade Math Instruction in Germany, Japan and the United States*. Washington, DC: National Center for Educational Statistics.

Truax, C., & Carkhuff, R. (1967). *Toward Effective Counseling and Psychotherapy*. Chicago: Aldine.

Vygotsky, L. S. (1978). *Mind in Society: The Development of Higher Psychological Processes*. Cambridge, MA: Harvard University Press.

Wassermann, S. (1976). Organic Teaching in the Primary Classroom: Sylvia Ashton-Warner Is Alive and Well and Her Work Is Flourishing in Vancouver. *Phi Delta Kappan, 58*, 264–268.

Wassermann, S. (1987a). Teaching Children to Think: The Abbotsford Project. *The Canadian School Executive, 7*, 3–10.

Wassermann, S. (1987b). Teaching for Thinking: The Principal's Role. *Principal, 66,* 17–23.

Wassermann, S. (1989a). Learning to Value Error. *Childhood Education, 65,* 233–235.

Wassermann, S. (1989b). Reflections on Measuring Thinking While Listening to Mozart's Jupiter Symphony. *Phi Delta Kappan, 70,* 365–370.

Wassermann, S. (1992). A Case for Social Studies. *Phi Delta Kappan, 73,* 793–801.

Wassermann, S., & Eggert, W. (1989). *Profiles of Teaching Competency* (rev. ed.). Unpublished manuscript. Available from Faculty of Education, Simon Fraser University, Vancouver, BC, Canada.

Wassermann, S., & Ivany, J. W. G. (1996). *The New Teaching Elementary Science: Who's Afraid of Spiders?* (2nd ed.). New York: Teachers College Press.

Wassermann, S., & Wigmore, J. (1999). *Tooker, the Remarkable Dog* [CD-ROM]. Vancouver, BC: Figaro Educational Software. <fffigaro.com>

Winchell, P. (1954). *Ventriloquism for Fun and Profit.* Baltimore: Ottenheimer.

Windschitl, M. (1999). The Challenges of Sustaining a Constructivist Classroom. *Phi Delta Kappan, 80,* 751–755.

Wiggins, G. (1993). Assessment: Authenticity, Context and Validity. *Phi Delta Kappan, 75,* 200–214.

# Index

# About the Author

**Selma Wassermann** is Professor Emerita in the Faculty of Education at Simon Fraser University, Vancouver, Canada. She is the co-author of two texts, *Teaching for Thinking: Theory, Strategies and Activities for the Classroom* and *Teaching Elementary Science: Who's Afraid of Spiders?* and the author of *Getting Down to Cases: Learning to Teach With Case Studies*, and *Introduction to Case Method Teaching: A Guide to the Galaxy*, as well as *The Long Distance Grandmother*. Recipient of the Award of Teaching Excellence at Simon Fraser University, Dr. Wassermann is now the co-director of Figaro Educational Software, creating innovative computer software for classroom use. She lives in Vancouver, with her husband Jack, and cat, the incomparable Mischa. Her daughter, Paula, and two grandsons, Simon and Arlo live-to-ski in Nelson.